MY CHIEF AND I
and
FIVE YEARS LATER

FRANCES ELLEN COLENSO

FRANCES COLENSO

MY CHIEF AND I

OR, SIX MONTHS IN NATAL AFTER THE LANGALIBALELE
OUTBREAK

(Originally published under the pseudonym Atherton Wylde)

and

FIVE YEARS LATER

A SEQUEL

Edited and introduced by
M.J. DAYMOND

UNIVERSITY OF NATAL PRESS
PIETERMARITZBURG
1994

© 1994 University of Natal

UNIVERSITY OF NATAL PRESS

PIETERMARITZBURG

Private Bag X01, Scottsville 3209, South Africa

ISBN 0 86980 886 9

My Chief and I, or Six Months in Natal After the Langalibalele Outbreak
was first published by Chapman and Hall, London, in 1880 under the
pseudonym Atherton Wylde. The sequel, *Five Years Later*, is published here
for the first time from a manuscript in the Natal Archives, Pietermaritzburg.

Cover design: David Moon

Typeset in the University of Natal Press
Printed by Kohler Carton and Print
Box 955, Pinetown 3600, South Africa

CONTENTS

ILLUSTRATIONS

ACKNOWLEDGEMENTS

The publishers are grateful for permission to include the photograph of Frances Colenso. The original is in the library at Rhodes House, Oxford. The Natal Provincial Museum Services, Pietermaritzburg, supplied the print used in this book.

NOTE ON THE TEXT

The text is taken from the edition published in London in 1880 by Sampson Low; inconsistencies in punctuation have been corrected and it has been slightly modernised. Zulu orthography has changed considerably since Frances Colenso's day; for *My Chief and I*, the spelling of Zulu words that Bishop Colenso used in his *Dictionary* has been followed. For other words native to South Africa, the spelling used by Frances Colenso in her sequel, *Five Years Later*, has been followed as the survival of the manuscript enables us to know her practice directly. This manuscript is in the Natal Archives. In the Introduction, modern practice is followed. Frances Colenso's own translations of many of the Zulu words were included in the 1880 publication and have been retained in the body of this text in square brackets; for convenience, any of these words which are not in the Shorter OED have been listed again in the Glossary. The footnotes are all Frances Colenso's own. The extracts from newspaper reports which she used have, where necessary, been lightly amended to reflect the appearance of the original.

GLOSSARY

Modern spellings are given in brackets.

after-rider (from *agterryer*, Afrikaans/Dutch):   a mounted groom or other attendant.

amasoja: soldiers.

amabele (Zulu):   sorghum.

Amarail: according to Frances Colenso, a Zulu nickname for Durnford.

bayete: the salute given to Zulu royalty.

Bluff: the sandy headland which forms the south-eastern side of the Durban bay. It was acquired by J.S. King from Shaka.

camp-kettles: volunteers (origin unknown).

Draakensberg (Drakensberg) (Afrikaans/Dutch):   dragon mountains. This escarpment divides Natal from the high inland plateau. Cathkin Peak and Champagne Castle are adjacent peaks on this range. Cathkin was so named by David Gray (the farmer in Chapter 8), in 1858, after Cathkin Braes, near his home town, Paisley.

Exeter Hall: hall in London where anti-slavery meetings were held; used as a derogatory epithet for interfering philanthropists.

Fort Napier: the garrison established to the west of Pietermaritzburg in 1843 when the Dutch handed over to the British. The last British regiment left in 1914.

head-ring: a ring of latex and fibre formally sewn into a Zulu man's hair soon after marriage as a sign of social maturity.

Helpmakaar (Helpmekaar) (Afrikaans):   help each other. Frances Colenso's mis-spelling was common; it reflects the pronunciation.

Howick Inn: the falls over the Umgeni river were a popular beauty spot and accommodation for the public was first available in the village in 1849.

Inkos; 'Nkos (Zulu):   title usually reserved for an important chief.

innyanga (*inyanga*) (Zulu):   a medicine-man, herbalist.

Isandhlwana (Isandlwana) (Zulu): the name of this distinctively shaped
    mountain at the battlefield has been variously interpreted. The most
    probable meaning is 'a little hut' which it resembles.
isijingi (Zulu): mealie-meal and pumpkin cooked together.
kafir (orig. Arabic): unbeliever. Often spelt 'kaffir', but Frances Colenso
    used 'kafir.' In the late 19th century the word was used by whites for
    Xhosa and Zulu people generally, but was becoming an abusive term.
    The prefix 'Natal' was used to distinguish the indigenous peoples who
    came under the jurisdiction of the colonial government from the
    'Zulu-kafirs' who lived under independent rule beyond the Thukela
    River.
kafir corn: sorghum.
Khahlamba (Zulu): the Drakensberg; usually interpreted as 'barrier of
    spears'.
Langalibalele (Zulu): literally, 'the sun is hot'.
Little Berg: an escarpment of foothills below the main Drakensberg range.
Maritzburg: abbreviation of Pietermaritzburg. The site was chosen in 1838
    for the capital of the Boer republic of Natalia; the town was named
    after the Voortrekker leaders, Piet Retief and Gert Maritz.
Nana Sahib: A prominent leader in the Indian Mutiny of 1857 whose name
    became synonymous with villainy because many British women and
    children, to whom he had promised safe conduct, were massacred in
    his palace.
Pontac: a sweet, red dessert wine.
Putini (*Puthini*): the name Frances Colenso uses for the Ngwe. Puthini, their
    late chief, was Langalibalele's uncle; his young widow is the
    Umkosaza who visits Durnford's party while they are in the region of
    the Zikali clan.
Tugela (*Thukela*) (Zulu): the startling one. The river which divided white-
    ruled Natal from the Zulu kingdom.
tshwala (Zulu): beer made from malted grain.
Welch's Half-way House: Welch took over the thrice-weekly Durban –
    Pietermaritzburg omnibus service in 1862. In July 1868 he acquired
    Halfway House; there his wife provided passengers with lunches of
    such excellence that they were cited as one of reasons why his
    competitor, George Jessup, ceased operating.

INTRODUCTION

Published under the pseudonym Atherton Wylde, *My Chief and I* was written by a young woman, Frances Colenso, in the colony of Natal in 1875 and appeared in London in 1880. Although it achieved some fame in its day, and although the Colenso family gave copies of it to visitors seeking to understand the dynamics of local politics, the book has long been out of print and forgotten by all but a few scholars. This republication more than a century later comes at a time when its author's concern with the political fate of the Zulu people, as one of the groups which make up the South African polity, is again of vital importance in South Africa. To this re-publication of *My Chief and I* has been added *Five Years Later*, the sequel which Frances Colenso wrote in 1882, shortly before her early death. It has never before been published. The story of Anthony Durnford which Frances Colenso tells is one which will fascinate all readers; as adventure fiction, as a polemic and as historical record *My Chief and I* establishes her as one of the most important pioneers of political fiction by women writers in South Africa.

Concurrently with her fictionalised account of events in Natal in *My Chief and I*, Frances Colenso produced two major historical studies of the Zulu-Natal region: *History of the Zulu War and Its Origin* and *The Ruin of Zululand*. In all of this writing—fictional and non-fictional—she tried to influence public opinion and the course of events in Natal. The precedent for doing so came most directly from her father, John William Colenso. He was the remarkable first Bishop of Natal who, in the 1870s, found himself compelled to intervene in the handling of the colony's affairs by the Natal and the British Governments. When Langalibalele and his Hlubi people, as well as their neighbours, the Ngwe, were severely punished for a relatively unimportant failure to comply with the authority of the local magistrate, the whole Colenso family became active participants in the Bishop's efforts to expose this injustice. Working as a team, they mounted what was virtually the only public effort from within the colony itself to challenge the official account of the Langalibalele 'rebellion'. The family entered the fray in 1873, possibly little realising at the time that they were engaging in events that were to escalate into the Anglo-Zulu war of 1879, a war which demonstrated that the British Government had been drawn into what seems to have begun as a colonial determination to crush the Zulu nation under its king Cetshwayo. From the British point of view, Natal, where white traders first settled during the reign of the Zulu king Chaka, had been one of the quieter backwaters of the Empire. In the 1870s, when Frances Colenso was writing, events in this colony had thrust it into the centre of imperial controversy.

Although *My Chief and I* is directly concerned with what had been done to Langalibalele and his people, the 'chief' of its title is not that unfortunate man; he is the British soldier, Colonel Anthony Durnford, whose actions and attitudes exemplify the spirit of benevolent authority that Frances Colenso believed should guide all imperial officials. The passionate conviction, the anger and the dismay with which she tells Durnford's story had its sources in public and in private life. He had been subjected to vicious public criticism by the white settlers in Natal for his part in the Langalibalele 'rebellion'; the colonial government was determined to make an example of the 'culprits'; and the British Government was reluctant to recognise and rectify a blatant miscarriage of justice. The passion of her narrative had a private source too, for Frances Colenso loved Anthony Durnford. Their relationship had to be kept secret because he was a married man, but her emotion could find expression as she took up the cause of the soldier and the man. In this way Durnford and Langalibalele formed the parallel objects of her crusading spirit as she, like her father, used her pen in the cause of justice.

The narrative of *My Chief and I* covers the six months which followed the so-called Langalibalele Rebellion of 1873. What the Natal officials saw as a major insubordination had occurred when, finding himself cornered by the colonial authorities, Langalibalele had escaped with his men and their cattle over the Drakensberg mountains and into Lesotho. As soon as rumours of the planned flight reached Pietermaritzburg, Durnford was ordered to prevent it by taking a mixed force to the top of the mountain pass itself so as to turn back Langalibalele and the Hlubi. Three young, white volunteers in Durnford's force were killed in the ensuing clash. In Natal, Durnford was blamed for the fiasco and roundly criticised in the colony's newspapers. In her defence of her soldier, Frances Colenso told the story of the next task that he was given—that of blocking *all* of the mountain passes which led from Natal into Lesotho. She used his deeds to demonstrate to her readers his skill as a military engineer, his dutiful, upright leadership as a soldier and his manly sense of honour.

Durnford himself had also used this task as an opportunity to plead a cause.

He took a hundred men of the Ngwe chiefdom into the mountains to work as pioneers and he did so in order to demonstrate to the colony's government that the Ngwe were reliable, obedient people who deserved to return to the land that had been taken from them as a result of the 'rebellion'. His actions epitomised the impartial concern with justice that the Colenso family believed should be the spirit of imperial rule. Thus it was that in writing her tribute to the man she loved, Frances Colenso could bring his story into the larger cause for which her family was fighting. In writing *My Chief and I*, she too was pleading for justice for a wronged people.

For a young woman to intervene in international politics and to take on the role of champion-at-arms is unusual even today. In Frances Colenso's day, particularly in a remote colonial outpost, it was extraordinary. It necessitated her disguising her identity, and so she followed the example of many other women writers—she created a male persona for herself. Her Atherton Wylde is a young Englishman who arrives in Natal just after Langalibalele's arrest. This disguise was necessary for many reasons. Propriety demanded that Frances conceal her own feelings for Durnford whose estranged wife was living in England. As no woman could have travelled with Durnford's work party in the remote mountain regions of Natal, plausibility demanded that she create an author-narrator who could have had first-hand experience of the events she presents. Finally, given Durnford's own exemplary purposes in employing the Ngwe, prudence demanded that the Colenso name should not be too closely associated with the publication of his exploits. At the time of Frances's writing, hostility in Natal to the Colenso family was such that it might have damaged, not furthered, Durnford's cause.

The decision to create an imaginary, male narrator entailed Frances Colenso's presenting her factual material in the form of fiction. This makes *My Chief and I* the first known instance of a South African woman's using fiction directly to influence political opinion. It predates Olive Schreiner's allegorised attack on the land-grabbing of Cecil John Rhodes, in *Trooper Peter Halket of Mashonaland* (1897), by some twenty years. Today, however, Frances Colenso is not similarly celebrated as a pioneering woman in this country's literary-political history. The nineteenth-century origins of this neglect probably have to do with her being overshadowed by a notable and controversial father. In this, gender attitudes played their part for women were not readily granted a role in public life or recognised as writers. Some British women novelists achieved fame in the nineteenth century, but non-fictional, historico-political writing remained a male preserve. In the main, this discriminatory recognition of women's work has continued into the twentieth century. The stereotype of feminine intuition and emotionality has made it possible to acknowledge that women have the imaginative power to write novels, but not to acknowledge that women also possess the power of rational judgment demanded for the writing of history and for intervention in national affairs.

In Natal, hostility to the religious and political views of the Colenso family was such that the family tended to close ranks and this in turn meant that the Bishop's wife and unmarried daughters were subsumed in his causes. By all accounts, theirs was a willing dedication, but it too has served to obscure Frances Colenso's own achievements. It is the interactions of a public stereotype and a personal demand for womanly selflessness that we can now see as leading to the task which faced her in writing *My Chief and I* as she sought to speak in her own right without breaking away from her role as her father's daughter. To date, Frances Colenso's work has been thoroughly neglected in literary circles, and the limited recognition that she has had amongst historians suggests that they read her only in her minor role, as a daughter.

As has been suggested, in much of her work Frances Colenso collaborated with her ancillary status. In writing her now better-known *History of the Zulu War and Its Origin* (1880) and *The Ruin of Zululand; an Account of British Doings in Zululand Since the Invasion of 1879* (1884 & 1885), she thought of herself simply as extending the attempts of her father to obtain justice for the African peoples of Natal. He first took up the cause of the Hlubi people and their neighbours, the Ngwe, in 1874, in a pamphlet *Langalibalele and the Amahlubi Tribe* (also published as an Imperial Blue Book, C 1141, in 1875) in which he commented on the official account of Langalibalele's trial and the events leading up to it. It is in Frances Colenso's fictionalised history, *My Chief and I*, that we can see her finding her own, individual way of fighting the Colenso family cause. It is an important testimony to a woman's struggle to find her own voice, to speak with a measure of independence, within the attitudes and customs which circumscribed her life.

One of the sad consequences of the way in which she had to write *My Chief and I*—adopting a male disguise—was that in her day Frances Colenso's achievement could not create a precedent for other women writers in southern Africa who might have wished to enter the public arena. For today's readers, the consequences of this disguise are probably less practical than emotional. It is an uncomfortable disguise to penetrate because it reveals so much undeclarable passion; but this discomfort is also a reminder that her self-sublimation is what tells us of the constraints within which she had to think and write. And then, although it is the most immediately striking note, the yearning passion that comes through Atherton Wylde's praise of Anthony Durnford is in fact only one of the many notes in the narrative. The tone of Frances Colenso's writing actually ranges from spirited satire to heartfelt pleading. Proper acknowledgment of this range of tones is crucial for today's readers for (as will be shown later) it reveals the several ways in which an informed, perceptive and actively involved woman felt herself to be positioned in and by the interest groups of Natal in the 1870s.

Besides her obscurity as a political figure and writer of history, Frances Colenso has also not been given her place in the literary history of South Africa. In fact she is not thought of as a literary figure at all. This is because in her lifetime her earlier writing, especially her romantic fiction, was not identified as hers and has since been forgotten. Today, *Two Heroes*, the novel which she published privately in London under the pseudonym Zandile, and the unpublished novel, "A Little Orphan", are quite unknown.[1] Neither can be called an unknown masterpiece, but *Two Heroes* meant enough to Frances Colenso herself for her to write it into *My Chief and I*. When Atherton Wylde is at a loose end one day, he tries a novel. It opens with scenes set in Hong Kong. He is soon bored by it and is led to conclude that "the writer was a woman, and had never been out of England in her life" (304). Those in the know would have enjoyed the joke, for he is clearly reading *Two Heroes*. Frances Colenso had in fact spent very little time in England, so her joke is many-edged and touches mostly on her narrator's male prejudices.

The existence of two early romances indicates that *My Chief and I* was pivotal in Frances Colenso's writing career. It is here that she consciously broke away from the realm that a woman writer was expected to occupy, that of introspective romance, to stride into what had been demarcated as male territory—adventure and politics. Although the influence of this break could not be immediate, we can now see that in making it she inaugurated the interventionist tradition of fiction for which South African women writers, from Olive Schreiner to Bessie Head and Nadine Gordimer, are now internationally so celebrated.

As the Preface signed by Atherton Wylde tells us, the bulk of *My Chief and I* was written in 1875 but did not appear immediately because Durnford did not want a vindication of his actions published during his lifetime. He was killed at Isandlwana, the first major battle of the Anglo-Zulu War, in January 1879. The occasion to publish must have come to Frances Colenso with a miserable swiftness, but she used it to add an account of his death which established that in Natal, if not in Britain, Durnford was now recognised as the hero that she had all along believed him to be. The substance of the long "Note" which she added in 1879 is repeated in Chapter 3 of *Five Years Later*—the sequel which she wrote some three years after Durnford's death. The differences between these two accounts of the battle and his heroism show that, in her later writing, Frances Colenso had shifted the focus of her anger on Durnford's behalf from the colony to the metropolis. The differences also tell us much about what had happened, spiritually and emotionally, to her in the interim.

For the 1879 "Note", she reproduces, word for word, a newspaper correspondent's account of the first official visit to the battlefield some four months later. It recreates what must have occurred during the last minutes of the battle and stresses the heroism of the Natal Carbineers, led by Durnford, as they attempted to halt the Zulu pursuit of the soldiers fleeing towards Fugitive's Drift. This stand cleared the regiment of the verdict of cowardice which had hung over it since the skirmish at Bushman's River Pass. In *Five Years Later*, when she narrates the battle of Isandlwana, Frances Colenso uses a different focus. A fictional letter-writer is now her source and her concern is more simply with Durnford, his integrity as a soldier and as a civilian. The changes were made because of what she believed to be an attempt by Lord Chelmsford, commander of the British forces in Natal at the time of the war, wrongly to blame Durnford for the defeat at Isandlwana in order to avoid military censure himself. In her first account of the battlefield, she was intent on vindicating Durnford in the eyes of the colony; in her second, as her despair at clearing Durnford's reputation grew, her target audience became much larger—the British Government and military establishment.

To our anti-imperial and less heroic age, Frances Colenso presents what might seem an awkward division in her Chief when she insists first on Durnford's civil wish to avoid a conflict with the Zulu nation and then shifts, when the war and his military role dominate her narrative, to an emphasis on his perfect conduct as a soldier and his supreme courage in battle. In a recent study of Durnford, R. W. F. Drooglever emphasises the strangeness of this division, concluding that Durnford himself was a man in conflict, the humanitarian with the soldier. Drooglever suggests that Durnford's family tradition of military service might have "forced [him] into a career that did not suit his temperament" (1992:251). While this description accords with our views of integrity, it does not seem to be how Frances Colenso saw matters. Within her ethos, she seems to have found no contradictions between the actions of the man and the soldier.

All accounts of events, by participants and historians alike, are inevitably, but not necessarily consciously, coloured by a particular point of view. In both of the narratives published here, Frances Colenso's account is angled so as to glorify Durnford. Whether or not one agrees with her, the battle-heroics in *Five Years Later* make stirring reading.

The contrast between these simply presented heroics and the quieter, more complex focus of *My Chief and I* also illuminates other narrative decisions that Frances Colenso made. Her primary one was that the task of blocking the mountain passes should be the central action of her narrative. Now, it is a task which seems somewhat ridiculous—the horse had already bolted. In her day, it was a strange focus for a vindication of Durnford, who had been vilified in the colony for military incompetence. At first it seems odd that she should have concentrated on Durnford's mundane work as a roads engineer when the obvious way of rescuing his military reputation would have been to retell the story of the 1873 skirmish with Langalibalele's men in a way that removed all hint of blame from him. And her wish to do just this is indicated when she stages a story-telling within the story, so as to be able to re-cast these events. The fact of the skirmish arises easily enough when Durnford takes Wylde over the "ground of the disaster"(94) after the roadworkers had reached the same spot. But then, because Durnford was modest and unwilling to talk of his own exploits, she has to use Jabez as the informant who recounts the details of the clash to Wylde. Jabez Molife was one of the Sotho guides that Durnford had taken with him on the expedition (Drooglever 1992:46). This comparatively complex narrative strategy indicates how much Frances Colenso must have wished to be able to locate her narrative (and perhaps herself) directly in the events and the controversy to which she was responding. But, even if Frances Colenso's primary wish to rescue Durnford's reputation had to be squeezed into the central action, some very good reasons for concentrating on the blocking of the mountain passes can also be seen. It affords her a plausible occasion on which her surrogate, the young civilian Atherton Wylde, could be shown accompanying the soldier Durnford. It also allows her to give lengthy descriptions of the remoter regions of Natal and its peoples—such information would have had great appeal to the families of men posted to South Africa as well as to colonial and metropolitan lovers of adventure. Above all, it enables her to demonstrate that her hero embodied the imperial ideal, the combination of civic and military virtue, in which she so ardently believed. In his concern for the hundred men of the Ngwe, the Putini of her narrative, and in his determination that through these men the tribe should gain restitution for the punishment imposed on it following the Langalibalele 'rebellion', Durnford is shown to be a perfect agent of firm but benevolent imperial rule. It was such a rule which the Colenso family believed could help lead all the peoples of Natal to the full benefits of civilisation. Finally, we can see that her choice of events provides Frances Colenso with a theme (as well as a story) which established

Atherton Wylde as an integral part of her design. The rehabilitation of the Ngwe runs in parallel with that of her narrator—for both, Durnford is the key agent.

The fascinations of *My Chief and I* are manifold. In telling Durnford's story, Frances Colenso put forward criticisms of the policies and practices of the colonial government of Natal, and of the British imperial government, which are a notable, early instance of protest against racial injustice in South Africa. What makes such protest unique is that it was penned by a young woman, and one who lived in the colony of Natal itself. For such reasons the story behind the story of *My Chief and I* is as fascinating as the book itself. It is one which brings together heroism, high-level intrigue and farce. It was sufficiently well known (if in distorted form) in Natal and in Britain to have needed little explanation in the 1880s. For today's reader, however, the events, the personalities, and the issues need rather more. They and Frances Colenso's treatment of Durnford will occupy the next sections of this Introduction. In the final section, the place of her work in South African writing will be considered.

*   *   *

Of the four key personalities who affect this narrative—Frances Colenso herself; her father, Bishop Colenso; his erstwhile friend, Theophilus Shepstone; and Anthony Durnford—only Durnford is given any fullness of treatment in the writing. But even in his case the factual basis of the story is assumed to obviate any accounting for his presence in Natal. Only the presence of the fictional narrator, Atherton Wylde, is explained. He comes to Natal in disgrace and recovers under Durnford's patronage, a sequence which forms a curious echo of Durnford's own story for, as a young soldier, he too had been a compulsive gambler and he too was rescued by a mentor—General 'Chinese' Gordon.

Frances Ellen Colenso, the second daughter of John William Colenso and Sarah Frances Colenso (Bunyon), was born in 1849 in Norfolk. When her father was appointed to the new Anglican Bishopric of Natal in 1853, the whole family (her elder sister Harriette Emily and her brothers, Francis Ernest and Robert John) moved to the colony. The youngest child, Agnes Mary, was born shortly after their arrival. They settled at Bishopstowe, some six miles outside Pietermaritzburg, which was then a small garrison town and the colony's capital. There the Bishop established the mission station, *Ekukhanyeni* (the Place of Light). Apart from a short period at school in England, 1862–1865,

Frances was, like her sisters, educated at home. Her brothers were also educated largely at home; good tutors were difficult to find in Natal so that, as Mrs Colenso says in a letter, they were often "quite on their father's hands . . . as to their studies" (Rees 1958:189). In 1869, both sons went to university in England. Francis became a lawyer and, on his marriage to an English woman, settled in Norwich where he worked for an insurance firm in which his mother's family had an interest; Robert, who married a Canadian-born Scottish woman, had a medical practice in Durban.

The Colenso daughters did not marry. They were active as teachers at the mission school and in following their own intellectual and artistic interests— but always at home. Financial considerations, the proprieties of the day and the meagre cultural resources of a small colonial society seem to have restricted their lives. Mrs Colenso's letters indicate her regret that her daughters had to be denied the friendships and opportunities they would have enjoyed in England, but her letters also suggest that theirs was an intellectually vigorous household. The origins of the family's energy were maternal as much as paternal for Sarah Frances Bunyon was a woman of considerable learning. During their engagement she introduced her fiancé to the religious writing of S. T. Coleridge and the theology of F. D. Maurice and Colenso found himself strongly drawn to the humanitarian universalism and the practical endeavour that Maurice advocated. His wife's influence also led to one of the earliest instances of Colenso's fearless disregard for himself (and others in his family) in pursuing his beliefs when, shortly before leaving for Natal, he dedicated his first published collection of sermons to Maurice. In doing so, he paid no attention to the fact that Maurice was considered a dangerous thinker by conservative theologians in the established Church (Guy 1983:43). He was to show a similar disregard for vested interests when, ten years later, he incurred the anger of the Anglican establishment by publishing his arguments that the Pentateuch was what he called "a series of fables" (quoted in Guy 1983:108). The story was notorious in its day, and has often been told since, of how the questions about Biblical truth raised by the Bishop's Zulu converts (he himself named William Ngidi as a key questioner) joined with his own deliberations on such matters and prompted him to begin, in 1862, the publication of his controversial seven-volume study of the Pentateuch.

The Bishop's capacity to learn from others, coupled with his willingness to incur controversy, meant that while the lives of his wife and daughters were dominated by his needs, theirs was not the pattern experience of being rendered passive under patriarchal rule. Instead, in adult life they found themselves actively engaged in all of his concerns. (This may be why Frances Colenso seems to have felt equipped to project herself, disguised but without a sense of undue trespass, into the all-male world of *My Chief and I*.) There were often practical reasons for the Colenso women's involvement in the Bishop's affairs. For example, although he had, immediately after arriving in Natal, made the first systematic study of the Zulu language, his daughters Harriette and Agnes were better Zulu linguists than he (amongst the Zulu people, Harriette was called *udhlwedhlwe*—her father's staff). Therefore their help was vital to him when he fought for the rights of two Chiefs, Langalibalele and Cetshwayo, from 1873 until his death ten years later. Mrs Colenso's letters of this period frequently mention the family's combined efforts in compiling the "Digests" (reports and commentaries) that were printed at Bishopstowe and sent to influential people and organisations in England so that the Zulu cause might be understood. Passages such as this (in which Mrs Colenso's spelling has been retained) suggest the spirit in which they worked:

> It certainly does exasperate me to hear from people at home, my Brother to wit, that he does not agree with us about Cetewayo. What can he know? The lies of Sir Bartle Frere and sundry interested persons, supporters of his, have been fully investigated and exposed by the Bishop and his Daughter [Harriette] and many others, and really we know the King and many of his people. You cannot think how much time and what pains have been expended in this house searching into every thing connected with the history of Cetewayo and of Zululand before, during, and since the late war. (Rees 1958:362–3)

Frances was in Europe for part of this time (October 1879 – October 1881) but she was quite as active in the family's cause as her sisters. During the voyage to England, she began the two-volume *History of the Zulu War and its Origins* which was published in 1880, a few months after *My Chief and I*. In writing both works, she had the assistance of Anthony Durnford's brother, Lieut-Colonel Edward Durnford. Her two-volume *The Ruin of Zululand: An Account of British Doings in Zululand Since the Invasion of 1879* which was written at her father's expressed wish, was begun after his death in 1883 and published in 1884 and 1885. A third volume was completed, but not published.

Her journey to Europe after the disastrous Anglo-Zulu war of 1879 was made because, in her mother's gentle phrase, "Fanny . . . wants change" (Rees 1958:345).[2] It is a protective phrase used to conceal her daughter's grief over Durnford's death. What Mrs Colenso could not know at the time of writing was that the illness which would lead to Frances's early death had probably already begun to affect her. Just before the outbreak of war, Frances had, with her friend Helen Shepstone, nursed a young British soldier who had died of consumption before being able to join his regiment in Natal. This was in 1878, but it was only after her return from Europe in 1881 that her family realised that she was suffering from tuberculosis. Frances died in 1887.

Propriety prevented Mrs Colenso from acknowledging the relationship between Frances and Anthony Durnford. By today's account they loved each other, but, as he was a married man and could not, as a professional soldier, hope to divorce his wife (from whom he had long been separated) they could not acknowledge their attachment. The family's published correspondence reveals nothing of a special relationship, and it is only as her own death approached that Frances allowed herself, in her letters to her mother, to speak directly of what she had felt and of the loss she suffered in 1879. In an unpublished letter of 1885, she writes from England, knowing that her family did not altogether approve of her dwelling on the sorrow of Durnford's death:

> I think I feel its loss, and regret more passionately the days when I had it and only half prized it, every year I live, as I grow older, and realise more fully what life *might* have been to me by this time but for the loss of a noble life, and the preservation of an unworthy one. (Natal Archives, Colenso Collection, Box 4)

It is probably her failure to clear Durnford's reputation after Chelmsford had implicated him in the disaster at Isandlwana which colours Frances Colenso's self-criticism. The knowledge of her own approaching death (which her family had not yet fully apprehended) probably also underlies the emphasis she gave to "what life *might* have been."

Anthony Durnford entered the Colenso family circle at a time when they found themselves increasingly isolated because of the Bishop's public support of Langalibalele. The two men shared similar views and ideals. They saw a strong sense of duty and personal honour, self-discipline, courage, humility and authority as the qualities necessary for the Christian missionary and the imperial soldier alike. Durnford was clearly regarded with affection by the whole family. In one of her last letters home, Frances recalls a special gesture of affection that she sometimes saw her father use when speaking to him; Harriette, in a letter to her grandmother, mentions him as "a new friend of ours, of whom you shall hear more" (Rees 1958:275) and Mrs Colenso often writes of "our Colonel Durnford".

Durnford was forty-two when he arrived in Natal and Frances twenty-three; he had had postings in countries such as Ceylon, Malta and Gibraltar but had not seen active service. Like Atherton Wylde, he seems to have been an impulsive, injudicious young man, and to have regained moral and spiritual strength through a mentor-figure. As an engineer, he was put in charge of roadworks in the colony, and was soon also employed in a civil capacity as Colonial Engineer. It was work that he thoroughly enjoyed. In view of the claim in *My Chief and I* that the opportunity to work under his guidance was a valued opening for a young man, it is interesting that Mrs Colenso's letters mention that Frank Lyell, the son of one of her correspondents, did in fact work with Durnford in 1874 and was "put . . . in charge of 40 of the rescued slaves" (Rees 1958:288). This snippet suggests, too, that the figure and experiences of Atherton Wylde were not entirely imaginary. All in all, Frances Colenso's presentation of Durnford, though avowedly adulatory, seems consistent with other sources of information: he was an idealist with an overriding sense of duty and a belief in the superiority of the 'true' English gentleman. The potentially humanitarian streak which the Bishop found so appealing is evident in a letter written soon after his arrival in the eastern Cape (before he reached Natal). In it he says of the Xhosa people, with whom the British army had been fighting an intermittent border war for nearly thirty years, "the people are at least honest, chivalrous and hospitable, true to their salt, although only barbarians. They are fine men, very naked and all that sort of thing, but thoroughly good fellows" (Durnford 1882:4).

In his stern refusal to compromise, Durnford was very different from the person that Theophilus Shepstone, the other major figure in the Colenso world at this time, seems to have been. Although he appears in Chapter 5, "The Minister for Native Affairs", Shepstone is not named in *My Chief and I*. His actions after the Langalibalele 'uprising' were an important influence on the mood of the narrative for Frances Colenso shared her family's anger over what they saw as Shepstone's betrayal of principle in putting settler interests above those of the original inhabitants of the colony. When the Bishop learned that Shepstone had actively discouraged the witnesses who could have explained to the court why Langalibalele was fearful of appearing when summoned to Pietermaritzburg, there was an abrupt and irrevocable break in their eighteen-year-old friendship. To some extent, Durnford seems to have filled the space in the family circle that was left by this break.

Shepstone was born in England, near Bristol. His father took up mission work soon after arriving in the eastern Cape with the 1820 settlers and, from the age of three, Shepstone was raised amongst the Xhosa people. He spoke their language fluently. When his career took him to Natal (he settled there in 1845), he set about learning Zulu with characteristic thoroughness and was said to have spoken it with a Xhosa accent. He soon made himself known throughout the country as one whose advice on 'Native policy' was invaluable. Frances Colenso's picture of him as a "Zulu despot in the midst of his savage retainers" (29) uses the exaggerations of the satirist to show her distrust of his imitation of tribal manners. But, as Secretary for Native Affairs in the colony, he does seem to have been an able and ambitious politician as well as being a secretive man of carefully cultivated dignity, a survivor who understood the political uses of expediency and adaptation. In comparison to him, Durnford seems to have been a steadfast, sensitive but uncompromising idealist. As can often happen, Durnford was picturing himself when he wrote admiringly of Colenso, "The Bishop is a man of men—[he] would go to his death for the *right*" (Durnford 1882:11); it is this moral conviction joined with an heroic sense of honour which seems to have set the Bishop and Durnford apart from Shepstone.

On the other hand Shepstone was an able man, as the following account of events in Natal will show. When he went to England in order to defend Natal's handling of the Langalibalele 'rebellion', he clearly impressed Lord Carnarvon with his vision and diplomatic skills.

*   *   *

The context of the events covered in *My Chief and I* is one in which many different interest groups can be seen to combine and collide. Among these groups were the Zulu nation led by their new King, Cetshwayo; Langalibalele and his Hlubi people; their neighbours, the Ngwe; the Colenso family; Natal's white colonists with their economic problems and racial prejudice; the Natal Government, which, under its newly arrived Lieutenant-Governor, Sir Benjamin Pine, was trying to attain greater independence from Britain; Shepstone who, with his locations policy (special settlement areas for African people living in Natal), was something of a law unto himself; Lord Carnarvon in London with his dream of a South African confederation; Durnford and the British military forces garrisoned at Fort Napier in Pietermaritzburg.

The angers which surfaced in the Langalibalele affair had, like most of the colony's problems, an economic base. To understand why Durnford was ordered to block the Drakensberg passes, why the Ngwe were severely punished for the actions of the Hlubi, and why Langalibalele was subjected to a trial, the conduct of which caused consternation in Britain as well as in the Colenso family, it is necessary to go back almost thirty years.

In 1848 the Hlubi, who had once formed a large and powerful chiefdom in Zululand, fled from the Zulu King, Mpande (the father of Cetshwayo), across the Thukela and into Natal. Led by Langalibalele, they crossed into the colony with all their cattle and settled in the Klip River district of northern Natal. Some eighteen months later they were moved by the Natal Government, acting on the advice of Theophilus Shepstone, to an area of 90 000 acres in the foothills of the Drakensberg where they were to act as a buffer between the white farmers and the San (Bushmen) cattle raiders. There they came under the jurisdiction of the Resident Magistrate, John MacFarlane, of Weenen County—it is his household which Durnford and Atherton Wylde visit on their way through Estcourt. Frances Colenso lays some emphasis on John MacFarlane's being a temperate man. At least in her picture he is more reasonable than his brother Walter, who, as speaker of the Natal Legislative Council, was on record as playing up racial fears when campaigning amongst the white electorate of Estcourt. His characteristic call was for a more effective militia for Natal and for the Council to take steps to end the shortage of (cheap) African labour.

Underlying all the factors which led to conflict between Langalibalele and the authorities in Natal was the labour question. On leaving Zululand, the Hlubi had had to enter the cash-based economy of the colony for, once in Natal, they were required to pay taxes and rents of various kinds. In this and in their task of protecting the colony's frontier, they were reasonably successful. As they prospered as farmers where they had been settled, they were understandably reluctant to work elsewhere for white farmers. Thus their successes served not to satisfy but to annoy the colonists. Moreover, as the *Natal Witness* put it in 1869, these peasant farmers were "coming into competition with the white man and [were] fairly beating them in the markets" (quoted in Manson 1979:19). The markets in question were created by the discovery of diamonds, in 1868, in Griqualand West. The white farmers of Natal had hoped to take advantage of this development, but without a supply of cheap black labour they could not do so. Rather than labouring on farms, many Hlubi men preferred work on the diamond fields where they were able, as direct or indirect payment, to obtain guns.

Although permission was sometimes given for these men to keep their guns, the Natal Executive Council seems to have been alarmed by rumours of the deliberate accumulation of firearms in the locations and of a planned uprising. The resident magistrates were reminded that all firearms had to be registered and John MacFarlane duly ordered Langalibalele to instruct his men to bring in their weapons. Despite repeated instructions, the Chief failed to comply with these orders to MacFarlane's satisfaction and eventually he was ordered to report in person to Shepstone in Pietermaritzburg. When the Chief failed yet again to obey, his shuffling amounted to "gross indiscipline, indeed rebellion" (Brookes & Webb 1965:113) in the eyes of the colony. From the Hlubi point of view, there was good reason to distrust the colonial authorities as they had found that guns sent in for registration were often returned damaged or not returned at all. They also remembered that some years earlier another chief, Matshana, had responded to similar orders and had been taken by suprise when the white official concerned (Shepstone's brother) produced a gun and attempted to arrest him. Several tribesmen were killed. But this distrust might have been overcome were it not for one of the "tragic misunderstandings" (Etherington 1978:24) which precipitated the confrontation at Bushman's River Pass. By an unlucky coincidence, the annual northern camp of the Natal Volunteer corps was held near Estcourt in June 1873 and Langalibalele thought that the military exercises were a threat directed at his people.

On the settlers' side, rumours that Langalibalele (who was connected by marriage with several powerful chiefs and who was revered throughout the region for his powers as 'Rainmaker') was planning a general insurrection, caused several farmers' families to leave the district. Moved by the "almost hysterical public opinion" (Brookes & Webb 1965:114) against Langalibalele, the Executive Council of Natal judged it necessary to teach the Chief a lesson. But, because Shepstone wanted no disturbances while he was arranging a coronation for Cetshwayo, nothing was done for the next two months. Then, after an ultimatum to Langalibalele produced no results, Pine issued a proclamation, on 11 November, which outlawed the chief. Finally, to prevent Langalibalele's escape, a large armed force composed of British troops, volunteers from the Natal Carbineers and several thousand African troops, and accompanied by Shepstone and Pine himself, was sent out against him.

The plan was to surround the Hlubi lands, to prevent the men escaping to Lesotho over the Drakensberg mountains with their cattle and so to bring Langalibalele to book. The section of the force under Durnford's command, was, as Atherton Wylde says, to form part of a pincers movement which would meet at the top of the Bushman's River Pass and so prevent the Chief's escaping that way. This pass was one up which cattle could fairly easily be driven. While the plan might have been good, the maps given to the pursuing colonial forces proved to be useless. Durnford, after a terrible journey during which he was injured when his horse fell, eventually arrived with two-thirds of his men at the top of the Bushman's River Pass, but was too late to stop Langalibalele. As the other half of the pincer movement, under Captain Allison, did not find its way up the mountains at all, Durnford and his men were alone in attempting to turn back those Hlubi men who were still coming up the pass with their cattle. Durnford had been instructed by Pine not to fire the first shot. As the men faced each other and tension mounted, the Zulu-speaking Carbineers, understanding the increasing ferocity of the Hlubi threats better than Durnford could, grew anxious and pressured him to give the order for a retreat. When he did so, the Hlubi took the troops' movements as an opportunity to open fire. Four men were killed: three Carbineers—Troopers Erskine, Potteril and Bond—and Elijah Khambule, Durnford's translator. The retreat then became "disorganised and precipitate", in the words of the judgment of the Court of Enquiry (Pearse *et al* 1973:69). Durnford later claimed that he managed to rally only his Sotho guides in order to halt the pursuing tribesmen. He stated that he saw some individual acts of bravery, but that most of his white troops simply fled back to the pass they had ascended. The details of what happened were vigorously contested by all involved. Several of the Carbineers, including their senior officer, Captain Barter, published their version of events in Natal newspapers (these are reprinted in Pearse *et al* 1973) but Durnford, as was required of a professional soldier, maintained public silence, reporting only to his commanding officer. The colony was horrified, particularly by the loss of life and the implication that the Carbineers had been cowardly, and publicly blamed Durnford for the disaster.

In the weeks which followed, the Hlubi people who had remained in Natal were hunted from their hiding places and were, it seems, often ruthlessly killed. One Carbineer recounted, in a letter that was published in the *Times of Natal* on November 15, 1873, that twenty volunteers came across "one fellow in a cave [who had] loaded his rifle with stones." When they "got him out . . . Moodie shot him through the brains." The writer's boast was: "We are gradually wiping out the three poor fellows who were shot; and all our men are determined to have some more." Although this paper's editorials supported such action against the Hlubi and punishment of the Ngwe (Colenso 1874:175), not everyone in Natal was as bloodthirsty. In a letter published in its next issue, another volunteer comments "it is by no means an honourable warfare, a few wretched men and women in holes and bushes, offering little, if any resistance, attacked by *hundreds*; certainly no *glory* can be got by it!"

This sense of shame was shared by Durnford, as is to be seen in the representation in *My Chief and I* of his response to the spread of colonial anger from the Hlubi to their neighbours, the Ngwe, who were accused of having aided the rebels. The colonists were persuaded that the Ngwe had thousands of Hlubi cattle hidden amongst their herds and were angered when Mbalo, the chief, did not produce them on demand. A 'sweeping' of the location followed. The men of the tribe were imprisoned, their lands and cattle confiscated and the women and children either left to fend for themselves or distributed amongst other 'loyal' tribes. There was a plan to put each adult into three years' forced servitude and much of the land, like that of the Hlubi people, was sold to white farmers. It was these measures which Durnford attempted to counteract by proving that when employed on roadworks, the Ngwe men were reliable and obedient, and that the tribe warranted restitution. It was also these measures that Lord Carnarvon, guided in part by Bishop Colenso's arguments, condemned most roundly in his dispatches to Pine, in December 1874. (Frances Colenso quotes part of this despatch in Chapter 16.)

Langalibalele's trial began on 16 January 1874, immediately following his capture in Lesotho, in mid-December 1873. After the Hlubi had been six weeks on the run, it was a Sotho Chief, Molapo, who betrayed them to the pursuing authorities. Langalibalele, his sons and several of his men were marched, in chains, to Pietermaritzburg, but one man did escape from captivity—the induna, Mabuhle [Mabudhle], with whom Durnford had exchanged "love tokens" (24) at Bushman's River Pass and regarded as "a brave man and one worthy of his steel" (79).

The manner in which Langalibalele's trial was conducted was what first alarmed Bishop Colenso. For it, most of the rules of procedure in British law and in what the colony understood to be tribal custom seem to have been ignored. The prisoners were made to plead but were not allowed counsel; all the witnesses were selected by the prosecution and were not cross-examined (Guy 1983:207). Pine, having outlawed Langalibalele before heading the military expedition against him and having also appointed himself Supreme Chief for the hearing, opened the proceedings. His address suggested that he had presumed the verdict, and its basis in fact, in advance of the court's findings. Even at the time, the horror of what was happening was evident to ordinary people in Natal; one colonist wrote privately that the trial was "the most wonderful case of blunders I can conceive possible for men past infancy to have made" (Guest 1976:63). Found guilty, Langalibalele and one of his sons were banished for life to Robben Island, six other sons and two hundred tribesmen were imprisoned. At this point of the farce, Durnford was sent back to the Drakensberg to block not just the pass that Langalibalele had used, but all of them; at this point too, Atherton Wylde arrives in Natal.

The British Government was clearly disturbed by the trial. The Governor, Sir

Benjamin Pine, was held responsible for Natal's mishandling of the Langalibalele 'outbreak' and was recalled; Carnarvon, deciding that the self-governing
status Natal had been seeking was inopportune, sent out Sir Garnet Wolseley as
Administrator with the task of steering Natal back to Crown Colony status. This
relationship to Britain would, he believed, make the colony's acceptance of a
future confederation of states in South Africa easier to ensure.

It was during Langalibalele's trial that the Colenso family's friendship with
Shepstone came to an abrupt end. Shortly after, when a petition asking that
Langalibalele be allowed to appeal against the sentence of banishment was
prepared, Colenso learned, through his Zulu assistants Magema Fuze and
William Ngidi, and through the Hlubi people who had taken refuge at
Bishopstowe, that the tribal elders who had signed the petition had been bullied,
intimidated and even threatened with jail by Shepstone and his men.

For many years, Colenso had believed that Shepstone's policies were based
on his own view of the common humanity of all people. He thought that as
Secretary for Native Affairs, Shepstone sought to lead the black people living in
the locations to their "rights as men & British subjects" (quoted in Guy
1983:204). These two men had often stood alone when colonial opinion was
either suspicious of the missionary Bishop's teaching that all people are equal,
or was angry with Shepstone's locations policy which, because it allocated
African people land on which they could be relatively self-sufficient, was held
to perpetuate the labour shortage. At first, therefore, Colenso was concerned
only because he believed that Pine (who was an indecisive man) was being used
to stir up confrontation by the party advocating responsible government for
Natal. This group would have found an 'outbreak' a useful opportunity for
damaging Shepstone's locations policy in order to bring about an increase in the
number of black labourers available in the colony. Once, however, he had
evidence of Shepstone's complicity in the "eating up" of the Hlubi and the
punishment of the Ngwe, Colenso was forced to accept that Shepstone's
policies did not have the interests of the African people at their core. He came to
see that in fact these policies were likely to prevent African people in Natal from
moving out of their tribal conditions. As Rees puts it: "whereas Shepstone was
solely interested in the tribal native, the Bishop was equally, if not more,
concerned about the Zulu who wished to become de-tribalised, to identify
himself with the white man's culture, and to integrate himself with the white
man's society" (1958:308). In the light of the break between the two men, their
African names seem peculiarly prescient: Colenso's was 'Sobantu' which
translates as 'Father of the People' while Shepstone's was 'Somtsewu' which
translates as 'Father of Whiteness' (Guy 1983: 198).

Despite the grief Colenso felt at the "failure . . . of truth and justice" in a man he had loved, he was, as his wife reported, now convinced that his opposition to Shepstone would have to be "war to the knife" (Rees 1958:283). When Colenso decided to go to London to plead Langalibalele's case, he was once again careless of his own interests. Following his controversial commentaries on the Pentateuch and following his lengthy legal battle against Bishop Gray of Cape Town who attempted to remove him from his Natal office in the 1860s, Colenso was receiving very little financial support from missionary bodies in London and had a much diminished circle of friends in the colony. Nevertheless, as one colonist said at the time, "When he had little left to lose he risked that little for their (the Africans') sakes" (Brookes & Webb 1965:112).

Although he had some success in his fight for the Hlubi and Ngwe people, Colenso must sometimes have felt that his efforts counted for little. Worse was to come. In the next four years, he was to see Britain embark on a war against Cetshwayo and the Zulu nation which he regarded as quite unjustified and a betrayal of "the sense of justice and right which defined the true Englishman" (Guy 1983:284). When he died in 1883, it must have been with the knowledge that despite his and his family's courage and sacrifices, his values and objectives (the missionary endeavour and the imperial example which were to teach a higher way of life to the Zulu people) had not been furthered in Natal. Twice in one decade, Bishop Colenso had felt himself called to defend an African chief who was a victim of the schemes of British officials in South Africa. He held Pine to be ultimately responsible for Langalibalele's banishment and Sir Bartle Frere, High Commissioner for South Africa, for Cetshwayo's. In each case, it was Sir Garnet Wolseley who was sent out to ensure that Britain's decisions were implemented as swiftly as possible. If the Colenso family had thought Shepstone was unprincipled, they thought this man far worse. Colenso wrote, in September 1879, that Wolseley's decision to banish Cetshwayo to Robben Island was "the crowning act of infamy to this iniquitous war" (Guy 1983:285).

In view of the comparative defeat of principle and ideal in the Bishop's life, Shepstone's fortunes after the Langalibalele 'outbreak' are also worth noting. Like Bishop Colenso, he went to London in 1874 where his presentation of Natal's case to Lord Carnarvon clearly impressed the Secretary of State. While Natal's Governor, Pine, was censured, his adviser, Shepstone, was given a knighthood; while Colenso's arguments were accepted, it was to Shepstone's advice that Carnarvon really attended. Impressed by his diplomatic skills and plans for the subcontinent, Carnarvon gave him the task of bringing the

Transvaal under British influence so as to make it, like Natal, amenable to the idea of confederation. (Carnarvon's scheme was ended by the Anglo-Zulu War of 1879 and the first Anglo-Boer War of 1881.)

In the long run however, Shepstone, who believed he 'knew' that curious colonial entity 'the native mind', must have been a disappointed man. Once he had annexed the Transvaal and was appointed its Administrator, his official function in Natal came to an end and, after three decades of rule, he ceased to be able to affect 'Native policy'. His new role in the Transvaal kept him in the thick of events for a time. It occasioned his remarkable about-face on the question of land rights, for Shepstone suddenly ceased to champion Zulu claims to an area of north-western Natal and supported the Boer farmers' attempts to obtain it. As Frances Colenso relates in *Five Years Later*, when a Land Commission considered the rival claims in 1878, judgment went in favour of the Zulu. Sir Bartle Frere managed to delay the announcement of the Commission's findings for six months and then to mask its implications in the ultimatum that he sent to Cetshwayo. This demanded an immediate and complete reorganisation of Zulu society, especially the military clan system. It was an unmistakable sign that war was intended.

As Shepstone's son, George, was killed at Isandlwana, the war must have been a sad event for him personally; a year later he himself was pensioned. Then, for the deliberations leading to the settlement after the war, Sir Henry Bulwer, the new Lieut-Governor of Natal, called him in as an adviser. He was firmly against the restoration of Cetshwayo, but at the same time he disagreed with Wolseley's proposed settlement of Zululand (it was to be divided into thirteen districts, each ruled by an appointed chief) on the grounds that it left the territory independent. But his advice was ignored by the Colonial Office, largely because the alternative he favoured was the expensive one of annexing Zululand. He was also alarmed by Wolseley's recognising the independence of the Transvaal for it threatened his "dream that British rule, through the agency of the colony of Natal, would extend northwards" (Guy 1983:315).

*   *   *

For much of *My Chief and I*, Frances Colenso's representation of Durnford and what he stood for entails a lively rendering of the attitudes and political interests current in Natal. One of the means by which she registers the colony's harmonies and dissonances is in her use of the title 'Chief'. Its source is tribal, military, religious, sexual and paternal and its use in the narrative indicates the way that the colony's interest groups must have interacted.

But at times the picture of Durnford thins down considerably and in the *Sequel* all but one of the dimensions of Frances Colenso's presentation have gone—the polemic is now single-minded and her Chief is seen simply as a man of heroic destiny. A rule of thumb which may explain this reduction is that the more confidence Frances Colenso felt in British justice and truth, the more presence she could give to the range of interests at work in the drama she was handling. This pattern would also explain why she sometimes draws attention to Atherton Wylde's gauche personality, thereby allowing her reader to attribute the idealism in the picture of Durnford to her narrator's youthful excess. Placing the tone of the praise in this way is to acknowledge that an author's feelings and attitudes may differ considerably from those of the characters and narrator that he or she creates. But the excess in a passage like this cannot be as comfortably contained:

> Gallant soldier! kind and courteous gentleman! There was not one amongst us—officer or man—who would not have followed him to certain death, or have gladly died in his defence, for we all loved as well as respected him. I might fill many pages with stories which would prove how well he earned our affection, what thoughtful care he exercised over our welfare, how kind, firm, and judicious was his treatment of us, so that never did one of his men fear to go to him for advice or help, nor dare to face him with a guilty conscience. (2)

It is a passage in which the author, not just the narrator, takes many risks; today, the adulation expressed in it speaks of complex needs. Frances Colenso must have believed that her use of a male narrator made it safe to venture declarations of the kind implied here. Otherwise, using a willingness to die (which is a long established literary metaphor for the fulfilment of sexual passion) as the index of loyalty to Durnford would have been unthinkable. Most commentators have been content to ascribe this ardour to 'poor Fanny's love' for Durnford, but the highly charged rhetoric, the invocation of chivalry, the confident use of absolutes, the blend of childlike respect with brave camaraderie all suggest that more than love, romantic as well as sexual, is the basis of such writing. The chafing of an ardent spirit in the confines of her womanly role may explain some of its excess, so too may Frances Colenso's personality (her mother's letters suggest that she was given to intense and lasting friendships with women as well as men), but even these possibilities cannot fully account for the note of strange, brave yearning that is struck in this writing.

When Atherton Wylde reports on matters in Natal, there is no tendency to idealise. As one might expect, what strikes him most forcibly is colonial bigotry and ignorance. He is surely speaking directly for his author when he observes of the perennial labour problem that "it was the old story; the black man did not care to be the white man's slave, and the white man could not endure the black man in any other position" (46). But Frances Colenso does not use him simply as her mouthpiece. She clearly enjoyed the opportunity to play with the idea of Natal as a moral sanitarium for delinquent young Englishmen and she is sometimes equally playful with Atherton Wylde's personality. Although he is deeply self-critical when he first arrives in Natal, a metropolitan sense of his innate superiority makes him not at all hesitant to condemn colonial self-importance. This ironic interplay of attitudes is often Frances Colenso's way of guiding her reader's judgment. For example, when Wylde questions the passengers in the coach to Pietermaritzburg about Langalibalele's being called "a bloodthirsty old rebel" (35) it is clear that he is attacking colonial prejudice. But then, when Wylde hears Durnford himself speak of "my rebels" (meaning the much wronged Ngwe), he does not recognise his Chief's ironic echo of the colonial label. He himself is caught up in prejudice when he longs for a fight against these "rebels" because it would enable him to rush valiantly to his Chief's rescue.

The narrative's targets are also sometimes unexpected. In Chapter 2 for example, even Durnford becomes a source of amusement when he engineers a mass marriage for the rescued slaves with the same efficiency that he would have shown in organising a road-working party. And then Wylde's own excesses are exposed to laughter when he defends Durnford's honour in the hotel diningroom in Estcourt. Frances Colenso uses a light touch for the narrative picture of herself too, when she gives a glimpse of the Bishop's daughter who, being "a lady [could not] . . . take part in a discussion with these rough men" (17) during the bus journey to Pietermaritzburg. She takes the greatest of her playful chances when she has Atherton Wylde comment, after the curious marriage of the rescued slaves, that, although he had been inclined to laugh at first, by its end "I could not have felt less inclined to laugh at my own wedding than I did at this" (9).

Had Frances Colenso been able to sustain such a lively sense of the tensions in her characters and their relationships, she might, given her insight into issues in the colony, have used her fictional methods to produce a work of great wisdom. As it is, when she turns to special pleading for Durnford the earlier liveliness of her presentation is overwhelmed by despair and a barely sublimated sexual passion. This has its own great interest and appeal, and it would be facile to suggest (as has often been done) that Frances Colenso's feelings for Durnford simply ran away with her. Understanding the forces at work in a text as remarkable as *My Chief and I* demands a more consciously historical effort. It requires too a willingness to speculate, perhaps even to intrude, on the underlying elements of a Colenso daughter's responses to her world.

The pressures on the Colenso family ethos in the decade following the Langalibalele affair were very great indeed. 1880, the year that *My Chief and I* appeared, marks a turning point in their judgment of Britain's role in Natal's affairs. Jeff Guy has outlined the Bishop's disillusionment; it must have been shared by his wife and children as they saw the failure of their ideals to guide imperial action:

> . . . the war, in destroying twelve thousand lives, had also destroyed the meaning in Colenso's life. The fact that the invasion had been initiated and prosecuted by Britain, negated the basic principles upon which his political, moral and religious existence was founded. (1983:286)

Her father's example is clearly the strongest influence on Frances Colenso's presentation of the man she loved and of the colony where he died. For this reason, it is important to note that Bishop Colenso did not set himself against war as such; it was the injustices of a particular war that led to his protest. Her writing suggests that Frances Colenso, like her father, did not think war to be inherently unjust. She too accepted that the military side of empire-building could be compatible with its civilising thrust and that the soldier and the missionary could unite in common cause. The conjunction on which her beliefs rested is evident in a phrase she gives to Atherton Wylde when he says that, having seen the terrain at Bushman's River Pass where Durnford's troops clashed with the Hlubi warriors, "I found that I could most thoroughly coincide with *those of my own cloth* who, having seen the place, asserted that the Colonel had been perfectly right . . ." (234, emphasis added). Here may be sensed Frances Colenso's blending of Durnford with her father, of the military calling with the pastoral. Here too is a sign that Frances Colenso may have allowed her veneration of her father to sanction her feelings for Durnford.

That Frances Colenso did not write simply as her father's daughter is, however, also evident. For example, Atherton Wylde accepts polygamy with a thoughtless alacrity which no Colenso could have displayed. Polygamy was such a contentious issue in British missionary and colonial circles that to raise it at all was risky. Although he did not approve of polygamy, Bishop Colenso had

incurred the wrath of other missionaries by refusing to demand that Zulu men
who wished to convert to Christianity should cast off all but one of their wives.
His argument that this would be to destroy the fabric of African life is an
example of the humanism he had taken from Coleridge and Maurice, and this is
what had led him to try to build on the moral sensibilities already present in a
person rather than to see conversion as demanding an absolutely fresh start. In
the guise of Atherton Wylde, however, Frances Colenso allows herself to
contemplate a much easier approach. When he meets Hlubi's wives, Wylde
employs none of the weighty considerations which guided Colenso, he simply
concedes that the favourite wife was "decidedly the best looking" (105). It is a
callow but sensible response; it suggests that Frances Colenso knew very well
how to enjoy the speculative freedom with which the writing of fiction provided
her.

The relationship of an issue such as polygamy to the Colenso family's larger
sense of their mission is also interesting to trace. As Jeff Guy has argued,
although Colenso believed in the common humanity of all people, and in the
potential for spiritual virtue in a heathen people, his thinking was not egalitarian
in the postmodern way. He was of his Darwinian age in his belief that just as
life-forms progressed up the evolutionary scale, so some human cultures had
achieved superiority over others. It is for this reason that he could accept talk of
'barbarians'; it is probably also why Frances Colenso seems to have felt no
difficulty in having Wylde comment that the rescued east-African slaves might
be "naturally inferior" to the Zulu people who were "far better-looking and
more intelligent" (10). Although Colenso's humanism may seem to us to have
its limitations, his wish to raise a heathen people to the higher standard of
civilisation which Britain represented seemed revolutionary in the Natal of his
day. There, black people were tolerated only as a source of cheap labour. It was
in the face of such attitudes that the family preferred to live in the relative
isolation of Bishopstowe from where Mrs Colenso wrote with amusement as
well as regret of their "social excommunication" (Rees 1958:370).

This literal, physical distance between themselves and Natal's capital would
seem to have translated very readily into an ironic vision of the colony's affairs;
the isolation it brought could also help to explain a certain inflexibility or
narrowness in their approving or disapproving of particular people. To sustain
them in their isolating views and work, the family seems to have selected
certain historical figures as symbols of the strength they needed. One such
figure was Martin Luther, whom they saw as the courageous reformer of a
stultified church. Mrs Colenso explicitly draws a comparison between her
husband and Luther when she writes of his selfless religious and political
campaigns:

I don't suppose [the world] . . . can understand a man's sacrificing his own private friendships and public supporters on account of a question of wide general interest, of justice or humanity . . . . I don't believe there are many in this world who can understand his single-mindedness. Whatever he has done, whether in criticisms of the Old Testament, or his protests against the action of the Government here against this poor chief [Langalibalele], it has always been because, like Luther, *he could not do otherwise*. (Rees 1958:283)

This belief in the heroic union of a calling and a personality seems to have been a sustaining one for all members of the family. That Luther's familiar phrase was their byword for courage and dedication is evident when Frances Colenso gives Durnford a rhetorically embellished version of the same words. Explaining that, after long consideration, he did not feel responsible for the deaths of three Carbineers at Bushman's River Pass, he says: "Thinking calmly over the matter at this distance of time, I say that I could have done no otherwise" (55). The propensity to find a complex set of ideals embodied in a single person would also have been fostered by the theology of F. D. Maurice who taught that "God was already present in all mankind" and that "Christ, the perfect man, had already redeemed the world" (Guy 1983:25). These teachings were viewed in England as dangerously close to the Unitarians' heretical denial of the Trinity, but to the missionary Bishop and his family, they were a powerful support which informed their personal relationships as well as their public ones. Mrs Colenso's sister, Harriette, was also married to a missionary bishop, Bishop McDougall of Labuan. When she assessed her sister's life, Mrs Colenso wrote in revealing terms:

. . . what a martyrdom her life has been to duty and to her love for her husband. She finds support in her loyalty to one, the *One* who in the idea of Christians combines all that is pure and high and perfectly loving with the capacity of suffering which is implied in the human frame. I doubt whether we are able to conceive (vividly) of virtue or of holiness apart from these conditions. (Rees 1958:249).

This sympathetic insight into the resources on which her sister had drawn indicate the resources that Mrs Colenso herself, and probably her daughters too, must have used in supporting the Bishop. Her phrase "the *One*" consciously performs a double blending—man and God, and then husband and Christ—through which she accounts for the wifely devotion that she too has practised.

It is not unlikely that it was from her mother, as well as from her father, that Frances learned her readiness to make of Durnford a figure of virtue incarnate.

In some ways, the love that this strong woman has for Durnford echoes the feelings suggested in Charlotte Brontë's novels where characters like Jane Eyre, Shirley Keeldar and Lucy Snowe all seek a man who will recognise their equality while also possessing a strength that will master them. Charlotte Brontë did not often achieve for her women characters the self-insights that would comprehend such contradictory tendencies; as often as not they eluded Frances Colenso too. Given the family's acceptance of the right of an empire to rule its subject peoples and, at times, to do so through the military, given also their faith in the 'true' British gentleman's embodying honour and justice, it must have been difficult, if not impossible, for her to question the authority, the power, of a man like Durnford—let alone that of her father.

The means that Durnford used to uphold his authority are also not always considered critically. When Atherton Wylde describes the flogging of a waggon-driver who had not listened to Durnford's instructions, the only view taken of it is that it was a fully warranted punishment, and very effective as a deterrent to others. Again, when Durnford is shown taking responsibility for a group of ex-slaves, he is presented as simply humane in his concern for their welfare. For example, he institutes a system of reward, rather than punishment, to persuade them to be obedient. The uniform he has devised for them is a clean and sensible garb. What gives us pause for thought today is that uniforms are always devised by those in power and, as such, are a badge of servitude. These are matters which the daughter of a missionary, one whose mother had herself devised a uniform for her servants, could probably not see to interrogate.

If Frances Colenso was too much at home in her family's ideology to question some aspects of authority, there are many converse signs that while her narrative demanded that she should embody in her characters some of her society's gendered stereotypes of authority, she was barely able to do so. The narrative takes care to show that Durnford has earned his status through the discretion and control which he exercises, but even while she does this, Frances Colenso has Atherton Wylde express himself in ways which show the difficulty she had with typically male attitudes to authority:

> No man of my acquaintance has a hotter temper, nor one under more complete control: and that, I believe, is the true secret of his undeniable power over those who serve under him. I have heard his voice sound like that of an angry lion, and have seen his eyes blaze, and his face rigid with

displeasure; but only at rare intervals, and under great provocation. As a rule his reproofs are administered in a calm but decided manner, without anger or impatience, while those who receive them look as frightened as though they had seen the devil. (8)

The awkward association of calm, benevolent authority with "the devil" may be ascribed to an attempt to give Atherton Wylde a suitably manly note. But the result is one which undermines the larger claim. The confusion could also be ascribed to Wylde's personality. He is given to excess and sometimes he acknowledges this—as when he is ashamed of being jealous of the assistance that the Sotho guide, Windvogel, gives to Durnford as they climb a difficult mountain path. On balance, however, it seems likely that it is Frances Colenso's difficulty with gender stereotypes that is revealing itself. Further testimony to this likelihood comes from the feminine note in Atherton Wylde's behaviour which is a counterpart of his moments of stagey masculinity. In the scene where Wylde defends his Chief's honour by flinging down the gauntlet (in the form of a glass of wine) before a young man of Estcourt who had posted "abusive placards concerning Colonel Durnford about this town" (34), the indignation and its expression seem to come from a feminine fantasy of manliness.

It is in the presentation of Durnford's death at Isandlwana that Frances Colenso most clearly lapses into one-dimensional thinking against which not even her family ideology could protect her. She gives his death as simply a glorious moment which "covered a life which had been blighted . . . with the memory of an undying glory" (59). To some extent, this verdict on Durnford is the result of a practical problem: to give her first account of the battle, in the "Note" to Chapter 8, Frances Colenso relied on a newspaper report, that of the *Natal Witness* of May 29, 1879, which she quoted, word for word, in its entirety. Using a secondary source was necessary as Atherton Wylde was by then back in England, and she, in her own guise, could not go near the battlefield. In fact, no one, not even the Bishop, was allowed there until the military burial parties had done their work, four full months after the actual battle. In those months the colony was filled with rumours that Durnford had committed suicide on the battlefield, and Pine spoke publicly of 'poor Durnford's misfortune'. Therefore, a newspaper's scotching of rumour must have meant a lot to Frances Colenso. But, in using this report, she had to accept its limitations of perspective and judgment. A colonial newspaper, however enlightened, was not likely to take the fuller view of the war (including a sympathy for the Zulu side) which was held by the Colenso family. She could have invented a correspondent more sympathetic to the Colenso view as a source of her "Note", but then she would

not have had an opportunity to show the change in Natal in public opinion of
Durnford. Thus Durnford's death remains simply a glorious example of
imperial and colonial courage; nothing appears of the injustices of the war. The
Colenso family had felt from the beginning how wrong it was that the might of
the British Empire should be brought against a king and a nation which seemed
to be trying to maintain peaceful relations with the colony. But, by having
Atherton Wylde use a newspaper report, Frances Colenso allows none of these
complexities to appear.

In *Five Years Later*, the simplifications are even more evident; Frances
Colenso rests her account of the build-up to war on her certainty that Sir Bartle
Frere, advised by Theophilus Shepstone, actively sought war, and she stresses
Durnford's opposition to it. But then, once her narrative engages with the war
itself, she takes the easy way out of the problem of where sympathy should lie
by looking only at Durnford's military zeal and prowess. His primary duty as a
soldier is all that counts. Thus she again allows herself to convey an intensely
emotional but incomplete understanding of the meanings of Durnford's
death.

Durnford was not all that died at Isandlwana for Frances Colenso. So too did
her faith in Britain. But she does not attempt to bring together her idealising
love and the anger and grief that she must have felt over Britain's betrayal of her
family's beliefs. There are moments in her narrative when she could have done
this. For example, when she added the "Note" about Isandlwana, which she
must have done just before the book's publication, she also added a footnote
acknowledging the bravery of the Carbineers in the battle (48). But she did not
at the same time alter her original claim that racist feelings in Natal would not be
allowed to result in war against the Zulus because "our English Government at
home keeps such a vigilant watch over her colonies, to prevent unjust and
unnecessary wars" (47). Leaving this claim without qualification is strange, for
by then Frances Colenso knew that the Anglo-Zulu war marked the end of
Britain's willingness or ability to control racism in Natal.

                              *   *   *

Durnford's death at Isandlwana is not, however, as paramount in *My Chief and I*
as it had become by the time Frances Colenso wrote the *Sequel*. Rather, her
tribute to his embodying the imperial ideal rests on his civic virtues—especially
on his concern for the Ngwe. Her picture of the man in action as he supervised

the blocking of the passes over the Drakensberg and campaigned for the release of the Ngwe, also enabled her to broaden her appeal from the politics of the day to the interest that many readers in England must have had in the adventurous side of daily life in a colony. To this end, she was fortunate in having Durnford's letters to his mother from which to work; these were subsequently compiled by his brother, Edward Durnford, and published as *A Soldier's Life and Work in South Africa 1872 to 1879: a Memoir of the Late Colonel A.W. Durnford* (1882). A comparison of this work with *My Chief and I* shows that for sequences such as the work in the Amapongwana Pass, when fires had to be lit so that the men could work in short relays in the intense cold, Frances Colenso used the exact wording of Durnford's letters. Many other details are also taken from the letters, such as the description of the more permanent camp that was built at the head of the Bushman's River. On this site, the remains of the fires which the soldiers built can still be seen today, along with a large 75 (for the 75th Foot Regiment) that was carved in the huge rock which Wylde describes as forming one wall of their mess. Minor events such as Durnford's horse being caught in a tree when it fell over the edge of a mountain path and accounts of actual people, such as Mr G. Mansel of the Natal Mounted Police and Umkosaza, widow of the late Chief of the Ngwe, also come directly from the letters.

The need for Frances Colenso's anonymity creates an interesting relationship between these two works. In editing *A Soldier's Life*, Edward Durnford quotes quite extensively from *My Chief and I* (which he names) and then does his best to deflect interest from its authorship. Obviously he knew the real identity of Atherton Wylde but his effort to protect Frances Colenso involves a different fiction from the one she herself had used. He says that the experiences narrated in *My Chief and I*, instead of being those of a "supposed author . . . [were] really the combined experience of several young men, everything related being true of one or other of those who furnished the materials" (Durnford 1882:282). Edward Durnford also says that the manuscript was sent to him by the "principal compiler" shortly after his brother's death, and that he (Durnford) added the portrait of his brother and the note on his death before the manuscript was published, "in November, 1879" (Durnford 1882:282). Although Edward Durnford seems to have been mistaken abut the date of publication, he may have been right about his degree of responsibility for its final form—if it was indeed he, and not Frances Colenso who inserted a newspaper correspondent's published account of what the battlefield at Isandlwana revealed. As Edward Durnford also worked to clear his brother's name from Chelmsford's criticisms, perhaps one can say he had equal reason to want the satisfaction of citing a public tribute to his brother's heroism.

Edward Durnford also adds a footnote which testifies to the pleasure that the account of Anthony Durnford in *My Chief and I* gave to a brother officer. A Colonel Brooke RE, writes:

> You teach your reader to love your chief. All who knew him well loved him when alive, and your book will, I think, make those who have not known him think of him with affection and reverence. Your picture is a wonderfully faithful one: it brought vividly back to my mind many an hour spent with him. I thank you as a friend for doing this, and I thank you equally as an engineer officer for so truly portraying to the world a man whose name adds such lustre to our corps. He was one of those who have lived in this world unrecognised by the multitude during life, yet leaving behind a name which must in time influence the lives of many. (Durnford 1882:282)

Colonel Brooke's praise is especially interesting in that he did not find the portrait of Durnford too adulatory or fulsome; it would also seem that he did not detect, or was not disturbed by, an incipient femininity in Atherton Wylde's expressions of affection. Nevertheless, for today's reader, perhaps unused to the heartfelt writing of the nineteenth century, *My Chief and I* is an unusual, demanding and often painfully raw narrative. What signs there are of its having been read in recent years suggest that it has not been treated to the historical, imaginative inquiry that it deserves. Such a reading is not simply a matter of being an historian. Many historians have indeed read *My Chief and I*; it appears in the bibliographies of most works about Natal at the end of the last century, especially those which focus on the Anglo-Zulu War of 1879, but it seldom gets beyond the footnote. This is perhaps because it has little to offer to anyone seeking what is customarily thought to constitute 'information' about events in Natal. And for those wanting to understand the Colenso point of view, the writings of the Bishop himself, and later of Harriette Colenso, have been felt to be more than sufficient. For the general reader (as distinct from the professional historian) the events which Frances Colenso depicted are not, compared with others of the day, momentous. The success of Durnford's personal objective in obtaining pardon for the Ngwe gives a pleasing shape to the story, but admirable and important as this endeavour was, historically it is thoroughly overshadowed by the cause of Langalibalele and the Hlubi and by what was soon to happen to Cetshwayo and the Zulu people.

It is not only a search for factual information or excitement which may close the reader's imagination. Some historians have been responsive to the emotional dimension of Frances Colenso's narrative, but they have usually seen it only through current stereotypes of gender. For example, Donald Morris, in *The Washing of the Spears*, is blinkered about his own style when he finds Frances Colenso guilty of "frequently allow[ing] her emotions to tinge her writing" (1966:214). His assumption that Frances Colenso did not use, or did not possess, an intellect surfaces explicitly when he says that when Durnford was killed, and blamed by Chelmsford for the disaster at Isandlwana, she "leaped like a tigress to the defense of the reputation of the man to whom she had given her love. All the pent frustrations of her life burst forth, and with burning and implacable animosity she set out to clear Durnford's name and to fix the onus of the defeat on Chelmsford" (1966:438). Morris is not alone in such prejudice, for his soap-opera view of daily life colours most of the popular histories of this period.

Some of the questions Frances Colenso's book can prompt have been raised in this Introduction. For a reader who wants to go behind the text as a finished product, there are many others. And many, by their nature, have to remain unanswered. Frances Colenso's decision to focus her story on Durnford in relation to the Ngwe raises questions of exactly whom she was writing for—did she imagine her readers as fellow-settlers in Natal, and what impact could she hope to have on them? Could she have hoped to influence the politicians in Britain, or Durnford's brother-officers throughout the Empire? And if direct influence was what she sought, why did she use the relatively slow means of writing a fictionalised story? The medium of print can never guarantee the writer a desired effect, but at least the impact of journalism would have been more rapid. If her purposes were not only to affect public affairs, but to please individual readers as well, to what pre-existing tastes was she appealing? Narratives (imaginary or otherwise) of travel and adventure in far-flung places had found, with the growth of the Empire, a ready audience in Britain, but if this was her ticket, the question which again arises is why she limited her action to the least heroic part of Durnford's story—to the relatively dull activity of road-making.

All texts are enigmatic in the ways that these questions suggest; the unusual qualities of *My Chief and I* and its positioning between fact and fiction mean that it will prompt these questions in a way that the more familiar novel or short story might not. Questions of form join with those of gender to make *My Chief and I* an important South African text: its republication should re-invigorate many of the questions about local writing, especially those concerning women's subjectivity and power and those concerning the relationship of fiction to history, which have been somewhat overshadowed by the need of the last forty years to combat the evils of legalised apartheid.

It is also perhaps easier to tease out the elements of the racial attitudes in *My Chief and I*, and to recognise what they meant and how they developed, than it is to ask these questions of texts closer to us in time. Through Durnford's actions, Frances Colenso argued for what would, in her lights, have been a just and humane treatment of the black inhabitants of Natal. While she was consciously at odds with most of the colonial players on her stage, there are, as has been said, many aspects of the ideology of empire in the late nineteenth century which she could not interrogate, let alone challenge. But those socially induced blind-spots and pieties have their equivalents today. The customs and attitudes by which gender roles are formed and sustained are a case in point. In Frances Colenso's day, women were not encouraged to intervene in public matters because, despite the enterprise and adventurousness that everyday settler life demanded of women in the colonies, public life remained the domain of men. By and large, this is still the case in South Africa. What *My Chief and I* represents in this respect is a woman's determination not to be constrained by the barriers of custom; Frances Colenso was a remarkable proto-feminist in the way that she carried her personal affections right into the public, political arena.

As the causes of Langalibalele's flight over the Drakensberg suggest, the ownership and control of land is a central issue behind the writing of *My Chief and I*, as it was in Olive Schreiner's later and better known work, *Trooper Peter Halket of Mashonaland*. Frances Colenso's narrative is thus also an important record of the way that colonisers imposed meaning on the land, literally re-shaping it and the lives of its inhabitants to their purposes. The terrible consequences of competition between two cultures' practical uses for the same territory, and between the meanings that they would give to it, are at their most painful when Atherton Wylde describes his ride through the devastated lands of the Ngwe.

The period of the Anglo-Zulu war gave rise to many fictional adventures set in Natal—as in G.A. Henty's writing for young people and in that of Rider Haggard, who appealed to older readers with an appetite for the glamour and romance of conquest. More recently Daphne Rooke has written about the war from the perspective of the Zulu people, in *Wizard's Country* (1957) and John Conyngham, in *The Arrowing of the Cane* (1986), has explored the bearing that a memory of imperial defeat such as that at Isandlwana has had on contemporary lives in Natal. Adventure, military and other, has long proved a compelling subject in South African writing, but the most significant of Frances Colenso's literary successors are not likely to be of this kind. It is undoubtedly the land question that will remain a crucial issue as South Africans remake their country, but the racial allocation of land is unlikely to stand alone as a subject. Writers will now have to give equal attention to the way that gender surrounds and inhabits all issues in daily life as it does the textual representation of life.

Surprisingly enough, contemporary fiction, especially that by black writers, has only recently begun to turn its attention to depicting the contest over land rights. After the depredations of the 1913 Land Act prompted Sol T. Plaatje to express the anger of loss in *Native Life in South Africa* (1916) and to write his visionary rejoinder to deprivation in his pastoral epic, *Mhudi* (written in the early 1920s but published only in 1930), fiction in English in southern Africa had to wait for Bessie Head's work, beginning with *When Rain Clouds Gather* (1969), for a powerful focus on the relationship of a people to their land. In contemporary black writing, this focus on land has been blended with the gender question in Lauretta Ngcobo's novel, *And They Didn't Die* (1991). She depicts the loneliness and helplessness of women who are left on the land because of the system of migratory labour. But these are still isolated instances of such writing in South Africa for, although the control of land has been a crucial struggle under apartheid, racism has been registered as a largely urban phenomenon in black writing.

The case is similar in white writing where the city dweller's view has dominated. This may be why, in commenting on the historical theft of the land in her novel, *The Conservationist* (1974), Nadine Gordimer made use of sustained metaphor rather than direct statement. She uses the presence of a black corpse which will not stay buried on the land now owned by Meiring, an affluent white businessman in Johannesburg, to indicate how an historical injustice will return to haunt its perpetrators. Although gender has not been an issue that Gordimer has avowedly espoused in her fiction, the dialogue between a novel such as *Burger's Daughter* (1979) and *My Chief and I* is a fascinating one. For her novel, Gordimer creates Lionel Burger whom she calls the last of South Africa's (white) heroes, and she has him explain his stand against oppression by using the phrase from Luther that both Mrs Colenso and Frances Colenso had used about their men of heroic destiny. Gordimer uses the German: *"Ich kann nicht anders"*(1979:26). It is in this novel too that so many of the questions about patriarchal control which arise from Frances Colenso's relationship to her father-figures are explored when Rosa Burger takes up the torch of opposition to racist, illegitimate rule in South Africa that her father, Lionel, had first carried.

It is probably foolhardy to predict contemporary responses to *My Chief and I* and the influence it may now have. Perhaps more than its identification of issues, its way of making the personal political will be most influential. If so, the note of brave defeat—of the author as well as of the man who formed her subject—will be telling. Given the complexities of the story and its context, the everyday phrase under which Frances Colenso imagined her story, "My Chief and I", speaks volumes. There is the ironic energy of "Chief"; there is, too, a mixture of assertion and self-subordination in "My Chief". Today's reader will also make the compassionate recognition that however brave it was for a (disguised) woman to have made that claim, it becomes a lonely and anxious one in the doubling of "and I".

M.J. Daymond
University of Natal, Durban.

NOTES

1. The manuscript of "A Little Orphan" is in the Natal Archives. Frances Colenso also published two stories, in the *Natal Colonist*, called "Playing with edged tools; a New Year's tale" and "Too Late!—fortunately". The latter tale was reprinted in Durban in 1876.
2. Fanny was Frances's name in the family—her mother did not like Nelly, which she herself sometimes used.

REFERENCES

Brookes, E.H. & C. de B. Webb. 1965. *A History of Natal.* Pietermaritzburg: University of Natal Press.

Colenso, J.W. 1874. *Langalibalele and the Amahlubi Tribe, being remarks upon the official record of the trials of the chief, his sons and induna, and other members of the Amahlubi tribe.* Printed by Spottiswoode & Co, New-Street Square, London.

Drooglever, R.W.F. 1992. *The Road to Isandhlwana: Colonel Anthony Durnford in Natal and Zululand.* London: Greenhill Books and California: Presidio Press.

Durnford, Edward. 1882. *A Soldier's Life and Work in South Africa 1872 to 1879.* London: Sampson Low, Marston, Searle & Rivington.

Etherington, N.A. 1978. "Why Langalibalele Ran Away." *Journal of Natal and Zulu History* I; 1–24.

Gordimer, Nadine. 1979. *Burger's Daughter.* Harmondsworth: Penguin.

Guest, W.R. 1976. *Langalibalele: The Crisis in Natal 1873 – 1875*. Research Monograph No 2, Department of History and Political Science. Durban: University of Natal.

Guy, Jeff. 1983. *The Heretic: A Study of the Life of John William Colenso 1814 – 1883*. Johannesburg: Ravan Press and Pietermaritzburg: University of Natal Press.

Manson, A. 1979. "A People in Transition: The Hlubi in Natal, 1848–1877." *Journal of Natal and Zulu History* II, 13–26.

Morris, Donald R. 1966. *The Washing of the Spears: The Rise and Fall of the Zulu Nation*. London: Jonathan Cape.

Pearse, R.O.; J. Clark; P.R. Barnes; G. Tatham (eds). 1973. *Langalibalele and the Natal Carbineers: The Story of the Langalibalele Rebellion, 1873*. Ladysmith: The Ladysmith Historical Society.

Rees, Wyn (ed). 1958. *Colenso Letters from Natal*. Pietermaritzburg: Shuter and Shooter.

FURTHER READING

Of the books listed above, that by Jeff Guy gives an invaluable account of Bishop Colenso; the oddly-titled collection of Mrs Colenso's letters, edited by Wyn Rees, is incomparable for its picture of how the family saw its place in Natal. A biography of Bishop Colenso that was written with the family's help is the Revd Sir George W. Cox's *The Life of John William Colenso. Bishop of Natal* (1888). A recent popular account (which draws extensively on W.R. Guest's scholarship) of Langalibalele's actions and trial is *The Bent Pine* (1976) by Norman Herd. The study of Durnford by R.W.F. Drooglever adds the insights of recent historians to the memoir published by Edward Durnford.

The most recently collected views of South African historians appear in *Natal and Zululand, from Earliest Times to 1910: A New History* (1989) edited by Andrew Duminy and Bill Guest, and in *The Anglo-Zulu War: New Perspectives* (1981) edited by Andrew Duminy and Charles Ballard. Jeff Guy's *The Destruction of the Zulu Kingdom: The Civil War in Zululand 1879 – 1884* gives a contemporary view of the history first written by Frances Colenso. The route by which Durnford led his soldiers to the top of Bushman's River Pass, and the skirmish which followed, has been traced in detail by R.O. Pearse in an appendix to *Barrier of Spears* (1973).

MY CHIEF AND I.

COLONEL A.W. DURNFORD, ROYAL ENGINEERS

MY CHIEF AND I

OR,

SIX MONTHS IN NATAL AFTER THE LANGALIBALELE
OUTBREAK.

BY ATHERTON WYLDE.

With Illustrations.

LONDON
CHAPMAN AND HALL, 193, PICCADILLY.
1880.

DURNFORD.

(From "The Cape Argus," April 5th, 1879.)

HIM best I love of that bright band
Whose bones lie white on Zululand;
Where "in one place" they fought, they fell,
They Died! my England, mark it well!

Brave, cheery voice! I hear it now;
As when, with battle on his brow,
Along the shining line he passed,
Death-doomed, yet steady to the last.

When 'midst the dying and the dead,
The colours from his charge he sped;
Stainless was every silken fold,
Unsoiled the crimson and the gold.

He knew the charge his sovereign gave,
Good glorious queen! that bold and brave,
Yet just and gentle, must be those
Who bear her standard 'midst her foes.

'Twas no command to disobey
With tongue in cheek when far away.
Sword, flag, commission, evermore
With Christian chivalry he bore.

Not his to catch, in savage feud,
The savage spirit, murderous mood.
A soldier! prompt at duty's nod;
But leaving vengeance unto God!

Not his vain vaunts of martial might,
Nor coarse, base brag of blood-steeped spite;
Nor heightened phrase, to darken foes
Whom Britain bids her sons oppose.

He preached not "war at any price,"
He practised high self-sacrifice;
He fought, "obedient unto death,"
And now he fears no censor's breath.

Briton and native, sleep they well,
Where, 'midst their swarming foes they fell;
Where weird Sandhlwana lifts his hand,*
For silence, o'er the awful land.

And 'midst the names that drift along
The golden tide of fame and song,
Seek DURNFORD'S.   In the troubled van
Of peace and right, he died for man!

T. W. SWIFT.

Wynberg Parsonage.

* Sandhlwana is said to mean the "Little Hand" mountain.

AUTHOR'S PREFACE

THIS story was written in 1875, when all the events of which it tells were fresh in my mind. While writing it I intended it for immediate publication, but by the time it was finished I began to feel great doubt as to whether he in whose honour it was chiefly written would like to see so much about himself in print. Finally I made up my mind to send my manuscript to 'my Chief,' and ask him to read it, and to give me leave to publish it. I knew that, at least, he would give it his full attention, and would not unnecessarily nip a young author's early efforts in the bud.

In due time the manuscript came back to me, with the evidence of having been carefully perused in the numerous pencil scores in the Colonel's handwriting which appeared upon its pages. There were various slight corrections of details of our expedition which he remembered more accurately than I. A few remarks of his own which I had quoted were struck out, and some suggestions for better-turned sentences written here and there upon the margin.

Besides this, however, he had, through the first few chapters, marked for omission every sentence in praise of or personal to himself, evidently trying to bring my book into a shape in which it might be at once laid before the public.

But he must soon have found that, were all personal to himself cut out, the mangled remains of my story would be worthless indeed, and his final decision was contained in these words, 'My dear boy, publish your book when I am dead and gone if you like; but not before.'

He told me, however, that the facts of my story were correct, and that it might do good for some of them (concerning the Putini tribe, etc.) to be made public.

And now that, alas! the day of which he spoke has come, and he is gone, I have taken out the old manuscript again, and with the addition of a few notes, referring to his glorious death at Isandhlwana, I lay before the public what is but a poor tribute of affection and respect from the humblest of his friends to one whose truly Christian life was as much honoured by those who came within its influence, as his heroic death by the world at large.

ATHERTON WYLDE

CONTENTS.

CHAPTER X.

MY CHIEF AND I

CHAPTER I

MY EARLY STORY

'My Chief and I!'—such is the title which I have chosen to give to my tale, although it is of my Chief principally that I shall speak, reserving to myself the post of chronicler, and speaking of myself only so far as is necessary in describing that part of his life which has been brought into contact with mine. Yet to accomplish this, some slight account of myself must be laid before the public, and with this I will begin before passing on to more interesting subjects.

My name is Atherton Wylde, and I am still a comparatively young man—young at least in years, although perhaps in little else. Fifteen years ago I was a subaltern of engineers, and went out to Gibraltar to serve under him whom I have since learnt to call my Chief, then Captain Durnford, of the Royal Engineers.

Well do I remember him as he was when I, wild in nature as in name, first came under his command. Gallant soldier! kind and courteous gentleman! There was not one amongst us—officer or man—who would not have followed him to certain death, or have gladly died in his defence, for we all loved as well as respected him. I might fill many pages with stories which would prove how well he earned our affection, what thoughtful care he exercised over our welfare, how kind, firm and judicious was his treatment of us, so that never did one of his men fear to go to him for advice or help, nor dare to face him with a guilty conscience. When he took his final leave of them upon the parade-ground at Gibraltar amongst one-hundred-and-twenty stalwart hardy soldiers, all admirably disciplined, fearless men, there was not—no! I do not think I speak beyond the fact when I say that there was not a single one whose eyes were dry. I think it no shame to my Chief to acknowledge that upon that day he himself was no stern unmoved exception to the general rule. I parted from him then, and did not think ever to serve under him again. Had not unkind fate removed me from beneath his influence I think that my own story would have been a different and a worthier one; for my desire to please him, and my dread of his displeasure were so great that, reckless youngster though I was, I never seriously offended while I was with him. From the time that he left us, however, my downward course began. I was an only son and much indulged. I had never known what it was to deny myself, or to be denied, in anything. My subsequent course of folly sprang less from vicious inclinations than from a gay and happy temperament, which combined an immense capacity and desire for pleasure, with an absolute lack of self-restraint, either natural or acquired. Thus much I may say in my own excuse, though I fear that it is hardly worth recording.

It is not necessary to enter into a detailed account of the idle, dissipated life into which I plunged as soon as ever my Captain's restraining influence was removed. The course, through every phase of folly into the deeper shades of vice, has been too often depicted, and is too well known to many, to need recapitulation here. It is enough for my purpose to state that not many years had passed over my head before I found myself a ruined man, without fortune, career, or friends worthy the name. My father had been both rich and liberal towards me when he first started me in life, and for some time my heavy demands upon his income were met without a murmur. But Fortunatus's purse alone could have held out against my wild extravagance. The day came when I received warnings and remonstrances along with the remittances; and then, a little later on, the latter failed entirely. Finally, I was obliged to leave the army, and returned home a disgraced and ruined man, to my well-nigh heartbroken father.

During the next few idle and miserable months it seemed to me that I had awakened from an insane dream. All that I might have been, all that I had forfeited by my own folly, rose daily before my mind's eye, contrasted with the degradation to which I had sunk, until I could endure the quiet inactive life that I was leading no longer, and determined to try that last resource for the desperate —a life in one of the colonies. I think that my relatives, with the exception of my poor father, were glad to get rid of me, and wished above all things that I should hide in a foreign land the disgrace which my misconduct had brought upon the family. Accordingly I was sent out to Natal, where I was to make my own way as well as I could.

I imagined that when I landed in Durban the colony contained no more desperate and reckless man than I. Life, without the respect of those around me, without self-respect—to the loss of which I had but lately become so keenly alive—without position, fortune, all that had made it desirable, was worthless to me. I was ripe for any mischief, and in a fair way to end my days at the lowest stage of humanity, when, providentially for me, I met once more with my old Captain (now Lieutenant-Colonel), and was saved by him from, and in spite of, myself.

One day early in 1874 I was strolling aimlessly down West Street, Durban, brooding over my gloomy prospects. In my depressed state of mind I had lacked spirit to seek for employment which, naturally enough, had not come out of its way to seek me. I had that day changed my last five-pound note and did not know where to look for another when that should be spent. In fact it was my darkest hour, and rightly so, for it was the hour before dawn to me, the dawn of a better and more useful life than any I had ever led before.

On what small chances our futures seem to hang! Since I had been in Natal I had carefully avoided any meeting with men of my own cloth, not so much from any fear of recognition as from what was, let me hope, a feeling of honest shame and compunction. Accordingly, upon this bright summer morning, I was listlessly watching the stream of people of many nations, English, Dutch, Indians, and Africans, etc., who passed me by, and wondering the while whether amongst them all there was one single individual so absolutely friendless and hopeless as I, when I observed two infantry officers in uniform walking up the street towards me. I immediately crossed over to the other side of the road in order to avoid them. I looked back at them as I went, however, and consequently I did not observe that, in escaping from two men whom I did not know, and who would not have taken any notice of me, I was placing myself immediately under the observation of just the one man in the colony whom I most desired to avoid. Yes! I knew that my old Captain was in Natal, in the double capacity of commanding officer of Engineers and Colonial Engineer. It was not long since the disastrous affair at the Bushman's River Pass, where he was wounded, and, knowing him of old as I did, I could appreciate at their true value the accounts of his conduct at that time, with which the colony was filled when I reached it. I could picture to myself his gallant behaviour, and while I longed to have been at his side, fighting with and for him, upon that day, so that the honour of standing by him should not have been left, as indeed it almost was, to the few *black* soldiers of his force alone; yet I did not feel myself worthy of his notice now, and dared not present myself before his gaze in my present degraded situation. Consequently I had given Colonel Durnford no hint of my existence, and now the meeting between us came unsought.

Looking behind me as I walked, I took no heed to my steps until I ran against an advancing figure, and turned to apologise. My apologies were redoubled as I observed the injured arm carried in a sling, and then, one moment later, I knew who it was. Great as was the change wrought by suffering and illness on my former Captain's appearance, it was undoubtedly he. Strong and broad was his tall upright figure when I saw him last, one to whom fatigue and illness were almost unknown words. Now he was but the shadow of his former self, and yet there was no mistaking him; I fairly quailed before the searching glance of those steady eyes, and felt as though a frown upon the pale worn face would annihilate me. I would have left him with the words of apology upon my lips and have escaped—anywhere to be out of his sight. But he was too quick for me, and had recognised me at once.

'What! Wylde? Atherton Wylde? Surely I am not mistaken!' he exclaimed, holding out his hand to me.

I could not choose but take it, although the kindly tones of the well-remembered voice caused me to tremble as I trust no fear could make me do. 'Yes, I am Atherton Wylde,' I replied in somewhat unsteady tones. 'I hardly thought that you would have recognised me now, Colonel Durnford.'

'I do not forget old friends so easily,' was his reply, while I felt that he was studying my downcast countenance to some purpose, and would fain have hidden it from his view.

'What brings you to Natal, Atherton?' he inquired presently, in rather altered tones, 'What are you doing here?' I had been a favourite with my Captain of old, and it seemed to me now that he had not quite lost his interest in me.

'I don't know; nothing,' I faltered in reply. And then, with some gleam of returning spirit, inspired by the very presence of my Captain, linked as it was with old associations, 'I should be glad enough to get any work to do.'

'Come along and walk back with me to the club,' he said, after a pause, during which I felt as though he was reading my inmost thoughts. 'You shall tell me all about it, if you will, and perhaps I may be able to help you.'

I turned, and we walked back almost in silence, during which I came to the determination that I would make a clean breast of it to Colonel Durnford, and abide by his decision. Should he consider my offences unpardonable and spurn me from him, I would give myself up, and make no further effort. Should he hold me out a friendly helping hand—was there not yet a chance for me?

Never, as long as I live, shall I forget the little back room at the club in which I told, and he listened to, my tale. Its every detail is riveted in my memory by the powerful emotions which mastered me within its walls: the tap of the billiard balls in the next room, and the cracked voice of Jelly, the waiter, in the passage, are all present to me while I write these lines. When about half way through my confession I saw a young lady leave the house opposite, at which I was vacantly staring while I spoke, in her broad garden hat and dainty dress. At that moment I was telling my listening Colonel how days and nights, and endless sums of money, had been played away by me in the hells of London. Since then broad flapping hats and little dancing steps are inextricably interwoven in my mind with wild wicked scenes and reckless companions.

My Chief—for such he has been ever since that day—listened to my story without further interruption than was necessary to the perfect understanding of my case, and with a certain grave intent expression upon his pain-worn countenance which betokened that he was giving his whole attention to the subject without prejudging its merits. There were some facts to be told in extenuation of my past conduct which I do not care to record here. It is enough that he thought them palliations, if not excuses, and gave me some sympathy as well as blame.

When I had told him all, and sat in breathless miserable silence awaiting his comments upon my tale, he rose and walked away to the window, where he stood apparently contemplating the waste of glaring sand which lies in Smith Street. It could have been but a second that he stood there, yet to me—poor wretch upon the rack—it seemed an age. At last he turned, and, venturing to raise my eyes to his, I saw there that I was saved. He came back and sat down again.

'Look here, Wylde,' he said in decided business-like tones, 'if you are really willing to *work* and can keep steady, I'll make a man of you yet. Let bygones be bygones, and begin afresh. There must be good in one who can speak the truth so fearlessly as you have done today. I know it is the truth, for I knew all about you before. Will you take a place on the roads?' he asked sharply.

'Certainly, sir,' I answered instantly. I thought he meant as a labourer. Had he even offered me the shilling I should not have hesitated to take it.

I think he was pleased with the promptness and earnestness of my reply, for a grave smile crossed his face. 'Well, I can put you in charge of a road party at Pinetown at once,' he said. 'There are some forty men there, liberated slaves from Zanzibar, whom I wish to keep together. When can you be ready to take them over?'

'At once! tomorrow; as soon as you wish, sir,' was my eager reply.

'Tomorrow I must go out to Umgeni Bridge, and the next day to the Point,' he said, rather to himself than me. 'The following day? Yes, I shall leave Durban on Friday, and you can go with me. I shall be driving and can take you in; but you must send your luggage up some other way. Now mind! we shall leave this by half-past six on Friday morning, for I have work to do in Pinetown, and must get up to Welch's Half-way House the same night, so as to be in Maritzburg in good time on Saturday morning.'

When, half-an-hour later, I left the club, and the friend thus suddenly raised up for me in my hour of greatest need, it seemed to me as though I had stepped into a new world. The very sunshine had a more cheerful and less sultry glow; and, for myself, was I the same dejected miserable man who had slouched along the pavement that morning, with but one refuge in view from my gloomy thoughts—the canteen or drinking-bar? I felt no temptation now to turn my steps that way. In fact, drink had never been a passion with me. I had but resorted to it for excitement's sake in the old gay days, and of late to drown my misery. But now the meeting with my former Captain, the very fact that, knowing the worst of me, he had yet taken me by the hand, and spoken to me with kindness unmixed with anything like contempt, had helped me back to some self-respect, to some hope for better things. I *would* do better. I resolved it as I had never done before. I would not disappoint his trust nor cause him to throw away his goodness upon an unworthy object. So resolving I took my way to my lodgings with a firmer step and a higher head than had been mine for many a long day.

CHAPTER II

HOW WE MANAGED OUR WEDDING

Pinetown has been called the Cheltenham of Durban, and is allowed by most to give a healthy change from the damp heat of the latter place. It is, I believe, a general resort for invalids from the coast; but I took up my abode there, not to recover health by quiet enjoyment of rest and fresh air, but to regain life itself— worthy the name—by good hard work, and earnest endeavours to do my duty.

I had never yet been beyond the Durban turnpike road in this direction, for, in my downcast helpless mood, I had not cared to take the trouble; and now, as we drove rapidly through the fresh air of the early morning, I looked with newly awakened interest upon the country around us. We were fast leaving the blue sea behind, in its soft haze of morning sun and mist, and glimmering here and there with white sails and whiter surf. The Bluff with its heavy brush, right to the water's edge, and shining lighthouse tower, and the town, pretty enough at a little distance, were soon lost to view; and, after a couple of hours' rapid driving upon a good road, through tangled bush, amongst which on every side Nature had flung her loveliest garlands in wildest profusion of brilliant and scented blossom, we passed through the long straggling village which calls itself Pinetown, and drew up at the excellent stables belonging to the Colonel as Colonial Engineer.

Here, as elsewhere in all stables appertaining to the department, I observed the good condition and kind treatment of the beasts. I could not help remarking upon it to the Colonel, who immediately upon his arrival proceeded to inspect every portion and corner of the establishment, while the men in charge seemed to be nervously casting glances round to make sure that all was right. My remark received no immediate reply; for at the moment when I made it the Colonel's eye was caught by a bad gall upon one of the stalled horses, evidently the result of careless harnessing. Was ever face susceptible of such changes in expression between the extremes of gentleness and severity as that of my Chief! I would not have been the man in fault, who stood shaking in his shoes, for any money. Not that the Colonel lost his temper, stormed, or even raised his voice.

On the contrary, he rather dropped it, and spoke as calmly as possible. I never heard a reproof given in a quieter, more courteous manner, nor one which I should less like to receive myself. There could be no doubt as to its effect upon the men, and, for my own part, I began to think that I should feel cooler outside, and was moving off, by no means desiring a reply to my last inopportune remark, when my Colonel turned to me with a smooth brow and genial smile, and answered, 'Yes, I don't care to see my animals neglected or ill-used; besides, it is always bad economy,' and then we left the place.

This is the Colonel's way. Not that he cannot break out into fiery indignation when occasion comes. No man of my acquaintance has a hotter temper, nor one under more complete control; and that, I believe, is the true secret of his undeniable power over those who serve under him. I have heard his voice sound like that of an angry lion, and have seen his eyes blaze, and his face rigid with displeasure; but only at rare intervals, and under great provocation. As a rule his reproofs are administered in a calm but decided manner, without anger or impatience, while those who receive them look as frightened as though they had seen the devil.

Our next visit was to the quarters of the married couples amongst the liberated slaves, my future charges. These quarters were a row of little rooms, very small, but clean and well-ventilated. The Colonel had just had them put up for the poor creatures, who had not long come into his hands, but were already showing signs of improvement in condition from the miserable skeletons, scarred and starved, who had been rescued from a captured dhow off Zanzibar a short time since.

'There are ten or twelve women belonging to this party,' said the Colonel to me, after he had inspected the men, mustered for that purpose near their barracks, about fifty yards from the married people's quarters. 'When the Protector of Immigrants first offered them to me with the men I refused the charge altogether; but upon second thoughts it occurred to me that these poor creatures would be much happier if they had some sort of home life, so I have determined to keep them together. The next thing to do is to marry them all round, as far as the small number of women will go. And that is what I have come here for today.'

I was about to laugh, thinking it a joke; but I immediately saw by the expression of his countenance that he was perfectly in earnest, so I retained my gravity, and waited for what would come next. 'None of them can understand a word of English,' continued the Colonel, 'so that a religious ceremony, or anything of the sort would be a mere profane farce. It is proper to add that I have consulted with "my clergy," and we have come to the conclusion that the more simply the thing is done the better. So now, Wylde, you are going to assist at an extensive wedding.'

The scene which followed was the most novel and curious that I ever witnessed. The Colonel and myself, and the principal road-overseer of those parts, stood in the open space before the little houses. On one side of us were the forty men, on the other the girls and young women. These latter were all dressed in neat costumes chosen and ordered for them by the Colonel himself, and consisting of dark blue cotton gowns, with crimson handkerchiefs upon the heads. Each wore a string of large beads, the special gift of my Chief, who evidently aimed, not merely at making the 'slaves' useful, but also at rendering them happy, or at least contented, members of society.

When all were assembled the Colonel called up the women, and, with the help of one of the men who had been longer in the colony than the others, and had picked up a little Zulu, and that of the overseer who could talk the latter language, he managed to make them understand what was required of them. Each in turn privately named the man whom she chose as her husband; the names were noted down on a slip of paper, and, with this in his hand, the Colonel crossed over to the men, who had been kept out of earshot, and required each of those who were down on his list to name his chosen bride. By this method all chance of any one of the girls being taken in marriage against her will was avoided, and it was satisfactory that in every case save one the choice of the men agreed with that of the girls. The one exception was that of the youngest girl—a mere child indeed—who named as her selected husband a man who refused to have anything to say to her. She seemed very disconsolate, but she was so young that it could be no great subject for regret. A separate little room was next assigned to each couple. Finally the bridegrooms were marched over towards their brides, and each man in turn was directed to take the object of his choice by the hand and to lead her away. This concluded the marriage ceremony. It was amusing to observe the modest air displayed by these dusky brides. They all covered their eyes and faces with a corner of their dress; yet their smiles showed plainly enough that they were well satisfied.

There might have been something ludicrous in this performance had it been managed by any one else. But there was something in the simple earnestness and quiet dignity with which it was conducted, which took away all desire to make a joke of it. I could not have felt less inclined to laugh at my own wedding than I did at this.

I must confess, however, that the impressiveness of the ceremony received no addition from the beauty of the brides. I have since seen many kafir girls with graceful forms, and not a few with pretty faces; but amongst these poor

freedwomen there was not one who could boast of any such charms. Whether it
is that the east-coast negroes are naturally inferior to their southern brethren, or
whether generations of cruel slavery have degraded them to their present low
type, I know not. But at all events, as far as I can judge, there is no comparison
between them and the Zulu kafirs of Natal, who are a far better-looking and
more intelligent race.

The freedwomen of Pinetown were neat and clean, thanks to the Colonel's
care in providing an English matron to take charge of and teach them; but I
cannot say much more for them. They were of a singularly low type, with
heavy, underhung features, and remarkably awkward figures. There was,
however, an occasional gleam of grateful affection upon the dark faces of both
men and women when the Colonel spoke to them which lighted them up
wonderfully.

We went into the schoolroom of the establishment before we left. It was but a
narrow slip of an apartment in the row of tiny sleeping rooms, but in perfect
order with its white table and two benches. Here presided the Matron who
showed us some very creditable work done by her pupils, sewing, ironing, and
writing upon slates. The Colonel inspected everything with interest, and I
followed him wherever he went. He inquired of the Matron which was the
best-behaved pupil, and which the second, and gave each a little present
proportionate to her merits, after which we left the place.

There were still two of the slaves captured from the dhow, whose recovery
from the effects of the ill-usage which they had received was doubtful. I saw
them, and wondered how such mere skeletons could exist at all. I heard the
Colonel give his directions concerning them, ordering wine for them, and
perpetual strong beef tea. No other treatment could have saved their lives I feel
sure; and, if life is a blessing, as I suppose it is, they were fortunate to fall into
the hands that received them.

One other little episode of the day must be recorded. While the Colonel was
inspecting the schoolroom and scholars, the Matron complained to him that her
charges were sometimes very refractory, and that she should like to have some
way of enforcing discipline. As she could not talk to them, nor understand what
they said to her, she thought that the best and shortest way would be for her to
use the rod at her own discretion. Here was a knotty point! The Colonel
considered it; while I, who had been watching the Matron's face over his
shoulder, hoped that he would not grant her request. That she was a clean and
active woman was evident, and the Colonel had confidence in her honesty; but,
like so many clean and active *poor* women, she evidently had a temper of her
own, and I did not like the notion of these poor creatures being committed to

tender mercies free of restraint. Probably the expression of her face, and the resentful way in which she spoke of her charges' delinquencies, struck my Chief as well as me, for he seemed unwilling to agree to her suggestion; nevertheless it was plain that there was some justice in her demand. How was she to manage all these young women if she had no power of punishing them for misconduct? In this dilemma the Colonel turned to me and asked me if I could suggest any way out of it. I was glad of the opportunity, for, as it happened, I *had* an idea. I ventured to remark that the very fact of the Matron's being unable to speak to or to understand her pupils* might lead to her thinking them ill-behaved; whereas, could they interchange ideas, she might possibly find that it was not so. But I suggested that a system of slight fines might meet the exigencies of the case. Suppose the girls were allowed some small pocket-money, which might be kept back in case of gross misconduct?

I confess that I was gratified that the Colonel adopted my suggestion instantly and without hesitation.

'Yes,' he said, 'that is a capital idea of yours, Atherton. They shall each have an allowance of sixpence a week, and anyone who disobeys her mistress shall be deprived of her week's money.'

A few months later, by the way, when the women had each accumulated a small sum, they all went to spend their money in Pinetown according to their own taste. The result of their purchases was that, upon the following day, in each little room without a single exception hung a *sunshade* of some description or other. In one there appeared a large green umbrella, in the next a small brown parasol, in a third a middle-sized white ditto, and so on along the line. Why they should all have fallen in love with this particular, and to them, one would have imagined, most useless product of civilisation, it is hard to say, seeing that their complexions are not much affected by the rays of the sun, and their heads are well protected from its power by a thick woolly crop. But so it was. I have since observed, however, that the African, as a rule, dislikes exposing himself to the heat of the midday sun, and suffers more in doing so than we Europeans are in the habit of imagining; while, as for their love of useless articles of costume, I have seen a native attired in what the ladies some years ago used to call a 'skeleton crinoline,' and nothing else! This last, however, was a kafir, and further advanced in civilisation than my Pinetown 'slaves.'

I did not see much more of the women during the short time that I remained at Pinetown; but, as far as the men are concerned, I can freely assert that they were a very well-behaved and manageable set, and worked well under my

---

*   The language of the east-coast natives is almost unknown in Natal.

superintendence. True, I was exceedingly anxious to give satisfaction to my Chief, and spared no pains to that end. The hardening of that portion of the main road to Pietermaritzburg progressed rapidly during the time I spent on it, and I honestly did my best to carry out my Chief's wishes in the spirit which he exercised towards these poor people, rescued from a life of horrible slavery indeed, but set down to work amongst a strange people, with whom they had no means of communication, and without any certainty in their own minds that the flogging, torture, and starvation, to which they had so long been exposed, might not any day begin again for them under their new masters. I had never any serious trouble with them; and I have often thought since that, in whatever small disagreements took place between me and my men, possibly the same reasoning applied to me as to the Matron in charge of the women. Could I have talked to them in their own language, and have understood what they said, perhaps I should have had no difficulties with them at all.

CHAPTER III

LANGALIBALELE

After all, however, I did not remain very long at Pinetown. When I had been working there for about three months I received a summons from the Colonel to join him immediately at Fort Napier, and offering me a post which was not only infinitely superior to that of a road-overseer, but was the one which now I would have chosen before all others. The Colonel told me in his note that he was about to start upon an expedition up-country, and wished me to accompany him upon it. I joyfully gave over my road party and instructions concerning them to the man sent down to relieve me, and started off without any loss of time for Pietermaritzburg.

Of the two modes of travelling open to me, as I had no horse of my own—namely, the 'bus and the post-cart—I chose the former, although the least to my taste, because I could not tell whether, if I let the 'bus pass at 8.30 A.M., I should find a place vacant in the post-cart at 1 P.M. I did not wish to lose a day in obeying my Chief's summons. Accordingly, I resigned myself to the terrible ordeal, which eight hours' jolting and semi-suffocation in that closely-packed and uneasy vehicle proved to be. The 'bus was as full as it could well be, without allowing for a well-grown and vivacious little child of about two years, whose remarkably pretty face and winning ways were an amusement to the company generally, but whose restless activity must have been sorely fatiguing to the tired, sad-looking young mother who held her upon her knee.

My travelling companions were all strangers to me; and, with an Englishman's usual taciturnity under like circumstances, I kept myself very much to myself for some time, amusing myself with taking notes of the people and of their conversation. The latter soon became general, and strongly political from a colonial point of view. All things colonial having as yet the charm of novelty in my eyes, I listened with considerable interest. On one side of the low, narrow, hard-seated vehicle sat two members of the Legislative Council, a Transvaal farmer, and a very little Roman Catholic priest, accompanied by two tall young ladies, who appeared to be travelling in his charge, and who, I concluded from their deferential manner towards their priestly friend, must be scholars from the convent school in Durban. On the other side sat the pretty young mother and child (by the way, I do not think I mentioned before that the mother was pretty as well as the child), a respectable-looking old gentleman, who appeared from the conversation to hold some civic authority in Pietermaritzburg, two more farmers or transport riders, a half-coloured St. Helena woman, and myself. Two men on the box with the driver completed the party.

During the first hour's drive my attention was chiefly occupied, and my indignation excited, by what I conceived to be the uncivil treatment received by the aforesaid coloured woman. Fresh from civilised lands as I was, and as yet uncontaminated by colonial prejudices of race, I was keenly alive to anything like ill-usage or discourtesy to a coloured person merely for their colour's sake; and it seemed to me to be shameful that this woman, who was clean and well-dressed, talking good English, and distinguished only by her brown skin, should be snubbed and browbeaten by the whiter passengers, and thrust into a corner and neglected while paying the same as the rest of us at the wayside inns.

I think so still, and that the latter proceeding especially was dishonest as well as unchristian. But I am bound to confess that the result of my constituting myself in a small way the champion of this particular dark lady, by making a point of giving civil answers to a remark or two made by her to the company generally, and completely ignored by our fellow passengers, was such as to make me more cautious for the future. I had no particular desire to be on familiar terms with any strangers, black, white, or brown; but, after once exchanging only the very smallest of civilities with my St. Helena friend, I found that there was no shaking her off at all for the rest of the day. She seemed to consider that I had taken charge of her altogether, appealed to me upon every occasion with the most embarrassing frankness, and favoured me occasionally during the remainder of the journey with short disconnected passages from her private history, delivered in an alarmingly sudden manner at every pause which occurred in the general conversation, so that the fragments of interesting information which she gave me concerning herself were comically out of keeping with what came before and after.

As I have already remarked, the conversation had a strong political flavour, and I listened to it with some curiosity and a desire to know a little more of popular feeling in Natal than I had as yet had any opportunity of doing.

The expedition against the native chief, Langalibalele, in which my Chief had been severely wounded, was not long over, and was constantly alluded to. With but one exception the speakers adopted a tone concerning it which would in itself have prejudiced any Englishman against the colonial side of the question; vindictive expressions against the unfortunate captive, eagerness for his death, and, if that could be, for the still more complete destruction of his unhappy tribe prevailed. I did not then know much about the matter, and put a few questions to the man next me as to the crimes for which this wicked old chief was so detested, expecting to hear that he was a second Nana Sahib, or, at the very least, that he had made a murderous assault upon some defenceless homestead or other. But neither then nor on any subsequent occasion was I ever able to discover that he had done anything worse than run away in a fright, a fault which, if worthy of death in a British soldier, is hardly deserving of so severe a correction in a poor untaught heathen.

'What has the man done?' I asked of my next door neighbour in the 'bus.

'Done! why, he has rebelled against the government! He is a bloodthirsty old rebel!' was the somewhat indignant reply that I received.

'Yes, so I hear,' was my quiet rejoinder. 'But, what I want to know is in what way he has shown his bloodthirsty rebellious disposition. What has he *done*?'

'Done! done! why, don't you hear me tell you that he is a *rebel*!' exclaimed the farmer to whom I had addressed myself, looking very hot indeed.

'I have heard you *say* it, but I have not heard you *prove* it, my dear sir,' I replied. 'What proof is there? What has convinced you that this man is what you say he is?'

'Why, why,' stammered the man, completely taken aback, 'he is a rebel because everybody knows that he is. Didn't he run away!'

'Oh! I see,' said I, in a tone of the most complete conviction. 'Thank you; I am a stranger here, and only asked for information.'

'And I'll tell you what it is, sir,' exclaimed a man opposite me, bringing down his clenched fist upon his knee with a resounding thump, 'when you have been as long in the colony as I have you'll know a little more about it. If I'd been the Governor a few months ago, the rebel chief should have been tried by court-martial, and have paid the penalty of his crimes, either by cord or bullet, at once. I'd have given no ear to the Exeter Hall cry of pseudo-philanthropists. The man was taken red-handed [*Anglicé*: running away? A.W.], and he should have been put to death with all the men of his tribe who resisted us. The others should be put to hard labour, and the women and children put out to service. That's what I would have done, and made it a good thing for the colony too.'

A moment's silence ensued upon this burst of legislative eloquence, and immediately my St. Helena friend remarked to me from the other end of the vehicle, 'My mistress gave me six new pair of stockings and this dress that I have on before I left.'

I hardly knew how to receive this and similar pieces of information, while the other members of the party appeared unaware that anyone had spoken, and the other Legislative Councillor took up his colleague's speech with emphasis.

'The whole thing has been bungled,' he said. 'All that was needed to make the farce complete was that a verdict of "Not Guilty" should have been given at the trial. Who would then have been responsible for the thousands of cattle that have been taken and sold by us, for the huts burnt down, and the property destroyed, for the blood shed on both sides, I should like to know! You are quite right, X——; there should have been no trial at all; the old fellow should just have been strung up at once. But this playing at justice has made the whole affair contemptible.'

I thought so too, when I came to know a little more about it, though not quite in the sense that the speaker meant. However, I made no further remark at the time, nor did I think it worth while to point out the confusion of ideas between that most just of all courts, a court-martial, and 'no trial at all,' as displayed by the last two speakers.

A house on the roadside was next pointed out to me where lived a man who ran out to spit in the face of the captive chief when he, a manacled prisoner, was on his way to Durban and when the cart in which he was being conveyed stopped to change horses. It appears that there was no one present upon that occasion who possessed manhood enough to knock the scoundrel down, nor has he since been lynched, or in any way taught what Englishmen think of such dastardly actions. I must also say that the deed, although censured by my fellow passengers of the 'bus, seemed to excite nothing more than mild disapprobation amongst the speakers, with the exception of the respectable old citizen of Pietermaritzburg before alluded to. I am bound to observe that the old man came out with a speech which displayed a manly and Christian spirit for which I honoured him.

I had not wished to embroil myself with my chance companions, and had therefore checked the indignant words which rose to my lips, although, in old Scripture phrase, 'it was pain and grief to me.' But the aforesaid citizen spoke in my stead. He declared boldly that he looked upon Langalibalele as an injured man who had done nothing to deserve the treatment that he had received, which was a disgrace to the colony. He went on to say that amongst them all there was but one man who had been wise enough to see the truth, and bold enough to declare it, although very much to his own injury, as he (the speaker) well knew. 'This one man,' he said, 'was doing all in his power to save the colony from the consequences of the fatal mistakes that had been made. He was Natal's best friend, both to black and white, but got nothing but abuse from the latter. And,' he concluded, 'you all know whom I mean—the Bishop of Natal.'

I have said that only one of the *speakers* seemed to feel for the oppressed tribe. But there was one other present who, although perfectly silent, evidently took a vivid interest in the subject. This was one of the young ladies in the charge of the Roman Catholic priest; and I had observed her with some attention as the rapid changes in her countenance evinced her intense dissent from the harsh sentiments enunciated, her indignation against the cowardly attack upon the prisoner, and her pleasure in the old man's defence. Now, when the Bishop was spoken of so highly—he had been alluded to already although not by name, in terms far from flattering in connection with this affair—she leant forwards to look at the speaker, with heightened colour in her face. It was manifestly as much as she could do to keep silence, but it was as evident that it would not be well for a lady to take part in a discussion with these rough men, and she sank back into her place, contenting herself with a whispered remark to her priestly escort, who, indeed, seemed to be rather nervous, and excessively anxious to keep her quiet. I could not help thinking that, if that young lady were to take the reins into her own hands, and speak out her mind, the priest would be rather like a hen with ducklings. However, she seemed submissive enough. I observed that an awkward silence fell upon the party after this direct mention of the Bishop, and wondered what could be the cause. A few minutes later we stopped to change horses, and I chanced to overhear a little conversation which took place between the same lady and the last speaker. He stood by the 'bus door to help her out; and, as she gave him her hand, she said to him, 'I do not know who you are, sir, but I cannot refrain from thanking you for the way in which you have just spoken of my father.' 'Ah!' he replied, 'my name is ———; of course you know me now?' My own private impression is that the name conveyed not the slightest information to her; but the momentary blank expression which crossed her face was instantly banished, and she replied promptly, 'Oh! Mr.——, of course, I beg your pardon.' 'Indeed,' he said, 'I feel that I ought to beg yours for speaking of the Bishop before you at all.'

I thought to myself, 'Bravo, old gentleman, there's true delicacy of feeling; *you* feel that it is not quite the thing to speak of her father in her presence, even in his praise, while these other fellows make no scruple of hinting abuse pretty freely.'

Before we started again I inquired of one of the legislators who had exchanged remarks with me before, who were the two young ladies with the Roman Catholic clergyman. His reply was, 'that one is one of Bishop Colenso's daughters, the other I don't know, but I believe she has something to do with the convent school in Durban.' So that my original guess was right about one of the two, though not about both.

Welch's Half-way House, where we dined, is certainly as good an inn as one can wish to find in a colony. It is neat and clean, and its mistress is thoroughly the mistress of the art of plain cooking. A cheerful incident occurred on our leaving Welch's, which seemed to enliven the journey a little, and to give me an insight into the method of horse-breaking in vogue in Natal. We were driving six horses, and one of the wheelers put in this time seemed to take an unusual number of men to hold and harness him. On inquiring I was told, 'Oh! he's only been in harness once before. We're breakin' of 'im in.'

Accordingly, the ragged-looking native grooms having let go the six horses' heads, we started. No! I mean we tried to start. Five animals bounded forwards, but our unbroken steed took a direction of his own, not contemplated by the rest of the party, and in two seconds he was down, all four legs kicking in the air, and then rolled beneath the 'bus. The passengers were requested to descend, the horse was dragged out and righted, and then we submissively got in again and tried once more. This time we made a fair start, though a rapid one, and tore along the road at a great pace for a mile or two, after which the wild horse settled down to his work, and the pace became more moderate. I was surprised at the *sang froid* exhibited by the women of our party, and concluded that rough travelling must be too common an occurrence in Natal to excite remark or alarm. Even the baby girl did not seem at all frightened, although much concerned as to whether the 'poor little horsie' was hurt or not.

During this stage of the journey one of the young ladies getting rather faint, as well she might, from the suffocating heat within the 'bus, was given a place in front by the driver, where she could enjoy the breeze. The men, though a rough-looking set, were civil enough in this matter; and the driver, a young fellow in corduroys, with his head tied up in a handkerchief, took great care about covering her dress from the dust with a cloak, and fastening the latter securely down. I was sitting next to the driver inside, and could hear every word that passed above me. I was at once struck with the perfectly free-and-easy style of his speech. He was not rude, and did not mean to be so, but he evidently considered himself completely on an equality with any passenger who might be in his charge. The young lady by his side, indeed, appeared a little surprised, and it was plain enough that this was a new experience to her; but she took it all in good part, seeing, I suppose, that the youth intended nothing but politeness, although her replies were slightly monosyllabic. For some time he entertained her with short accounts of the conduct of his passengers on such and such occasions of danger, and his own driving experiences, delivered in a spasmodic and occasional manner, in the intervals of controlling his horses, and making a point of telling her not to be frightened whenever he had time to think of it, that is to say, whenever there was the least occasion. To do her justice she did not seem to require the advice. He next expatiated upon a topic highly interesting and gratifying to me, namely, the great change and improvement in the condition of the roads since they had come under my Chief's supervision. Never before had they been kept in such excellent order. At last, after a short silence, the driver, turning to his fair companion, inquired, 'Have you such a thing as a pin about you?' There was an astonished look from a pair of blue eyes, and then, after a moment's deliberation, the pin was produced from some mysterious fold or other, and gravely presented in silence. It was immediately used as a toothpick, the young man remarking the while, 'I've got a tooth here that has been bothering me all day.' After which he proposed to return it. My young friend of the blue eyes, however, did not seem to view the proposition with favour, and replied, 'Had you not better keep it in case you should require it again?' Whereupon he stuck it into his coat sleeve.

I was wondering whether such familiarities were matters of course in Natal between young ladies and omnibus drivers, when I became aware that she at all events did not look upon them as such, for her face, turned perseveringly away as though she were intently observing the scenery, showed signs of so much amusement that her final victory over her sense of the ridiculous struck me as highly commendable. At the next wayside inn the driver pulled up, dropped his reins into her hands with the words, 'Just hold them a minute, will you?' and was off the box in a second. I heard her murmur to herself, 'Suppose they go on!' The next time we changed horses, she resumed her place inside.

CHAPTER IV

THE REBELS

My fatiguing, but not entirely uninteresting, journey came to an end by half-past five, at which hour the 'bus drew up at the Plough Hotel. Here we all alighted; and, glad enough of our release from confinement and each other's very close companionship, we went each our several ways. I must confess that I experienced a slight sensation of relief at seeing my St. Helena *protégée* received and taken away by her own friends; for the thought had crossed my mind more than once how remarkably embarrassing it would be should she prove to have no friends, and should she appeal to me for assistance and protection.

Pietermaritzburg is approached from the Durban side by a wearisome length of flat, dusty, uninteresting road. The slight undulations over which the way passes for the last fifteen miles strike one as doubly monotonous after the wild and beautiful broken country through which the middle stage is cut. The little city—extremely pretty at that distance which lends enchantment to the view—had seemed close at hand for a long while. Lying in its basin, amongst hills, it showed a picturesque mass of houses and trees, amongst which the tall feathery spires of the bluegum stood out conspicuous. The white buildings of Fort Napier, rather bare but business-like, rose boldly above the town, the greater part of which it commands, against a background of loftier hills, dim in the gentle haze which prevails through the Natalian winter months, when only foreground objects have a sharp, decided outline. But such charms as the scenery possessed had lost their power long before we had passed the last undulation of the road, and drove rapidly down to the Victoria Bridge. Past the Park, we rumbled over the dustiest bit of road that we had yet encountered, running—melancholy entrance to the capital of a country—right through the public cemetery. On either hand, tombstones, shrubs, and trees were alike whitened and stifled by the heavy dust; and, amidst a cloud of the latter, which rendered us invisible to the passers-by, and them to us, we drove up to the Plough Hotel.

Hiring a native to carry my portmanteau, I walked straight towards Fort

Napier, where I knew that the Colonel lived. I was in so dusty a condition that I hardly liked to appear in the streets, which, somehow or other, in spite of the dry, dusty weather, managed to preserve an air of cleanliness and freshness, at least in the less public thoroughfares. Probably, however, this was greatly due to the many trees and running streams of the town. The trees are now fast being cut down and the streams covered over by the municipal authorities.

However, there was no help for it, as the streets of Pietermaritzburg boast of no public conveyances whatsoever. So, giving myself one good shake, to get rid of what superfluous dust I could—much as a dog does on coming out of the water—I started off at a brisk pace for the Colonel's quarters. His *home* I did not feel that I could call it, for there was nothing homelike about it, save for the two baboons, who had a comfortable establishment of their own in the courtyard, the horses in their good stables, and the dogs and native servants. But for the master himself there was but little attempt at comfort. Strict military order and cleanliness reigned from end to end of the little domain, but nothing more. His sitting-room and dining-room was his office; his bedroom a narrow slip behind it, or, in fine weather, a tent set up in the garden. The garden itself was of a considerable size, and contained a number of old trees. It was all freshly laid out when I saw it for the first time, for the Colonel had only lately come to live there, and his plants had not yet had time to grow and embellish the place. I wandered about it for some time, more and more depressed by its deserted and melancholy appearance, until at last I came back unconsciously to the garden gate and halted there. How long I remained thus wrapped in a brown study I know not, but I was roused by a cheerful voice close behind me, which exclaimed, 'What! Atherton Wylde! you moralising over a gate at this time of day!' I turned to find that I had been so absorbed by my own meditations that I had heard nothing of the Colonel's approach on horseback, until he had ridden up so close to me as to overhear some sudden outspoken words which had escaped me.

'We shall have no time for moralising now,' said he again, as he sprang from his horse, and gave me his hand with a kind welcome. 'Our work is cut out for us for the next few months. Of great importance I think it, for many reasons of which you shall know more shortly.'

At his arrival the silent deserted habitation seemed to spring suddenly into life, and to assume an entirely different air. A couple of native men—servants, clad in suits of spotless white canvas, edged with scarlet—rose as it were from the earth to take his horse and his orders, with a respectful salute of '*Nkos!*' [*Anglicé*: 'Chief,' 'Master.'] A splendid dog of the kangaroo-hound species had followed in his steps, and now stood watching for the caress which was presently accorded him, and casting at me an occasional glance of that polite reserve with which a noble dog commonly treats his master's stranger-guests. And, as we went indoors, various other meaner dogs started up on either hand to greet their master, who had a kind word for each, although evidently full of thought and business.

'Now, Wylde,' said he in brisk business-like tones, 'I have some despatches here to attend to which will occupy me for half-an-hour, after which I must ride up the hill to my rebel working party there. Take something first,' as his servant brought out wine and glasses at a signal from his master, 'and then, if you can get rid of the dust and fatigue by the time I start, you may as well take my second horse and ride with me. I will tell you something of my plans on the way.'

By the light of later experience I see now how particularly absurd was the excitement into which I was thrown by the Colonel's speech. But I must candidly own that, utterly forgetting the lesson I had already received that very day upon the force of such expressions as used in Natal, that one word 'rebel' sent the blood flying through my veins, and my thoughts running ahead with all the eagerness natural to a hot and foolish young soldier. I immediately concluded that some body of men working upon the roads had turned insurgents, and that we were to quell them by force of arms. As to asking any questions, I did not dream of such a thing, nor would I allow myself to show the excitement that I felt, the Colonel's own calmness, and quiet, unconcerned manner inspiring me to assume the same.

After the day's heat and dust, a bath and a change were most welcome; but I was in too great a hurry to enjoy the relief as thoroughly as I should have done had there been no 'rebels' on the hill, in prospect. I had observed that numerous weapons of all descriptions adorned the walls of the outer room, or office, and I came out, when fresh dressed, eager to have some assigned to me, and to see what force was to accompany us. My Chief had just finished his writing, and two horses stood ready saddled at the door. But the warlike preparations, which I had fondly expected, where were they? The Colonel, truly, was in uniform; but that was nothing unusual, and he bore no visible weapon, nor were there armed retainers of any sort in view. I was puzzled. However I kept my curiosity to myself, and we mounted and rode away.

We proceeded for some little distance in perfect silence. The Colonel's mind was plainly engrossed by whatever he had in hand, while I would not speak upon the subject which occupied my thoughts, and could not speak on any other.

He broke silence first by saying something more of the importance in his opinion of our present enterprise. Whereupon I ventured to inquire whether he intended to enter upon it unsupported. My readers will probably conclude that either I was mad myself, or else that I thought my Chief so; but in fact I had given him an allegiance so complete that I should not have dreamt of questioning the reasonableness of any proposition of his.

'No,' he answered carelessly, 'Captain B—— of the 75th, and his company go with me, and the young Basuto chief, Hlubi, with some fourteen followers, besides the Putini men.'

I thought that I now understood the matter, and that we should presently join our force. The Colonel probably carried a revolver, and did not wear a sword because it would be worse than useless to him on horseback with his injured left arm. And as for me, I supposed that it had escaped his notice that I was unarmed. I must therefore make shift to snatch some weapon from the enemy, and if I fell in the attempt—well, one could only die once. Nursing these heroic resolves I rode on while the Colonel resumed his discourse. 'We shall give confidence to the people of Weenen County, who are certainly in a horrid fright,' said he. 'Poor things! as Dr. Livingstone says of the Dutch Boers, they are very brave when kafirs have no guns. You see we shall penetrate into odd holes and corners of the country. The natives of Zikali's and Somadula's tribes will see the "Ama-soldiers" for the first time, and the result will, on the whole, I expect, be good.'

I was more mystified than ever, for, having once lost the right clue, I was getting farther and farther away from the truth at every word; and, as there were limits to even my dutiful want of curiosity, I tried to make a dash out of the fanciful labyrinth in which I had involved myself, by asking where we should get to that night.

It was now the Colonel's turn to look astonished. 'Tonight!' he exclaimed, 'back to my quarters, I hope.'

'I give it up,' murmured I to myself, while he continued.

'Did you imagine that we were making a start in this style? I cannot get off for another day or two yet. Ah! here are my rebels.'

I looked up eagerly as we rode round a sharp turn in the road which concealed the next two-hundred yards from our view, and made ready for the dash with which I was to secure my weapon, when——! But blank surprise and disappointment fell upon me as the 'rebels' came in sight. About a hundred men were drawn up at the side of the road under a corporal and four privates of infantry with some military precision, although they were truly a ragged regiment; but all bore picks and shovels ready for the legitimate work, and saluted my Chief with the utmost respect and submission.

'The outbreak seems thoroughly quelled, sir,' remarked I rather awkwardly.

'There never was any,' was his startling reply as he put his horse into a canter, and rode up to the party. Plainly we were still at cross purposes, and he imagined my remark to apply to the late 'rebellion' of the whole two tribes. And now, having inspected the men, and given some directions to the corporal in charge, he turned his horse's head homeward again, and we retraced our steps.

By this time the sun was sinking; but, as it vanished, the colder light of the moon high in the heavens made all around almost as distinct as by day. As we rode back my curiosity finally got the better of me, and I could not help saying to the Colonel, 'Excuse me for asking, sir, but why do you call these poor creatures "rebels"? What have they done?'

'What have they done? Nothing, I believe from my soul,' was the reply. 'I call them rebels in derision of those who are afraid of them. They are prisoners of the Putini tribe, which was "eaten up," as they call it themselves, on a charge of complicity with Langalibalele. They were given over to me at my urgent request to work upon the roads. The whole thing, as far as they are concerned, is now allowed to have been a mistake, and their freedom, and that of their tribe, is one of the chief objects that I have in view in our expedition up-country. The poor creatures have been as good and quiet as possible, and work well. I am endeavouring to persuade Government to promise them their freedom on their return from the Draakensberg mountains, where we are about to destroy the passes, supposing that they do their duty well, of which I am well assured. And I hope the release of the whole tribe may follow. You understand, of course, Wylde, that these things must not be spoken of. I have confidence in you, and trust you to keep counsel well; but discretion is most important now. A word from you, were you to get talking amongst your friends, might do much mischief and perhaps upset my plans.'

I hastened to assure him that I should look upon any confidence which he might be good enough to repose in me as a trust, to violate which would be most dishonourable; and I remarked besides that, even if I were inclined to be indiscreet, I should have no temptation in that line at present, as I did not know a single soul in the place, except himself alone.

In return I learnt from him much which I can safely say never passed my lips nor left my pen until long after the plans of which he told me had been either carried out or abandoned.

'The main object of this expedition upon which we are going,' said he, apparently satisfied with my assurances, 'is to restore confidence to Weenen County, which is shaken to its foundations by fears of an attack from the young men of the Hlubi tribe, who are reported to be collecting on the borders under the command of my friend Mabudhle, one of Langalibalele's chief captains, with whom I have already exchanged "love-tokens," ' (with a glance at his wounded and still useless left arm). 'There are also supposed to be parties of marauders lurking in the county. One or two houses have already been attacked, two persons stabbed, and an attempt made to treat the Resident Magistrate in the same way. I rather imagine that these are individual acts of personal vengeance, committed perhaps by men whose women and children were killed during the expedition last year, and that they must not be considered as systematic attacks upon the white population. Nevertheless, the state of panic to which they have given rise must be checked at once. It is also desirable to destroy the passes in the Draakensberg, bordering Weenen County, of which I believe there are many, although upon that point I can obtain but little information from those who have long lived in the colony, and who certainly ought to know. These passes once destroyed, it will for some years be impossible for horsemen to enter Natal on this side, or for cattle to be carried off over the range. I intend to take this party of so-called "rebels" with me to act as pioneers, in which capacity I have no doubt but that they will render valuable service, and thus enable me to claim from Government the pardon of the whole tribe, and their restoration to their old location. Government, I think, must by now be fully aware of the mistake that has been committed in "eating up" this innocent tribe; and the good services of my hundred pioneers, in closing the passes adjoining their own location, will afford a fair excuse for setting the whole tribe free, and for making restitution so far as may be possible. By this means the colonial authorities will extricate themselves from the very unpleasant dilemma in which they now find themselves placed, as I am convinced that the Imperial Government will never sanction such gross injustice as has been perpetrated, and it is necessary that the matter should be promptly taken in hand.'

Such was the substance of my Chief's discourse, to which I listened in attentive silence, feeling excessively anxious to get hold of matters by the right end at once, and knowing that such opportunities as this might not often fall in my way.

It struck me then, as it has often struck me since, for how very little he himself went in his own estimation of whatever work he had in hand. The liberty of these unfortunates, the peace of the country, the calming of fears for which he certainly had a lively contempt, were all objects for his utmost exertions. So also was even the honour of the Colonial Government, the late actions of which I rather fancy went shares with the aforesaid 'fears' in this respect, although while under it he served it as truly and energetically as he has all his life served that Imperial Government which has always owned his highest allegiance.

With these objects in view, he formed, and he carried out, an enterprise

involving the severest hardships to himself at a time when he had not
sufficiently recovered from wounds and consequent illness to endure them with
impunity. Yet, never then nor since, have I heard him claim the slightest credit
to himself in the matter. To the outside world he held himself as the servant of
the Government, obeying its orders, and carrying out its plans—plans which he
alone had made, and to permit the accomplishment of which he had with the
greatest difficulty to persuade an undecided Governor, and the crafty
unscrupulous men who governed him. Later on—as I saw with my own eyes—
he had also to force the same rulers to keep the promises which they had made to
the Putini tribe, and which they would have broken had not my Chief's stern
uncompromising sense of honour kept them, with the greatest difficulty, to the
mark. But of this more hereafter.

I dined that evening with the Colonel, his fine dog Prince sharing the banquet
with us, evidently quite as a matter of course. His behaviour was most
irreproachable and gentlemanlike. He sat at his master's side; his tall graceful
head above the level of the table, and his beautiful eyes gravely surveying the
dishes. He patiently awaited his share of each. If he thought himself forgotten he
made no sound nor disturbance of any kind, but raised one great paw, and laid it
gently upon the Colonel's arm in mute entreaty which could not be resisted. His
master told me that Prince was his constant and only companion, and evidently
thought a good deal of him, while Prince as plainly returned the compliment.

I slept that night in a second tent pitched in the garden, which, as the weather
was not yet chilly, I found extremely pleasant. It was the first time for some
years that I had slept under canvas, but it was not to be the last; and during the
next few months I had ample opportunities of comparing such comfortable
camping out as my Chief's thoughtful kindness and hospitality afforded me at
Fort Napier with the bitter cold of lying under canvas on the Draakensberg in
winter time.

CHAPTER V

THE MINISTER FOR NATIVE AFFAIRS

The next day was Sunday, and upon the following morning I was sent up the hill to direct the non-commissioned officer in charge of the 'rebels' to have them paraded at ten o'clock. It had been arranged that at that hour the Head of the Native Department should address them, and inform them of the duties for which they were destined, promising them in the name of the Government that they should be released on their return, should they have conducted themselves to the entire satisfaction of the *Inkos* under whose orders the operations were to be carried out. I was glad of the opportunity of witnessing this ceremony; and had, besides, some little curiosity to see the Minister for Native Affairs, whose character and importance to the country I had often heard discussed by the colonists, amongst whom opinions varied to so great an extent that whether, as some said, he was the wisest and best man of his age, the saviour of the colony, commanding the most absolute respect and affection from the whole native population whose many years of peace were entirely due to his wise and strong government—or whether, as others asserted, he was a crafty scheming man, bent on increasing his own power, and whose policy for years had been dishonest, unprincipled, and rotten to the core—was an open question to my mind, and one upon which I did not venture to question the Colonel.

I had a pleasant four miles' ride through the fresh yet sunny morning air that May day, reaching the 'rebel camp' in good time for all arrangements. The hundred Putini prisoners had now been for nearly five months at work under the corporal in charge of them, and during that time he, whether by his own choice or owing to the military spirit which presided, had contrived to drill them into no despicable condition of order. They marched in sections of four, and took up their position in line by the roadside in a manner which surprised me.

Punctual to the minute my Chief appeared on horseback, accompanied by the Head of the Native Department, and several native chiefs and *indunas*.* There was a great deal of saluting and respectful shouting as the party rode up and

* *Indunas* – head men; in the army – captains.

dismounted, and a general condition of anxiety and excitement prevailed, from which, I am free to confess, I was by no means exempt. Chairs for the two white Chiefs were now placed in the shade at the end of the building which formed the 'rebels'' barracks, the accompaning native dignitaries sitting on the ground to their right and left, whilst the 'rebels' formed a semicircle at a little distance in front. As for me, I took up my position a little behind the Colonel, and as close to him as possible, determined to see and hear all that I could; although, had I been aware of how long I should stand there, and how little wiser I should be at the end of the proceedings, perhaps I might have spared myself the trouble. I understand now that the whole thing was done in true native style, and that it is the custom of the Head of the Native Department to imitate as much as possible the habits of a Zulu chief in dealing with his people. Accordingly, he first held a consultation with his own special followers, which to my English ideas lasted a most unreasonable time, seeing that not one of them had a voice in the matter in hand, or would have ventured to do otherwise than say 'Amen' to their lord and master's remarks. Certainly, there was a good deal of snuff used on both sides, the natives taking large quantities in their curious bone or horn spoons, whilst the Head of the Native Department at intervals gravely tapped an elaborate silver snuff box; but it did not seem to hasten matters, and might as well have been done at home as far as I could see. But then, I, being an Englishman, and once a soldier, was accustomed to a prompter method of doing business, and was not so well-versed in kafir customs as the Head of the Native Department. His manners were those of a paramount chief, his habits of thought evidently running in the same groove; and I confess the scene appeared to me to be a solemn farce, and nothing more. I stole an occasional glance at my Chief, trying to read his opinion of it all in his face, but it was imperturbably calm, and not more weary-looking than usual in repose.

After a conversation with his own followers which seemed interminable, the great man at length addressed the expectant Putini people, who up to this time had preserved a decorous silence. Another lengthened parley now ensued, in which some half-dozen of the captives took a respectful part. Knowing no Zulu, of course I could not tell what passed, but the outward appearance of proceedings was as follows: a few words fell from the lips of the great white Chief, upon which a discussion took place amongst the hearers, one of whom then took upon himself to rejoin. After a pause—with snuff—more words of wisdom flowed from the lips of the great Chief, when the same ceremony was repeated, and so on, again and again, until, I confess, I was very weary. From tone and manner I concluded that commands and promises were being dribbled out to the poor creatures piecemeal, and that their replies were thankful acceptations of whatever justice and mercy they might possibly receive. But why should it take so long? The prisoners had nothing to urge; there was nothing for them to talk about; they were simply to be told so and so, and there should have been an end of it. But no! kafir-like, the great man considered it necessary to talk. Surely the whole thing might have been settled in five minutes, instead of which it took nearly two hours!

My mind was certainly unfavourably impressed by my first experience of the official method of managing native matters in Natal. It seemed to me that I was in the midst of an assemblage of savages only, whose modes of thought and ideas were different from anything to which I had been accustomed. I could hardly believe that I saw before me the man who has for so many years controlled, in England's name, the destinies of the native races of Natal. I felt, rather, that I saw the Zulu despot in the midst of his savage retainers, and to me it has long been inconceivable that England's honour should have been entrusted, since the birth of this her colony, to one who at heart was but a Zulu chief. At last it was over, and the ruler of the blacks departed with his retainers. I looked up at my Chief and thought I saw relief painted upon his countenance.

'What was it all about, sir?' said I.

He shrugged his shoulders. 'What matter so long as I carry out my plan?' said he, and turned at once to his work.

The men were sent to eat their midday meal, which had been prepared for them during the conference, and the Colonel then inspected the whole of the entrenching tools which had been laid out in order and ready for the march, directing some trifling alterations to be made, and satisfying himself that everything was in complete condition for service.

How different he was now from what he had appeared for the last two hours! Then he was silent, bored, yet quietly resigned to his fate, and to Mr.————'s tardy operations. Now he was full of life and energy, seeing into everything with his own eyes, forgetting nothing, overlooking nothing, and doing all as rapidly as thoroughly. I stood by and took lessons, ready at any moment for an order to myself.

Presently appeared, ready to start, a procession of five two-horse carts, the leading one flying a red flag denoting danger—and properly so, for it was laden with barrels of gunpowder to be employed in purposes of demolition.

The other carts were laden with tents, implements, and provisions, and all passed our Chief for inspection. Now the signal was given by the corporal in charge of the 'rebels,' when they fell in as if on parade, each man clad in a serviceable greatcoat and having a good warm blanket, rolled and worn horse-collar fashion over one shoulder and under the other. In addition every man carried his rolled sleeping mats, and a couple of long native sticks. The Colonel narrowly inspected this party, and noticing that several of the greatcoats looked worn and thin, he directed fresh ones to be given out from a supply which he had sent up for the purpose. It was pleasing to observe the satisfaction evinced by some of the recipients, who, having come from the locality to which they were now bound, fully appreciated the sufferings from cold and exposure which they were about to encounter. My Chief further observing that ten of the men did not look so robust as he considered necessary to encounter the anticipated hardships, directed them to fall out and to remain in barracks during the absence of their comrades.

All being now ready, each man shouldered his pickaxe and shovel; and, the signal being given, the party marched off apparently in high glee, and singing one of their national war songs.

Having seen little or nothing of the natives in their wild state I felt a great curiosity and interest in them, and was somewhat struck by this war song, which, proceeding from so many, had an impressive effect. Not that all sang, or rather shouted, together the whole time. One man, a leader, whether from his rank amongst them, or from his powers of voice, commenced, and chanted alone for a few minutes a monotonous dirge-like song, which was presently chorused by the whole body with a loud long shout of 'Hau! Hau! Hau!' and then the solo commenced again.

CHAPTER VI

ESTCOURT

Leaving the 'rebel' barracks behind us we slowly climbed the long steep hill which, rising above the town of Pietermaritzburg, forms the first and most difficult stage of the journey to Estcourt.

The Colonel's orders to us were to make short marches at first, in order that both men and horses should gradually be inured to hard work, and our first day's march, accordingly, was one of twelve miles only, to Howick, an inn close to the Falls of the upper Umgeni. This is a general halting place for travellers up-country, as well as a common resort for picnic parties and visitors to the Falls.

We reached Howick at about 8 P.M., marching having been but slow. But then, besides the fact that much of the road was uphill and our men heavily laden, we met with various accidents which caused delay. We could not have started in better order than we did, and the Colonel's careful forethought and personal attention to every detail of our equipment, etc., should have saved us from mishap, if anything could. But it is in the nature of expeditions, however well planned, that something should go wrong, and we were not exempt from the general rule. That unlucky ammunition cart in particular seemed bound to come to grief, whether from its weight, or that the driver was not as careful as he ought to have been. At all events the 'danger-flag' struck twice during our two first days' march, the cart upsetting, and in one instance a keg of powder bursting. However, no serious damage was done except to the wheel-horse's knees, which were badly cut.

Then there was delay at Howick in waiting for slaughter cattle; delay again at Currie's, our next halting place; and another twelve miles' march, owing to a report brought by one of the drivers that the Colonel's marquee had been lost or stolen from the waggon in his charge. There were two waggons belonging to our party which had been sent on a couple of days before us, and it was from one of these that the marquee had vanished. All our efforts to recover it were in vain. We never saw it again.

Such, however, were the most serious disasters which we had to report when, during our fourth day's march, the Colonel overtook us, and preceded us into Estcourt, the chief village of Weenen County, where we remained four days before starting for the mountains for which we were bound.

On the morning after our arrival our camp was visited by our Chief, who had lodged for the night in the village. He inspected the party, making minute inquiries as to the health of the men and the fitness of the horses for service; and, I am glad to say, finding everything to his entire satisfaction. He next ordered all the stores to be unpacked, carefully surveyed them, and had them repacked so that we should be ready to start at the shortest notice. That would be as soon as the infantry detachment, which was to accompany us under Captain ———, should receive a fresh supply of boots from Pietermaritzburg, which they were awaiting, and without which the British soldier could not be expected to march any great distance.

His business at the camp concluded, the Colonel turned to me, saying, 'Now I shall go and report myself to the Acting Resident Magistrate, Mr. M———, as it is only right that the chief civil authority in the County should know of all the movements of the troops therein. You may as well come with me, Wylde.'

Accordingly we walked across the Estcourt Bridge and turned our steps in the direction of the Magistrate's office, when we were overtaken by that gentleman in person on horseback and accompanied by an armed native escort, without which, I was afterwards told, he never stirred a yard by night or day. This fact was very significant of the feeling of the Magistrate as to the state of the County, and his subsequent speeches showed the condition of unreasoning terror to which men's minds had been reduced.

My Chief saluted him with courtesy, and the deference due to his office, making himself known to him in the following words, 'Allow me, sir, to introduce myself to you as the officer commanding the troops in this County. I am about to patrol the line of country immediately under the Draakensberg, and to destroy the passes leading out of Natal.'

The Magistrate's reply to this courteous address astonished me not a little. 'I should like to know, sir,' he said, in very angry tones, 'under whose advice Government has sent these rebels up to ravage the country. Not one of them will be with you in a week, and we shall all be murdered in our beds.'

I confess that I felt very indignant on hearing my Chief so rudely attacked; but he replied, 'I do not think, sir, that you have any reason to be alarmed. As to the men whom I have brought with me as pioneers, I can answer for it that every one of them will return with me when their work is accomplished. If there are marauders in the County they will fly before us. Nothing but good can possibly result.'

Forebearance and condescension in explaining matters were quite thrown away upon the Magistrate; so, with a quiet remark, my Colonel turned upon his heel and left him.

As we returned to the camp he exclaimed with an indignation which Mr. M———'s incivility to himself could not rouse in him, '*They* know how to treat the natives! Up here they would enslave them if they could. And now,' he said, 'I must go and pay my respects to the family of the Resident Magistrate, who is himself away in England on sickleave. He commanded the volunteers and native levies of the County of Weenen during the recent disturbances, and I made his acquaintance then. You can come with me, if you like, Wylde.'

I could not help telling him that, ready and willing as I was to accompany him anywhere, I sincerely hoped that I should not often be obliged to stand by and listen to uncourteous language addressed to him without the power of resenting it.

He laughed, telling me that, were I to quarrel with everyone who spoke ill of him in Natal, I should have my hands pretty full; for that just now he was about the best-hated man in the colony.

I knew it well enough; but it was grievous to me all the same, even although I knew also that it was for exactly those qualities which I respected most in him that the colonists and their newspapers reviled him.

'If we had our own men here, sir, as in the old days, I hardly think the curs would venture a second time,' I exclaimed with some heat. 'They would have had the houses of some of these wretched editors down about their ears long ago, and have ducked them in the nearest stream.'

My Chief could not help smiling a little at the recollection I brought up of the hundred-and-twenty bronzed and stalwart men of his company, each and all of whom would have looked upon an insulting word to their Captain as a wrong to himself, not to be passed over without punishment; and who would, undoubtedly, in such a case as this of the colonial newspapers, have taken the law into their own hands, careless of the consequences to themselves. But none the less did he reprove me for my intemperate language, warning me against allowing my indignation to get the better of me, and pointing out that, as his own personal follower, I must be doubly careful, as whatever I did or said would undoubtedly be laid to his charge.

I promised obedience and discretion the more readily as I had already had a little opportunity of relieving my feelings on that point, which I did not think it necessary to confess to my Chief, as no mischief had resulted. The facts were as follows: immediately upon our arrival the previous afternoon, I had fallen in with a private of infantry who had known me by sight during the time that I was hanging about Durban. Finding me now attached to the service of the Colonel, whom, in common with his comrades, he held in the highest estimation for his gallant and soldierly conduct during the expedition of 1873, he hastened to inform me of the state of mind prevailing in Estcourt towards my Chief. The Acting Magistrate's speeches were fair examples of this. The people were mad with foolish terror, and looked upon the Colonel as their deadly foe, about to bring death and destruction upon them at the hands of our poor peaceful, docile pioneers. The condition of panic which our operations would finally allay was at this time only augmented by our appearance. The man told me that numerous abusive placards concerning the Colonel were posted about the town, and that he knew who had done it.

'What is his name, and where does he live?' I inquired sharply. His name was X———, and he was staying at the Estcourt Hotel, was the information that I received. Consequently I came to the wise resolve of dining at the Estcourt inn myself that night, on purpose to pick a quarrel with Mr. X———. I wonder what my Chief would have said to me had he known of my intention!

At the hotel that evening we sat down to dinner some dozen men, amongst whom I was the only stranger. As such, however, my companions addressed me occasionally, with the lack of ceremony natural in a colony. They talked freely amongst themselves, and I soon discovered that the adversary that I sought sat exactly opposite me on the other side of the table. Nor was I long in finding an opportunity for the remark that I had to make. The conversation very soon turned upon my Chief and his doings, and the tone of the comments made were such as to lead me to think that I should presently have twelve quarrels on my hands instead of one. A momentary pause in their talk gave me the opportunity I required. Looking steadily across the table at Mr. X———, I said very deliberately, and in a voice loud enough to be heard by all present, 'By the way, I should much like to know the man who has been posting abusive placards concerning Colonel Durnford about this town. Could I see him before me I would certainly fling this glass of wine in his face.'

A dead silence followed my defiance. I had expected Mr. X——— to spring to his feet, and hurl it back again; but he only turned very red, and shifted uneasily in his chair without meeting my eye, and presently began to talk very fast to his right-hand neighbour upon some matter of farming.

Whereupon the rest of the company fell to feeding again, and to talking upon indifferent subjects; and I, feeling that my dinner would certainly choke me on the top of so much unexpended indignation, rose and left the room and very shortly returned to camp, which I had much better not have left at all. I never heard any more of Mr. X———.

In order to pay our visit to the family of the Resident Magistrate we mounted our horses and rode for about a mile-and-a-half by the riverside, through an undulating grass country, covered with mimosa bushes, arriving at a long thatch-roofed house, embowered in trees.

Here we were received by the ladies of the household, and by a brother of the gentleman from whom we had lately parted upon Estcourt Bridge. I suppose I must have been long enough out of the society of ladies to become shy; for, although I used not to be afflicted in that way, I was certainly so far overcome by being suddenly brought into an assemblage of the fair sex, that I had only a very confused notion of the names and number of those to whom I was introduced, and hardly knew what I was about until I found myself seated on one side of the room, being entertained by a young lady—name unknown—who owned a pair of fine dark eyes, and the Colonel talking to several other ladies and Mr. ——— opposite us. Our conversation had not got very far when that upon the other side of the room became so interesting to us both that we simultaneously stopped talking, and turned our attention to what was going on.

The Colonel had just discovered that, in consequence of the supposed dangerous state of the country, the ladies were about to leave Estcourt and take refuge in Pietermaritzburg; and he was entreating them not to adopt such a measure, knowing full well that, did they do so, a universal needless panic would prevail. He called upon the eldest daughter of the house (the mother was in England with her husband) to behave as became her father's child, and to set the example which she knew he would approve. After some persuasion, his arguments, more especially his appeal to Miss ——— as her father's daughter, prevailed. The young lady of the dark eyes, who I now found was a visitor from Pietermaritzburg, expressed herself as quite ready to take her share of the expected dangers; and the Colonel dispelled any doubts that might remain by promising to leave a corporal and three men of the infantry as a guard to protect them.

I soon observed that Mr. ———'s attitude towards my Chief was very different from that adopted by his brother, the Acting Magistrate, for the former seemed as friendly as possible. He was just concluding some agreeable speech or other with these words, 'And I hope, Colonel, if you ever pass our way, you will do us the pleasure of stopping the night at our house'—'we' standing for himself and his elder brother—when, to my great amusement, that unfortunate old gentleman entered the room in time to hear every word of an invitation which he certainly would not have ratified.

His look of horror, and his extreme discomfort at again so soon meeting the Colonel—whom he evidently looked upon as a firebrand of the hottest description—and finding him on such excellent terms in the family with which he himself was residing *pro tem.*, were so marked that my anger against him almost evaporated in delight at his discomfiture.

Our visit had already lasted sufficiently long, and we shortly took our leave and returned to camp, in the appearance of which a considerable change had taken place during our absence. The place was now thronged with native women and girls—the wives, mothers, and sisters of our captive pioneers.

These poor women had seen all the men of their tribe torn from their homes some six months before, their homes burnt, and their land laid waste, while they themselves were sent to live in a sort of half-captivity under the guardianship of so-called 'loyal native' chiefs.* They knew not what were their offences against the Government. To them it must have seemed that the white forces, and their native auxiliaries who came out against Langalibalele, disappointed of their prey, finding nothing worth confiscating, and comparatively little to kill, had turned their arms against a peaceful well-to-do little tribe, an easy unsuspecting prey, that they might not return home empty handed.

Ah! seeing how well the Putini spoils would have 'paid expenses,' and the Putini prisoners supplied 'cheap labour,' if only a convenient veil could be drawn over the little transaction to the eyes at home in England, I no longer wonder at the unpopularity of my Chief, who did so much towards tearing off that veil, and who, behind the scenes as he necessarily was, would not consent to the plan of 'every man making his own little game.' To him duty alone was clear, and he could not comprehend this 'working round crooked places,' as I have heard him term it.

Most of the Putini women had probably never expected to see their male relatives again, after they were carried off by the *impi* [army]; for according to the customs of savage warfare, which were carried out to a lamentable extent by us in that unlucky expedition of 1873, they would expect them all to be put to death. So now hearing, in the speedy way in which news always flies amongst the natives, that some of the long-lost ones were so near again, they poured into the camp to see them, all bearing offerings of native luxuries, such as pots of *tshwala* [native beer], mealies, pumpkins, etc. etc., for their respective relatives. The joy of the poor creatures on both sides was most affecting to witness, and no one present on that occasion could have doubted that warm family affection exists amongst the kafirs.

It was, however, but a short-lived happiness, for those precious colonial authorities seemed to have no vestige of human feeling towards their

---

* There are facts connected with the treatment of these women by the said 'loyal natives,' permitted and supported by the British authorities, which are hardly fit for these pages, but may easily be learned by those interested.

NATIVE COUPLE IN THEIR OWN COSTUME

unfortunate victims. For that one afternoon content reigned in the camp; and I need hardly say that our Chief was heartily glad that his *protégés* should have their hearts cheered and their spirits raised by a meeting with the families to whom he hoped to restore them in a few months' time. But on the following day a complaint was made to him by one of the 'rebels' that while taking a pot of *tshwala* from the hands of his sister, a native policeman, belonging to the magistrate's court, had snatched it from him and struck him over the arm with a *knobkerrie*. The Colonel directed the complainant to go at once to the magistrate's court then sitting, and attended himself, making the complaint that one of his men had been thus assaulted. The Magistrate dismissed the case as one founded on insufficient evidence. But this was not all. He considered that in any case the policeman would not have exceeded his duty in taking the pot from the 'rebel'; and he forthwith ordered that, in future, any women of the tribe of Putini found in Estcourt should be brought before him, in order that he might commit them to gaol, as, he said, *there was no knowing what mischief and fresh rebellion might not come from their being allowed any communication with their male relatives.* He further requested my Chief to give orders that no women should be allowed to enter his camp while at Estcourt, in which the Colonel acquiesced in deference to the civil power; although, in conversation with me afterwards, he freely expressed the indignation and contempt which he felt for the want of manliness and humanity which alone could dictate such tyrannical orders.

I must not forget to mention here that the party of Basutos, headed by their chief Hlubi, whom the Colonel had previously mentioned as forming part of his intended force, joined us upon the first day of our stay in Estcourt. These were some of the men who had so gallantly stood by him at that disastrous affair at the Bushman's River Pass; and I was not a little anxious to see them after hearing the high terms in which the Colonel spoke of their valour and discipline. They were small active men, upon small active horses, to which they seemed to belong almost as completely as did Attila's Hunnish followers to the steeds from whose backs they were reported never to descend. Each man of the Basuto party carried a blanket rolled behind his saddle, and a greatcoat rolled before him, and each man was armed with a breech-loading carbine. This was the whole of their equipment, and they looked what they afterwards proved themselves to be, a most serviceable body of scouts.*

---

* These Basutos are a far more civilised race than the Zulu kafirs. They dress in European clothes, live in square-built houses instead of huts, and can most of them read and write in their own language and in Zulu—not a few of them in ours also; but they are inferior in physique to the Zulus.

While we were at Estcourt, or soon after our departure, there appeared in one of the Pietermaritzburg newspapers an article which so exactly illustrates the feeling of the public concerning our expedition, before time and circumstances had proved our harmlessness, that I cannot do better than quote it entire, especially as it is a very amusing composition.

It will be in the remembrance of every reader that, during the last session of the Legislative Council, a scheme proposed by Major Durnford for drilling the Kafirs for road parties was submitted to the Legislative Council, and was unanimously and peremptorily rejected. Of course everybody considered the matter settled, and that the scheme had passed into the limbo of oblivion. But such we find is not the case. The Governor had the good sense to bow to the decision arrived at in the Council, because it was his duty to do so, especially when it was so well known that the Council had echoed the unanimous voice of the people. On the other hand, if the information we have received from Estcourt be correct—and we cannot doubt its truth—Colonel Durnford has deemed it to be part of his duty to disregard the authority of the Council, to insult it, and through it, the people, by placing a large body of natives under military drill. Two issues ago we informed our readers that Colonel Durnford had taken a large band—about one hundred and twenty—of the Putini tribe to blow up the passes in the Draakensberg. It was not sufficient for this recalcitrant Colonel, that sympathisers with, nay, members of the rebel tribe should have been chosen for this purpose, which gives them abundant opportunity to escape from the surveillance under which they are at present held, but that they may be the more formidable when they do escape, the Colonel has been taking the trouble to drill them. We are told, on good authority, that the Kafirs were drawn up in two lines, and ordered to dress, take open order, march—all which they obeyed with considerable precision, which showed that the instruction had been going on for some time . A drill-sergeant accompanied the party. This process of instruction was gone through *near to the magistrate's office at Estcourt*! and Mr. ———, who was lately so nearly assassinated, very wisely remonstrated with Colonel Durnford for pursuing such a course, and, in particular, that he should have chosen a place in close proximity to the magistrate's court to make such an exhibition. The Colonel, who has an infinite opinion of himself, replied with much *hauteur*, 'It is no business of yours, Mr. Magistrate, I know my duty.' The Colonel seems to be one of those high-minded persons who look upon the people of the colony as so many dogs as compared with himself, and who deems it good fun to insult a helpless Council, that may talk and pass resolutions, but can do nothing more, and which it is the duty of the officials to disregard and treat with contempt. Whether the people will quietly permit such open defiance of their will, and such barefaced violation of their orders, remains to be seen.

This effusion, amazingly incorrect, both as to fact and as to grammar, in spite of its comic magniloquence, afforded the 'recalcitrant Colonel' and myself immense amusement. One could not help wondering with what object the colony supports its 'helpless Council.' Can it be from pure benevolence to the members?

CHAPTER VII

OUR PERILS ON THE ROAD

The next few days were spent by the Colonel in inspecting us, our men, waggons, carts, horses, stores, etc., and in seeing that all our arrangements were perfected, until at last, upon the afternoon of the fifth day after our arrival at Estcourt, the troops were ready to march. The boots had arrived, and the detachment joined the expedition. The carts set off by one route across country, the waggons by the road, we ourselves keeping with the former. All promised a fair day's journey, when a messenger, sent across to us from the road, brought us the unwelcome intelligence that one of the waggons had stuck fast in a mud-hole, in which it remained immovably fixed. We camped for the night at a native kraal, near which the news of the accident had reached us, having made but seven miles that day.

Of course no further advance could be made until the unlucky waggon was on the road again. So the next morning saw a working party engaged in digging out the wheels, which had sunk above the axle-trees in mud.

No pleasant piece of work at any time is that of getting a heavily laden South African waggon out of a hole. The patient suffering oxen, struggling under the repeated lash against a dead weight upon which their strength makes no impression—the shouts and oaths of the drivers and crack of the whips—all under the blazing sun of an African midday, intensely hot even in winter, and surrounded by a parched brown-looking country—all this forms no agreeable picture for the memory to dwell upon. We, of course, prevented as much as possible the ill-treatment of the beasts; and when they—fourteen or sixteen great creatures, with humped backs and wide-spreading horns, harnessed (or 'inspanned,' as they say in Natal) two-and-two with huge wooden yokes—fell back exhausted and in confusion, the men seized pick and shovel and worked away at the buried wheels; and then, after ten minutes' toil, we tried once more what the results of our labour, and the recovered strength of the oxen, urged on by voice and lash, would do for us—yet still in vain. The work must be done. There was no help for it. We off-loaded the waggon at last, and even then the attempt was repeated a dozen times, before, with toiling, straining cattle, groaning and creaking timbers, and hot tired drivers, the huge lumbering machine stirred from its muddy bed. Then, with another effort, the spent oxen urged once more to full exertion, all hands pushing and tugging at the wheels, the waggon was on dry ground. The men loaded-up again, and it proceeded slowly on its way, with the chance of sticking fast in like manner in some other mud-hole before the day's journey was over.

Such is waggon travelling over most roads in Natal; and such, I have often been told, was the case even on the main road between Durban and Pietermaritzburg, until my Chief took it in hand as Colonial Engineer. Since that time such scenes have not occurred upon that section of the road. Our own experience was what I have described, though it was not the same waggon which stuck fast a second time that day. The latter accident occurred to another very heavy one, called in South African parlance a 'buck-waggon,' which was laden with the equipment of the troops, and which came to grief at the first muddy stream we crossed.

'This won't do at all,' said my Chief, and next day he sent out a working party to repair about four miles of road, which was in a particularly bad state, crossing a stream with very muddy banks. This was done on the principle that a stitch in time saves nine, and that it is easier to mend a hole than to pull your waggon out of one. Indeed, although the work delayed us another day, it was time well spent, and saved us much in the end.

The change in temperature, after leaving Pietermaritzburg, had been very great. There the nights were still warm when we left, but they were very cold by the time we reached Estcourt, where we found frost nightly, and saw snow upon the hills about seven miles off, an unusual occurrence, I believe, so early in the year.

Naturally we found it colder as we approached the mountains, and we were all of us, white and black, glad enough to sit round our blazing camp-fires at night.

Upon the last evening of our encampment at the kafir kraal, all were thus resting and warming themselves when a suspicious incident occurred. Round one of the fires sat some half-dozen pioneers, their dark faces and white teeth lit up by the glare, and brought into strong relief against the black moonless night. They were talking fast, but in subdued tones, for close by, although in the shadow, sat the Colonel, attended, as usual, by myself, while at a little distance stood a British soldier on guard, also shrouded in darkness.

To anyone arriving in camp the assemblage would have appeared to be merely one of natives belonging to the kraal, for there were not even 'white voices' at this particular fire. My Chief and I were equally silent, while we chanced to be the only Europeans close at hand except the sentry. The rest were either distributed around the other fires, or asleep in their huts.

Suddenly we were aroused—my Chief from his thoughts, myself, I confess, from a doze—by the sound of horses' feet, and next minute three natives, armed and mounted, appeared within the fire-lit circle. They saw neither us nor the sentry, and, evidently looking upon the party as a gathering of their own kind only, dismounted without more ado.

From where we were sitting their every motion was visible to us, and I never saw faces express greater consternation than did theirs when they caught sight of the Colonel's tall commanding figure, clad in uniform, as he advanced into the light of the blaze and demanded who they were. I kept close to him, meanwhile, under the influence of that vain hope of some day coming between him and danger, which throughout our expedition caused me to follow him as closely as his shadow whenever the work he gave me to do permitted it.

Without making the slightest attempt at an answer or explanation, the men rushed to their horses, endeavouring to mount and escape; but under such suspicious circumstances, and the still unsettled state of the country, that could not be permitted. My Chief sprang forward to arrest them. The sentry and I immediately following his example, and the fugitives, seeing that they had no choice but to submit, made no resistance, but laid down their arms and surrendered. They seemed unable to give any satisfactory account of themselves, or of the arms in their possession, consisting of five guns besides native weapons; nor had they any passes, without which it was at that time unlawful for natives to travel. Accordingly the Colonel detained them for the night, but released them on the following morning upon their being identified by Hlubi as retainers of the chief Zikali, a well-known 'loyal' subject, and one who had rendered service to the Government during the late disturbances. They were of a class whom I had already learnt to know as 'Government devils,' on account of the savage character of the acts perpetrated by them in the name and under the protection of the Government. I confess that I looked upon them and their kind as far more worthy of being kept prisoners and punished than our poor peaceful 'rebels,' except that after all they did but follow the example and carry out the orders of their white masters, who, not being ignorant savages, were therefore far more guilty than they.

Nor was this our only experience of the same sort. On the afternoon of the following day, as I was riding with my Chief and the advanced guard of Basutos, we saw about two miles distant a party of five armed natives on foot, running towards some rocky and broken ground, as if for concealment. The Colonel immediately ordered two of the Basutos to ride in one direction, and two in the other, for the purpose of cutting them off, while he himself rode straight for the flying men, followed, of course, by me.

The country was open and undulating, affording capital galloping ground, over which our horses went at full speed, doubtless sharing with their riders the exhilarating effect of rapid motion through the fresh, almost frosty air. I was enjoying myself to the utmost, feeling that I should never care to draw rein, when suddenly and unexpectedly I found myself brought to a standstill in a way which I by no means relished. My horse had plunged up to the girths in a morass, from which I extricated him and myself with considerable difficulty. Much annoyed at the delay occasioned by my accident, I pressed on again as quickly as possible, and breasting the heights beyond, I saw, at a few hundred yards' distance, my Chief alone, parleying with the fugitives, who appeared indeed to have turned at bay. I made all haste to reach the Colonel's side, but, as I galloped down the gentle incline towards the spot, I became aware, to my no small alarm, that the demonstrations upon the other side were decidedly warlike. Those men who had guns were beginning to handle them in a suspicious manner, while the others were unmistakably brandishing their assegais.

'One against five,' thought I, as I urged my horse to his utmost speed. 'He with but one hand for weapon and reins, and I out of the way as usual. Just like my ———— luck!'

But before I reached the spot my anxieties were relieved. My Chief had quietly dropped the reins upon his horse's neck, and drew the revolver which had hitherto been carried in his holster. The sight of it intimidated the foe, and, a couple of Basutos galloping up with cocked carbines in one direction, and I in another, the men laid down their arms and surrendered. We kept them with us for a couple of days, until we could identify them. After what has gone before, my readers may not be surprised to learn that these prisoners also turned out to be 'loyal natives,' also without passes, and carrying unregistered guns. They proved, however, to have been out upon Government service, and to be on their way home after escorting a Government official from one place to another; under which circumstances one would have imagined that they would have been carefully supplied with the passes requisite for their safety, which, however, was not the case. Of course the Colonel released them, while we rather wondered why they should have given us the trouble of chasing them, still more, why they should have resisted the Colonel's authority.

Their behaviour puzzled me considerably. At first I was inclined to think that their fear of us was a plain evidence of guilt of some sort. Were they, I argued, on a little expedition of their own, hunting out stray fugitives of the dispersed tribes for purposes of plunder or murder? Were they, perhaps, tacitly permitted so to do by their white captains, some of whom are known to have called for 'no prisoners,' with a bloody significance in the words, during the late 'rebellion'? My mind, I confess, was in a state of suspicion, owing to the tales of wrong and cruelty which I had already heard, and I was ready enough to believe anything of 'Government devils' and their masters. After the full explanation which we received from these five men, however, that little theory of mine was destroyed in this individual case; and upon further consideration I could only arrive at one conclusion as to the cause of the behaviour of both parties of would-be fugitives from our path. The conclusion left upon my mind is that these men, although one party at least was in Government employ and doing no wrong, were afraid to trust themselves in our hands, because the native experience of white men's justice and mercy, especially during the late disturbances, was such that they felt that no innocence on their part was a safeguard against cruelty and oppression. They had lost all faith in their white rulers; and my Chief was a stranger to them, who, for aught they knew, might promptly have them stripped and flogged, if not even put to death, as rebels, and no question asked or answered. Before we left this part of the country, the tribes residing in it learnt to know the Colonel better, and to fear no wrong or injustice at his hands; although, at the same time, they learnt to fear his just displeasure, and to pay prompt and entire obedience to his commands.

CHAPTER VIII

OUR JOURNEY ON

On the afternoon of the following day we arrived at Cathkin, a farm occupied by one of the true old colonists, Mr. ———. This farm is situated at the base of the Draakensberg, close to the location lately inhabited by the Putini tribe, the well-known peak, called Cathkin, or Champagne Castle, towering magnificently above the general line of the mountain range.

The Colonel rode on in front of the party to ask the permission of Mr. ——— to camp upon his farm, which the latter accorded; protesting, however, the while that these desperate 'rebels' whom we had brought with us would soon be dispersed over the country. Nevertheless to us he showed himself most hospitable, and, only stipulating that the 'rebels' should not be allowed to approach the house, he invited us all in, and soon set before us an excellent repast. ——— might be taken as a good type of the hard-working successful colonist. Settling in Natal many years ago, he has, by steady industry and perseverance, realised no inconsiderable fortune, in adding to which he was now assisted by his sons, whom, with excellent common sense, he has brought up to follow such trades as are useful in a new and sparsely inhabited country. Of the two at home while we were at Cathkin, one was a good waggon-builder, the other we found to be an experienced blacksmith. The house in which the family lived was substantially built, the signs of the times evident in the strong shutters attached to every window, to be closed at sundown, the heavy bars to the doors, the care with which the cattle and horses were kept in their kraals at night, and the guard of armed natives, provided by Government, which was posted every evening in the verandah.

I have been told that formerly, that is to say before the expedition of 1873, doors and windows were not even closed either by day or by night; and I believe that in most parts of the colony such is still the custom of the white inhabitants, except in the towns or in their immediate neighbourhood. This fact in itself seems to me to prove the peaceful and honest character of the uncivilised natives, amongst whom I believe thefts are absolutely unknown.

At the time, and in the locality of which I write, however, the bars and bolts were no unnecessary adjuncts. Peaceful and inoffensive as are the Zulu-kafirs when unmolested, they are not devoid of spirit, still less, as I have mentioned before, of family affection; and some of them had lately been driven by their wrongs to take vengeance upon their white oppressors.

Terrible stories there are, known to many but suppressed by most, of atrocities committed upon the so-called 'rebels' six months before—women and children killed, caves containing fugitives of both sexes fired into, and the unhappy occupants finally smothered by the smoke of fires lit outside for the purpose. These deeds were done by white and black on 'our' side—with shame I say the word—and vengeance had been attempted more than once by some of the unhappy survivors. Therefore it was as well that the houses in this part of the country should be furnished with bolts and bars.

One of the young men accompanied us as a guide when we left Cathkin, as he knew the country well; and I had some opportunity of conversing with him, and of eliciting his 'young colonial' views of matters. I thought that from him, living as he did close to the scene of the late disturbances, I should at least be able to learn in what way Langalibalele earned the title of 'bloodthirsty rebel,' which I had so often heard applied to him, and what his people had done to deserve the severe punishment which had fallen upon them. I confess that I was disappointed by the answers that I received. I hoped to find that at least our cause was good. I wished to think that we English had reason in the main for what we did, and that, although acts had been perpetrated by 'us' which all Englishmen must condemn, yet that they were but the individual instances of cruelty almost inseparably connected with a savage warfare, in which savage auxiliaries and independent volunteers are employed. Could tales have been told of attacks upon farmhouses and the white families living in them, of murder and insult to women and children, of any such injuries as would naturally put the fire of indignation into our hearts and brains, I should have been satisfied that punishment was justified, harshness excusable, and even cruelty not much to be wondered at, although deeply to be regretted.

But of any such justification or excuse I never heard a word. Not a single outrage had been committed of any description, not a head of cattle even stolen from the isolated farms in and close to Langalibalele's location. In answer to my questions our young guide had plenty to say, and all the usual complaints to make. The kafirs were lazy and 'cheeky,' they had been getting more and more so, and thought themselves as good as the white men now. In fact it was the old story; the black man did not care to be the white man's slave, and the white man could not endure the black man in any other position. This feeling, and this only, I believe to have been the cause of the expedition of 1873; and this same feeling would very soon bring about—what would prove a very different matter—a war with the Zulus, were it not, fortunately for all concerned (even for those who most resent the restraint put upon them), that our English Government at home keeps such a vigilant watch over her colonies, to prevent unjust and unnecessary wars. Otherwise, the very existence upon our borders of a large body of natives whom we cannot tax, who are not our servants, nor obliged to treat us with any especial respect, would certainly sooner or later bring about aggressive acts on our part, which in their turn would irritate our neighbours into giving us some handle for undertaking a war of invasion against them. Such a war would certainly be a bloody one on both sides, entailing consequences hardly to be calculated either in sorrow or duration. May just and wise rulers, under Providence, spare us such an evil!

As to Langalibalele himself, I must distinctly assert that although I have taken some trouble in making inquiries from those likely to know, I have never been able to gain a clear notion of what constituted either his long course of disrespect towards Government, of which I have heard so many vague assertions, or the 'rebellious' conduct for which his tribe has been destroyed. That he ran away instead of coming when he was called, under a well-founded fear of treachery from the whites, seems to be the extent of his offence. The more I heard of the expedition of 1873, of the reasons for it, and of the way in which it was carried out, the more did I hate to think that in such a cause, and in company with such men, was my Colonel sent to fight, and receive the wounds, one of which permanently disabled him. He simply did his duty, and I need hardly say, perhaps, that he had no share in the cold-blooded butchery—I can call it nothing else—which went on for weeks after the one fight at the Bushman's River Pass. All that time, regardless of his own wounded and shattered condition, he was away upon the mountains, in pursuit of the main body of Langalibalele's men, and for the purpose of intercepting another tribe supposed to be about to follow in the steps of the first. It is indeed to be regretted that he was not present to prevent such scenes as that which took place at the cave, since known as 'Colenso's Cave,' where for two hours one of the tribe held his own in a crevice amongst the rocks, against a force armed with carbines, revolvers, and rockets, surrendering only when covered with wounds, and unable to defend himself longer. Then, appealing and trusting to the white man's mercy, he came out, and, instead of being honoured as a gallant warrior, he was, after a short consultation amongst his captors, then and there shot! The place where this occurred has been called 'Colenso's Cave,' because it was the Bishop of Natal who raised his voice against this unworthy transaction. He had got his information from the accounts given of it in the papers by some of the

men present, who indeed were chiefly white men, and seemed, from their own
story, to see nothing unusual or base in their performance.

Our guide was thoroughly Natalian in his ideas on other subjects besides the
'Rebellion.' His remarks upon 'volunteers' amused me. He evidently thought
but little of the regulars, and had unbounded faith in his own kind—for he
belonged to a volunteer corps himself. The late failure of the Carbineers at the
Bushman's River Pass in nowise shook his faith.* Either they were quite right
to—*retreat*, let us say, when they did, or else their having done so too soon was
the fault of those who placed them—free independent volunteers, with a right
each to his own opinion!—under the command of a regular officer, who
actually expected them to obey his orders, and to behave like soldiers! Such, in
fact, seemed to be the prevailing opinion. One of our white drivers, I remember,
expressed himself much in the same tone, but in worse English, than my young
friend from Cathkin.

'Volunteers is not like reg'lars,' said this worthy gentleman. 'They oughtn't
to be expected to obey like them soldiers. They're all as good as another, and
ought to be axed their opinion, and not ordered.' I have often heard like
sentiments expressed by Natalians; nor have I ever, in conversation, found that
the word 'discipline' conveyed the slightest idea to their minds. Theoretically,
martial ardour had, I believe, been excessively rife before the expedition in
which it was first put to a practical test; nor had the dangers and discomforts of
that campaign entirely extinguished it; although it certainly was a pity that it
failed so entirely at the first sight of the faces of an armed foe.

We left Cathkin early on the morning of the second day after our arrival, and
effected the passage of the Sterkspruit, about three miles from the house, with
some difficulty, owing to the nature of the ford, or 'drift,' as it would be called
in Natal.

Both the track into the river—I cannot call it 'road'—and the road itself
passed between high and steep banks. The water ran with excessive rapidity;
nor was it possible to cross it in a direct line, as, owing to the impracticability of
the shore on either side, and the interposition of a heavy sandbank, the landing
place on the opposite side was some fifty yards higher up the stream than the
point at which we entered it. Nor was any more direct passage feasible.

It would be difficult to imagine a scene of greater apparent confusion than

---

* This was written in 1875; since then Natal has received a severe lesson as to what war really
means, and her volunteers have learnt a soldier's duty; since then, also, the Natal Carbineers
have retrieved the honour lost by their corps at the Bushman's River Pass, by the gallant conduct
of those other members of the same corps, who fought and fell under and with the same leader at
Isandhlwana. See note to this chapter, pages 54 to 59, for full account.

that at which I assisted on that day in the transport of our heavy waggons and carts over the Sterkspruit. Each waggon was drawn into the water by its own team of eighteen oxen, when, a sharp turn being made up-stream, a second span was required to drag it up along the sandbank to a position opposite the 'pull-out.' And now a third span is added, for it takes the united efforts of fifty-four oxen in all to drag the lumbering vehicle up the steep broken bank on the other side, and to land it safely on level ground again. As to the carts, their horses were powerless to effect their passage. The animals were all taken out of the shafts and led over alone—even that not without considerable difficulty. And then the whole of the ninety pioneers seized each cart in turn with a right good will, and, by dint of pulling, pushing, and shouting (a great deal of the latter), foot by foot they gained the opposite bank.

The difficulties of the day's march were so great that we had only accomplished a distance of eight miles when we encamped for the night. Nor was the next day's journey less arduous, at the close of which we pitched our tents at the foot of the Little Berg. This is a short range of mountains running parallel to the great Khahlamba or Draakensberg, and which we had to cross in order to reach the passes of the larger range leading from Natal into the broken and almost uninhabited country beyond, in former years the haunt of the predatory Bushmen, a race now almost extinct.

Our last day's march was of the most difficult description imaginable, the hills being often so steep, and the track—if track there were—so broken and rocky, that it was only by the most strenuous exertions on the part of every member of the expedition that the carts and waggons could be forced over them at all. Occasionally, when we had to take the latter up some more than usually steep incline with half-loads upon them, the united strength of the whole fifty-four oxen only sufficed for one at a time; whilst the only chance for the carts was to have them taken up by hand as, previously, across the drift.

But farther than the foot of the Little Berg not even thus could any vehicle be moved. It was very evident that pack-horses and oxen were our only means of transport over the range. Accordingly a camp was formed at this point in our journey, to which we should have to return after destroying the two passes for which we had been bound in the first place—Gray's, No.1, and the Old Bushman's (not the Bushman's River Pass, which lay about fifty miles distant).

At this camp, then, we left our carts, waggons, and oxen in charge of a few Europeans, whilst arrangements were made for the ascent of the Little Berg without them.

For this purpose pack-saddles were fitted to the horses, well padded with sheepskin, as the animals had already fallen off in condition, from work and exposure. Sacks sewn together formed a substitute for saddles for the oxen, which, with breast-straps, crupper, and overhaul girth, made a fairly efficient equipment, each ox carrying a load of about two-hundred-and-fifty pounds of meal or flour.

These oxen were trained to carry loads, and had been obtained from the chief Somathla (a near relative of the celebrated Langalibalele), who had been directed by the Colonel to send him all beasts capable of such service, with men accustomed to their care. The men were rationed with the pioneers, and the chief was well paid for the use of the animals, without the assistance of which, indeed, we could not have caried sufficient food supplies for our party.

The ox is a capital beast of burden. He is sure-footed, docile, carries a heavy load, and, being of gregarious habits, requires but little care in driving; as, if the first animal is led in the right direction, all the others will follow. His climbing powers also are remarkable. Give him but his own time and he will take a load over almost any country. An untrained ox is, of course, troublesome. It is necessary to throw him, in the first instance, in order to put his load upon his back, and when this is firmly secured, and the ox allowed to rise, he immediately commences a series of evolutions—bucking, kicking, and plunging—highly calculated to burst any but the strongest tackle. Yet, after he has indulged himself for a few minutes in this recreation, finding himself unable to get rid of the load which oppresses him, he subsides into a state of stolid endurance, and quitely takes his place amongst his better-trained companions.

The ascent of the Little Berg was by no means an easy one under even the best of circumstances. The mountain sides were clothed with long rank grass, which the extreme dryness of the winter atmosphere had rendered as slippery as ice, and it was very difficult for either men or animals to keep their feet. However, in due time it was accomplished, with no further casualties than the roll of one pack-horse and two oxen for a considerable distance, but without much damage done, and the total disappearance of one of the wildest of the pack-oxen, who, having performed a series of somersaults for about four hundred yards down a grassy slope, thought he had had enough of it, and having got rid of his load during the descent, disappeared at full speed in the direction of his customary feeding grounds. As for ourselves, we slipped, slid, and rolled, and picked ourselves up again, in a manner calculated to try the endurance of the strongest and most active amongst us, but nevertheless without any worse accident occurring to any of us than a few bumps and bruises.

A British soldier, indeed, was somewhat unceremoniously disposed of by one of the cattle driven with the expedition for slaughter purposes. The man happened to be the last of his party, and was cautiously picking his way at a very narrow point upon the mountain crest, when the animal behind him, possibly excited by the dangers of the passage and the sight of the man's scarlet coat, and pressed upon from the rear by the other oxen, rushed at him, and, fortunately passing his wide-spreading horns one on either side of his body, propelled him, with considerable velocity, into a thick growth of underwood, which, luckily for him, broke the violence of his fall, and he escaped unhurt.

We camped for the night of the fourth on a grassy spur, running from the base of the Champagne Castle peak, under a hill with a most extraordinary hole in its crest, through which the sky can be seen on the other side. The cold was considerable here, and we were glad enough to crowd round our blazing fires. Our appetites, too, were somewhat keen, and it was not unpleasant to witness the preparations for dinner which were carried on by our soldier-cook under the stars of heaven, with as much equanimity as if he were officiating in the mess-kitchen of his regiment.

The pioneers, meanwhile, were enjoying themselves immensely after their own fashion. Seated round a number of great fires, they were engaged upon their meal of fresh meat just singed in the flame to their taste. A beast had been shot for them that evening, of which but little remained till morning except the horns and the hide. During the intervals of mastication the tide of conversation flowed freely among them, and one was glad to see from their contented faces and frequent laughter that, although hard-worked, they were not unhappy, and were probably cheered by the hope of freedom held out to them by my Chief.

Indeed nothing could exceed the zeal and good will with which these poor fellows fell to whatever work the Colonel set them to do. Perhaps they might not have done as well under other masters; of that I cannot speak; but I do not believe that there was anything so difficult or seemingly impossible that they would not have attempted at the command of one whose mingled kindness and firmness had won their respect and affection.

With the fifteen Basutos this was still more evident. They, of course, were in more fortunate circumstances than the captive Putini people. They were free followers of the Colonel, who had led them to the fight, at the end of which they undoubtedly saved his life. To so warlike a race as they are, the kind master was doubly dear who was also the dauntless leader, and of its sort I never witnessed anything more touching than the mute devotion paid to my Chief by the Basuto warriors.

Of those fifteen who were with us upon the mountains, the names of two besides that of the young chief, Hlubi, are specially impressed upon my mind—

namely, Jabez and Windvogel. And of those two men I was jealous, although I liked them.

Windvogel aroused that feeling in my breast by a little action which for some time escaped my attention, but which after a while I discovered to be a constant practice of his. During those days of painful climbing and scrambling on foot over well-nigh impassable mountains, along precipices, through rocky defiles, by-ways and no-ways which none less enterprising than Colonel Durnford would have attempted, his wounded helpless arm and injured shoulder placed him at a great disadvantage, doubling the toil for him and the danger of accidents as well. I often wondered how he could climb in safety over places where I, with two strong arms to help me, felt life and limbs to be insecure. I thought a good deal about it, but Windvogel did something better than think. I soon discovered that whenever I looked to make sure that the Colonel was not in difficulties, Windvogel was always close to him, between him and the edge of the precipice, or just where he would be of use in case of a slip. As soon as I became convinced that there was a set purpose in this on the part of the Basuto, I felt aggrieved that what had escaped my thoughts should have occurred to him. I should have liked to send him away and to take his place myself; but I felt that on the one hand that would be neither fair nor generous, and on the other hand that such a course would defeat my own end. Windvogel could do unnoticed what would be instantly apparent were I to attempt it; and the result of my interference would probably be that both of us would be dismissed from such close attendance upon the Colonel, who very likely was quite unaware of Windvogel's guardianship, being entirely engrossed in the passage of his little army. Besides, I candidly confessed to myself that Windvogel, with his lithe agile frame and unshod feet, was fitter for the post than I, with my heavy boots and want of mountain practice. So I felt a little sulky for the rest of the day upon which I made the discovery, and made a point of giving Windvogel some of my best tobacco when we camped for the night.

As for Jabez, I remember him rather for his words than for his actions, for he was the only one of these silent undemonstrative men whom I ever got to talk freely or to speak of his devotion to our Chief. Jabez had lately visited both Estcourt and Pietermaritzburg, and those visits must have loosened his tongue; for he was in a state of hot indignation at the way in which he had heard the Bushman's River Pass affair, and the Colonel, spoken of in those towns, especially at the latter place, and by the friends and relatives of the volunteers. A very little encouragement from me would cause him to pour out a flood of eloquence amazing for a Basuto.

'Why these *Wolumteers* say Mr. Major make them all run away!' he would cry. (Our Colonel was Major then, and will long be known by that title amongst the natives.) 'All people say so; I very angry. I tell them I *hear* Captain B———— tell Mr. Major wolumteers frightened and *must* go home! I tell this. Then all the people say, "Oh! I never hear that before." I wish everyone ask me. I come—I tell them all! I speak out! I cry loud! *All lies!* Why do them wolumteers say this, and speak bad words of Mr. Major? I see *all* run away; leave Mr. Major all alone. Hlubi cry, "Come back! you leave Major behind!" They never come; and then Mr. Major and Basuto they come behind. Wolumteers run in front. When Basuto see wolumteers run away some begin to go too; and then Hlubi cry out loud, "Basuto! you too going to run like girls, and leave our Chief to die?" Then all Basuto come back again, not one man leave Hlubi and Mr. Major.'

My readers will forgive me for softening Jabez's broken English in repeating what he told me next, for I do not care to spoil its meaning. He said that upon that unhappy day, when my Chief had done all that mortal man could do to stay his flying troops, and to make them face the *now* pursuing foe, and done it all in vain; when his voice was gone with shouting, and he himself exhausted, shattered by a fearful fall the day before, and bleeding from fresh wounds received from the foe, he stopped at last and turned.

'I saw him turn his horse's head,' said Jabez, 'and ride straight back towards the enemy alone. Then some of us made haste to follow him, and I rode up beside him, saying, "Where are you going, *Amarail* [Chief]? What do you want?" for I thought he might have dropped something, and wanted to find it. He did not answer me, but he turned his head and looked at me as we still rode back together towards the pass. And then I looked into his face, and knew what he was about. He was going back to die, because that his soldier's spirit could not endure that he should ever turn his back upon a foe. Then I caught his bridle-rein, and turned his horse's head; for though he was my Chief, and I must fight at his command, I could not let him fling away his life by riding back alone amongst three-hundred fighting men who had tasted blood. We all cried out, "Come back with us, Chief, you must not die for nothing." He was too weak from loss of blood and great exertion to resist us, and so we brought him off safe amongst us, and we all went back to camp.'

Need I say why I was jealous, though with no unfriendly jealousy, of the Basuto Jabez?

I asked the Colonel later on whether this account was correct; but all the answer I could get from him was a rather short, 'I suppose so,' and an immediate order to set about some work or other which must be done at once.

NOTE

While preparing this volume for the press I have received from a friend in Natal a paper containing an account of the battlefield of Isandhlwana, which is so much to the purpose that I insert it complete in this place.

It proves that upon that unhappy yet glorious day, the Natal Carbineers won back again the honour lost by previous members of their corps at the Bushman's River Pass. It would be an injustice to the memory of my late beloved Chief to omit the true story of the 4th November, 1873, from this narrative. It would be equally unjust to the memory of those who fell beside him at Isandhlwana to omit the true story of the 22nd January, 1879.

One further remark I must make upon the subjoined article. The editor, towards the close of a brilliant and truthful record, says that if the Carbineers could have made choice of a commander, Colonel Durnford would have been the last man they would have named. I must venture to observe that the converse statement would have been more correct, namely, that if he judged them by his old experience in 1873, the Carbineers would naturally have been the last men whom the Colonel would have chosen to command. Probably he did not judge them thus, but the moral remains the same. I believe I am right in saying that not a man of those who fled from the Bushman's River Pass was amongst those Carbineers who went to Zululand; and I will venture to assert that Colonel Durnford was precisely the commander under whom men, as ready for the post of honourable danger as the Natal Carbineers of 1879 are generally admitted to have been, would choose to serve. In support of this assertion I may mention that the friend who sends me this paper tells me also that the first man who went up to Colonel Durnford, when the Natal Native Contingent was being formed, and offered to serve through the Zulu campaign under him, was the only one living of the four Carbineers who responded to his demand, 'Will none of you stand by me?' at the Bushman's River Pass. The other three chanced to be the very men who fell.

This brave fellow left the corps after that unfortunate expedition, and was with Colonel Durnford as Lieutenant N.N.H. on that fatal day at Isandhlwana; but not at the last, for from that 'last' none escaped alive.

My friend, who knew Colonel Durnford well, also tells me that, deeply as he regretted the death of those three Carbineers, and bitterly as I myself know he always felt the simple fact of having been forced to retreat before a foe, he knew himself to be so guiltless in the matter that he never felt himself in the least responsible for their death. He said, speaking of the Bushman's River Pass, not long before he left for Zululand, 'Thinking calmly over the matter at this distance of time, I say that I could have done no otherwise. Were it to happen again I must do the same, with the one exception that I should not return.' Yet, in spite of all he suffered, mentally and physically, in consequence of their failure, neither the friend who writes to me nor I myself have ever known him speak harshly of the Natal Carbineers.

Bearing the above in mind, I offer the following article from *The Natal Witness* of May 29, as giving the facts of the case, and the inferences to be drawn from them, as I should desire to give them myself:

> The field of Isandhlwana is beginning to give up its secrets; the mists of fiction are being dispersed by the dry light of fact. It has not been through mere idle curiosity that there has been a desire to know what passed during the final moments of that fatal struggle. There were difficulties to be explained, reputations to be cleared, allegations to be contradicted. There was the desire to know how those who were lost had died—to be sure that they died with their faces to the foe—to be satisfied that their death was not attended with any excess of cruelty or suffering. And there can be little doubt that it is the very anxiety to be assured of all this that stands responsible for the numerous fictions—as we must now hold them to be—which have been circulated with regard to what passed on that memorable day. Men who had been present in the early part of the day— and it is now evident that there has been as yet no reliable account whatever of what passed at the close of the tragedy—were largely influenced by their beliefs and their wishes, and, very naturally, were confused in their own minds as to what they had actually seen and what they thought must happen. As it is, the result of the recent sad visit to the camp completely reverses not only every story that has been afloat, but also every expectation that might have been formed. The report of what was actually found comes upon us as a surprise, and a surprise which, when it is carefully considered, lessens the pain that had previously been associated with the catastrophe. All the pictures—pictures both of pen

and pencil—that have been before the public, have represented certain broad features of the final conflict which, had it not been for this visit, might have been for ever accepted as true. They have represented the men of an Imperial regiment as standing back to back, and with their bayonets resisting to the last moment the pressure of the Zulu onslaught. They have represented the colonial forces, such as there were of them, as scattered hither and thither, acting, if bravely, quite without organisation or guidance. They have represented a commanding officer either as lost in the general *mêlée*, or, worse still, as having, with a coward hand, put an end to his own life. All these impressions will have to be reversed. 'The greater number of the soldiers were found one by one, in the long grass which covers the ground between the camp and the river. Colonel DURNFORD'S body, surrounded by fourteen of the Carbineers, and their officer, Lieutenant SCOTT, with a few Mounted Police and about thirty soldiers, was discovered at the mouth of the neck in rear of the Camp.' There is no mistaking the significance of these words, which occur in the telegraphic report sent us by our correspondent, who was himself on the spot. And equally unmistakable is the significance of the position in which the bodies of Colonel DURNFORD and his companions in death and in honour were found. Justice both to the dead and to the living demands that the real meaning of these facts which have come to light, after four months' suspense and doubt, should be fully pointed out. And it is satisfactory to be able to feel that, while these revelations add honour to names that have hitherto been unhonoured, they take nothing away from the reputation of those whose acts have already been recognised.

Let us go into the history of that fatal day, first so far as we know it from those whose narratives have been before us. That the attack on the camp came originally and mainly from the left front, seems to be a well-established fact. It was in this direction that the rocket-battery and mounted men went out to meet the enemy, with the immediate result, apparently, of forcing them to retire. The parties that had been out in this direction returned into the camp, and, as it would appear, the danger was regarded as so far surmounted that the men were allowed to fall out for dinner. And it is not a little remarkable that this account coincides, in a very striking manner, with the narrative of what passed while Colonel HARNESS, with his artillery and the three companies of the 2–24th were on their march after the General. The firing was heard, and the bursting of the shells was seen, by Colonel HARNESS, who at once, on his own responsibility, resumed his march towards the camp. His fears were derided; his movement countermanded; and about this time—somewhere corresponding with dinner-time at the camp—Lieutenant MILNE, who was on Lord CHELMSFORD'S staff, reported that the camp appeared to be all as usual. In all probability he was right. The enemy had retired on observing the retrograde march of the troops under Colonel HARNESS, and did not resolve to attack again—for it would appear that there were two distinct attacks—until Colonel HARNESS, unwillingly yielding to Lord CHELMSFORD'S special injunction, conveyed through Major GOSSETT, was well on his way after the rest of Colonel GLYN'S column, and too far away for his aid to be of any avail. Then, and not till then,—probably between one and two o'clock,—the second attack on the camp was made, and it remains a very grave question whether that attack would ever have been made if Lord CHELMSFORD had relied rather on Colonel HARNESS'S report, received through Major GOSSETT, than on Lieutenant MILNE'S field-glass. The second attack was made, and it must be remembered under what circumstances it was made. An urgent message had been sent after the General in the morning that the camp was threatened, and it must have become plain to everyone in the camp, by the time the second attack was made, that this urgent message had been disregarded. Owing to the neglect of the officer commanding the column—we leave it to others to decide as to whether that officer was Colonel GLYN or Lord CHELMSFORD —the camp had never been entrenched, and Colonel DURNFORD, when the second attack was made, found himself left to his own resources in a position which it was impossible to hold, unentrenched, against the force that threatened it. What was, under these circumstances, his duty as officer in command? He had successfully—owing doubtless to the distant and (to him) unknown co-operation of Colonel HARNESS—repulsed the first attack, and now saw no chance of holding the camp against a second attack, possibly, if not probably, made in greater force. His duty was, clearly, to sacrifice the camp, to save his men, and to cover, as far as possible, the line of communication with the base of the column at Helpmakaar. The situation was most critically dangerous. The Zulus were pressing on in large numbers, and the only thing to be done was to endeavour to hold the 'neck' with what men could be got together—for it must be remembered that, according to Captain ALAN GARDNER'S evidence, numbers were already 'on the road to Rorke's Drift.' The holding of the 'neck' was the place of danger and was therefore the place for the commanding officer. There was no appearance, at the moment, of any enemy in the rear of the camp between the hill and the river, and there might be, it seemed, if time could but be gained, a safe line of retreat for the whole force. The concentration—as Captain GARDNER'S evidence also shows—was accordingly ordered, and Colonel DURNFORD, gathering round him the few men who were willing to stand by him, prepared, as it would seem, with the assistance of the two guns, to make a bold stand in an advantageous position, and thus to cover the retreat of the bulk of the force. But it was too late. The Zulus were already in large numbers at the other side of the hill; the brave little band was surrounded, and was probably being exterminated, man by man, as the two guns made their dash through the 'neck' in the endeavour to reach Rorke's Drift. The rest of the story is soon told. Those who had before passed through the 'neck' found themselves surrounded by crowds of Zulus, through whom it was almost hopeless to attempt to force a way. And only when all was lost— when there seemed no chance of holding half-a-dozen men together—did the two gallant officers, who have lately received their well-deserved posthumous honours, make an effort, happily successful, though fatal to themselves, to save the colours of their regiment from capture.

We find no fault with the distinction thus conferred; but who, in the light of these recently discovered facts, were the real heroes of that day? Surely the two officers who commanded in that narrow pass at the rear of the camp—'poor' DURNFORD, whose 'misfortune' was so speedily telegraphed about the Colony, and Lieutenant SCOTT, of the Natal Carbineers. Surely, too, no smaller heroism was that of the fourteen Carbineers—the best part of those who were missing—who, mere boys as they were, gave their lives away in order to afford their comrades in arms a chance of retreat. The defence of Rorke's Drift has been compared to the Pass of Thermopylæ. But was not the holding of this pass by the Camp, in which every man shared the fate of the brave LEONIDAS and his companions, much more like that memorable action? The odds were greater; the choice more deliberate. Any one of these men might have had a chance for his life, had he chosen to follow the example set by so many. They remained, however, and they died; and only after four months of doubt, contradiction, and despatch-writing is it made known to the world who they were who have most deserved the coveted decoration 'for valour.' COGHILL and MELVILLE,—yes; CHARD and BROMHEAD,—yes; but more that all DURNFORD and SCOTT. 'Poor DURNFORD's misfortune' turns out to be no misfortune at all. The camp was lost through two causes—first, the neglect of the officer, be he Colonel or General, who neglected to see that it was entrenched; and next, the fatal error which led to the countermanding of Colonel HARNESS's retrograde movement, which contained the one chance of saving the camp. 'Poor DURNFORD's misfortune!'—but it was the best fortune which Colonel DURNFORD could possibly have looked forward to. Five years before his military reputation had been assailed, his judgment called in question, his name rendered unpopular in a colony to which he was peculiarly bound. The grave of the three Carbineers, at the head of Bushman's River Pass, was a grave in which seemed to be buried his own pride in his profession as a soldier. If the Carbineers, who on that former occasion believed that three of their number had been sacrificed through Colonel DURNFORD's blind obedience to a humanely meant order, could have made choice of a commander to be under in an hour of imminent peril, Colonel DURNFORD would have been the last man they would have named. By a strange—almost a startling —turn of events, however, the Carbineers found themselves again under Colonel DURNFORD's command in a moment when death seemed almost a certainty. Can we believe, however, that the old feeling of distrust remained with them? It is impossible. In moments when death is imminent—moments which, probably, no man ever survives to speak of —there dawns upon the mind a clearer light than is ever possible amid the worries and petty interests of ordinary life. And we may depend upon it that, during the short time that those gallant men stood together in the pass, while the enemy were pressing nearer and nearer, and while first one and then another fell death-stricken to the ground, there was a mutual recognition of worth which would have made up for a far longer period of misunderstanding. Could any man wish to die more happily that this?— covering a life which had been blighted with the memory of an undying glory, and receiving the affection of those who, by force of tradition, were most prejudiced against him? We have said this visit to Isandhlwana has brought us down to the dry logic of facts; but there is a solemn pathos and a poetry about this incident which passes expression. We grudge no honours either to the dead or to the living; but we claim for these two, and for all who fell with them, an honour greater than any that has been or that can be conferred. DURNFORD and SCOTT—there is a sermon in the coupling together of these two names which no colonist will ever forget. There lies in it the inculcation of those two noblest, and perhaps rarest, virtues under the sun—the high honour of the gentleman and the broad charity of the Christian. There is talk of erecting a memorial church. But what church that could be erected would be more sacred than the spot where these fourteen young heroes were found sleeping the last sleep of honour between their two officers?

CHAPTER IX

THE MOUNTAIN PASSES

We marched before daylight upon the fifth, as I remember well, for it was a new and unwelcome experience to me. I was roused from the sound sleep consequent upon the previous day's severe toil by the bugle sounding the reveille, and dressed as hastily as the bitter cold would permit, by the dim light of a lantern, which I lit as soon as I could persuade myself that it was not still the middle of the night. Then, after rapidly putting my things together, I turned out of my tent—which was warm in comparison to the freezing outer air—to find a crisp hoar-frost lying on the ground, and the stars twinkling from a cold and wintry sky.

It was not yet daylight, but all was alive in the camp. Through the darkness lights flitted in all directions, oxen lowed and men shouted, white tents were struck and packed, beasts of burden laden, and arrangements made for the morning's march. Hard by a tiny camp fire was struggling with the mists of night, and at it a servant was preparing coffee. One was glad enough to crouch beside the little blaze, and to warm one's hands for a moment, while fortifying oneself with the fragrant beverage, before hastening away to do one's share of the work in hand. Not that there were many minutes to spare in loitering over the fire. Our Chief was here, there, and everywhere, and shamed one's inclination to play laggard by his own incessant activity.

But half-an-hour was allowed from the time the bugle sounded the reveille until the 'advance' rang out, during which time we had all to turn out, pack up our things, strike the tents, and load-up the animals, an operation of no little difficulty in the darkness of the early morning. Gradually the lights appeared less brilliant, and the figures more distinct, as the darkness became more transparent with the coming day. Then suddenly it was light, the eastern clouds glowed rosy for but a moment, and the sun came bounding up with that singular swiftness and suddenness which it has in these latitudes. Its rays slowly dispelled the mists which lay lightly upon the hills but heavily piled as it were in the valleys, and instilled a little welcome warmth into our frozen frames.

At the sound of the bugle half the Basuto scouts galloped to the front as an advance-guard. Then came a section of the pioneers with their tools, to smooth the way for the pack-animals, wherever the ground became too difficult for them. Close behind these followed the infantry, with Captain B——— at their head; then the pack-horses and pack-oxen, followed in their turn by the remainder of the pioneers, the slaughter-cattle bringing up the rear, with, however, the usual rear-guard of Basutos, riding a few hundred yards behind the column of route.

At the head of all rode our Chief, attended by the faithful pair Jabez and Windvogel, and with the white guide at his side. At every place of more than usual difficulty the Colonel halted, and watched until the whole party had defiled before him, so as to make sure that no avoidable accident should take place. Then, galloping past over such rocky ground that it seemed a wonder how any horse could keep his feet, he and his orderlies were soon in their old places at the head of the column. As for me, I had my own place assigned to me; and, although out of working hours I looked upon myself as a somewhat privileged person with the Colonel, during them I should no more have ventured to leave my post without an order from him than any private in the ranks without his captain's command.

Our order of march was conducted with strict military precaution, as, from the reports which we had heard at Estcourt, it seemed very probable that at any moment we might find ourselves face to face with Mabudhle and his warriors. The country was a most difficult one, and the track which we followed led over great spurs running from the Draakensberg, with deep valleys between, the sides of which latter, bordering on the mountain streams, were generally clothed with a thick underwood, through which we had to force a passage, and which afforded admirable concealment for an ambuscade. As we advanced we came upon numerous indications of the presence of men; traces of fires, rude bivouacs formed of branches of trees and shrubs planted in a circle, the spoor of horses and cattle, etc., all showed clearly that there were fugitives from the scattered tribes still lurking in these secluded spots; for in this part of the country there are no settled inhabitants. In one place, indeed, on the banks of a sparkling stream whose icy-cold waters take their rise in the mountain, we found half-a-dozen low huts, fairly constructed, with all the signs of a settled habitation. It had been deserted, probably, at the rumour of our approach, for there was no living thing to be seen in it. Poor creatures! They must have thought their enemies most relentless, and I, for one, regretted that we had passed that way.

Such were the incidents of the day's march, diversified towards its close by a not entirely unsuccessful hunt after six eland, which we first beheld about half-a-mile to the left of our march.

These pretty, and now rather scarce, animals, which are about the size of ordinary cattle, remained perfectly quiet for some time, yet evidently watching the unwonted sight presented to them by our party with curiosity, if not with reasonable alarm.

Of course we could on no account have passed them by, for the eland is looked upon as especially deserving of the huntsman's attention; nor might we ever fall in with such a chance again. Half-a-dozen of the Basutos were promptly dismounted and sent on foot up the almost precipitous sides of the ravine, in order to drive the game in the direction in which we had taken up our post; the 'we' in this instance comprising the Colonel, Hlubi, Jabez, Windvogel, our guide, and myself. All six of us crouched down amongst the rocks, while our horses were carefully concealed in the brushwood, so as to give the eland no premature alarm.

Before long the game was afoot and moving in our direction, the Basutos having driven it most judiciously. The eland appeared heading towards a small pass within forty yards from where we had taken our stand. They did not see us, and all promised well. But alas! the luckless Windvogel, in his anxiety to learn whether they had yet come within range, exposed himself to view, and the eland, catching sight of him, turned short off, and, recrossing the stream, made off in the direction from whence we had all come. They gave us, however, fairly easy shots at about two-hundred-and-fifty yards' range, all of which, save one, proved unsuccessful. One beast staggered and fell, but, rising immediately, followed its companions, who were disappearing at that easy slinging pace peculiar to their kind. Just as they were vanishing from our sight, over the crest of a rocky hill appeared the head of the infantry column. Half-a-dozen of the men threw off their coats, dashed up the hill and, opening fire with their rifles, brought the wounded animal to the ground. There it was despatched by an assegai thrust, delivered with great satisfaction by one of the pack-horse leaders, all of whom—some twelve in number—on seeing the game, had simultaneously dropped their bridles, and, leaving the animals to take charge of themselves, had dashed off in hot pursuit.

Very shortly the eland was skinned and quartered, furnishing us with an ample supply of venison for the next few days.

Next day we camped about three miles from the old Bushman's Pass, where we were to commence our labours of demolition. This pass is so called owing to its having been the route by which almost the latest raid was made by the Bushmen. These were followed by a hastily collected party of farmers, who tracked them by the dead bodies of the cattle and horses which had become their booty, but never came up with the marauders themselves, except in the case of one straggler, who was overtaken and shot.

It was as a sort of frontier guard against these same Bushmen that the chief Langalibalele and his people were settled, five-and-twenty years ago, in a 'location' bordering upon the Draakensberg mountains. His land lay, however, not near this Bushman's Pass, but near the Bushman's River Pass, some fifty miles away, where my Chief was wounded in 1873.

In reference to this I may borrow a paragraph quoted by the Bishop of Natal: 'It must be admitted that the AmaHlubi* discharged well the special duties imposed upon them by the Government, and that, in consequence, the farmers in Weenen County conducted their operations, and guarded their flocks, with comparative ease. Langalibalele performed his part of the compact, and protected the county of Weenen from inroads of Bushmen by the passes he commanded.' (Parl. Blue Book, 1874, p. 10.)

One might have imagined that if it was convenient to post this tribe so as to protect the country from the Bushmen, they would not have been so hardly dealt with for possessing guns† to defend themselves and us.

Our camp was pitched about three miles from the actual pass, or rather from the actual passage on to the top of the mountain, for pass, properly so called, there was none. There were two approaches to this, one to be made by following the course of a stream for a considerable distance, and then turning off up a watercourse, dry at this time of year, but a roaring torrent in summer time. Near the mountain top this track joined the only other one possible, which followed the watershed line of a high and broken range of very difficult country. From the point where these two ways met it was but a hand-and-foot scramble of the most arduous description to gain the top of the mountain. Yet, in the old Bushman days, stolen cattle were frequently carried off by this pass, and that, during the flight of the AmaHlubi, men, women, horses and cattle had followed the same route was evident from their spoor.

We blasted no less than eight scarps out of the solid rock in order to render these approaches inaccessible, and we were engaged upon the work four days altogether.

This pass was supposed to have been destroyed in 1866 on account of the Bushmen. But the work done then would have been utterly useless had it ever been put to the proof. It consisted simply of a cutting about six feet deep in the turf across a great spur running from the mountain ridge, and leaving an easy passage to the right. It appears, however, that the very report of the operations

---

* The tribe of which Langalibalele was chief.
† The original cause of dispute.

was sufficient to keep the diminutive and crafty, though daring, foe away, for no more cattle were driven over the spot.

While we were at work upon this pass our camp was visited by one of the corps of volunteers who had followed the Colonel to the Bushman's River Pass the previous year. He remained with us two days and nights, during which time, of course, he was entertained with as much hospitality as our temporary camp afforded. I suppose his heart was opened by the friendly manner in which he was received, and the courtesy shown him by the Colonel, whom he approached at first with a somewhat suspicious and doubtful air, as though not certain of a kindly reception in that quarter, after the occurrences, and more especially the newspaper letters, a few months before. Possibly he even expected to be personally recognised and repulsed by the Colonel, not understanding that to him one of a party who were simply troopers for the nonce would be the same as another, especially as they had served under him for so short a time, and had never been seen by him, to his knowledge, before or since. But the gentleman in question became very friendly indeed when he found that no difference was made even after he had introduced himself as a member of the gallant ——— corps. On the second evening of his stay, the Colonel having left the fire to write in his tent, he turned the conversation towards the affair of the Bushman's River Pass, and argued the whole thing out with a private of the 75th, who happened to be well up on the point. I sat by and listened, for I was greatly interested in the matter, and glad of an opportunity of learning whether there was anything at all to be said upon the other side, which I very much doubted. I cannot say that any argument brought forward by our guest in support of his case struck me as being worthy of record, or even of remembrance; but I do recollect very distinctly that he was obliged to give up one point after another to his opponent, and that finally he fairly allowed that he and his comrades had run away in a panic. Some of them, he said, would have stood after the first shock was over, but, seeing the others streaming away a mile ahead, they all followed suit. He further declared that he would stick to this, whoever questioned him, for it was the truth, and nothing more.

I have often wondered since whether he kept his word, and whether he spoke out so boldly at the 'Court of Enquiry,' of which I have heard, but which took place after I left Natal. If he spoke then as he did beside the camp fire at the Old Bushman's Pass, he would be a valuable witness upon the Colonel's side, and an awkward one for his brother volunteers.

Next morning, after breakfast, he came up to the Colonel and made him a little speech about his kindness, but went on to inform him that many of the members of his corps had been much hurt and offended at finding that he did not recognise or notice them when he met them. Some of them, he said, did all they could to keep up the feeling that this was intentional neglect, but he himself saw now that the Colonel was 'not that kind of man at all,' and wished to take the opportunity of clearing up the matter. My duty carrying me away at this point in the conversation, I heard no more, and am not in a position to report the Colonel's reply; but as the volunteer remained talking to him with an air of gratification for some little time, I conclude that it was a satisfactory one, and that Colonel Durnford succeeded in impressing upon his mind the fact that he might possibly fail to recognise men whom he had commanded as troopers upon one solitary occasion without having any intention of wounding their feelings.

On Thursday, June 11th, we marched a distance of seven miles to 'Gray's Pass, No. 1,' so called because discovered by a man of that name while in charge of a native party in search of fugitives early in the year. His 'discovery,' however, was limited to the fact that a party of some half-dozen fugitives had fled in this direction and escaped over the mountain. We camped about two-and-a-half miles from the pass itself, which was as near as we could get the pack-animals, owing to the broken character of the ground.

Here we found three approaches leading on to the mountain top, of which two were the beds of streams coming from the mountain crest, and the third the watershed line between. It took us a couple of days to secure them, by scarping the rock and blasting, and I will not attempt to describe the difficulties that beset us in every yard of ground over which we passed. The excessive wildness and ruggedness of these little-used mountain passes must be experienced in order to be realised. None but fugitives in danger of their lives, or desperate men, reckless what they did, would attempt to cross them. Nothing short of the indomitable courage and determination of our Chief could have caried him and us through our tremendous undertaking. The hearts of many of us would have failed had we ventured to think of turning back before our work was done. Sometimes amidst our own severe toil and great difficulties we came upon spoors which were indubitable proof that some of the unhappy fugitives six months earlier had passed this way; and the hardest amongst us could not but feel pitiful at the thought of them—not men only, but women and children— without food or shelter, flying over these awful mountain wilds. That they had here found a temporary place of safety, however desolate, was also plain; for we found upon the mountain top some rude stone kraals, recently constructed, and evidently made for the shelter of human beings. Looking at these dreary relics of six months ago, I wondered what had caused them to be built; no man would needlessly remain in such a spot, none could exist there without provisions brought from afar; it was no fit hiding or resting place for the fugitives, nothing but the direst necessity could have kept them there. Was it for the protection of some sick man or feeble woman that these rough stones were piled together in this bleak barren place? Had wounded frame and weary spirit parted company here, with the roar of Africa's summer thunder for a dirge and heaven's scathing lightnings for the funeral volley? Or did here some less happy little mortal first awake to consciousness and life at such a bitter hour for babe and outcast parents?

Surely only such as these could have tenanted these rude bivouacs, for strong men would have hurried on in search of better cheer. I own that such thoughts oppresssed me, although I kept them to myself; nor, perhaps, was I the only one, for, standing near my Chief that day, beside the deserted shelter, I heard him ejaculate, *sotto voce*, 'Poor things! how cold they must have been!'

Luckily for them, however, they could not have had such cold to bear as we experienced now, for it was summer weather then, although, as it happened, wild and stormy. Cold and wet and comfortless they doubtless were. The Colonel told me that he found it bitterly cold when encamped at the Bushman's River Pass, upon his second visit during the summer of 1873. But such cold as we endured in the winter time would not have left one of them alive, entirely without resources as they were.

Nevertheless, we considered ourselves truly fortunate in our weather, as, up to the last day on which we worked at 'Gray's Pass, No. 1,' though cold, it was perfectly fine. We worked under a cloudless and warm sun by day, and protected ourselves with rugs and blankets from the hard frost which reigned nightly from sunset to sunrise.

But on the day before we left the second pass we had a fall of snow, a phenomenon which most 'old colonists' have lived their twenty or thirty years in Natal without witnessing, as one must go up the Draakensberg in winter time to meet with snow.

The sun shining out again made a pretty scene enough from our camp ground. The immense dark frowning precipices, of which the mountain range seems chiefly to consist, were touched on every crest with glistening snow, and falling clean over the highest perpendicular surface, a waterfall of no inconsiderable volume, but frozen into a column of ice, was glittering in the sunlight. Every other waterfall, of which there are many smaller ones, was similarly turned to ice; but the one above mentioned, near Gray's Pass, was the most striking from its size and prominent position.

On the 13th of June we left these passes, and marched over more very broken country, intersected by many streams which ran through deep and rocky beds, either bank of which was well-nigh impracticable. Indeed without the aid of the pioneers they could not have been crossed by our beasts of burden at all.

After about twelve miles of such travelling we got back to our old camping ground on a spur leading from Champagne Castle, under the remarkable hill before mentioned with a hole in its crest, and, on the following day, recrossing the Little Berg, we found ourselves once more at the camp where we had left our waggons, etc., without any other casualty than the fall of one of the oxen over a cliff, in consequence of which it was so severely injured that it had to be shot.

We rested here for one whole day, and the next morning marched for Cathkin, which place formed a sort of principal depôt for us, from which we could take up fresh stores of provisions and ammunition, and make fresh starts for the various mountain passes to which we were bound.

CHAPTER X

AGAIN ON THE MARCH

The first stage of our arduous journey was over. The first section of the work we had in hand completed. We had had a fair sample of the dangers and difficulties which it was our lot to encounter during the winter months of 1874, and imagined that we could fairly estimate what would be their sum total by the time we returned to warmer and less savage regions. But we had some bitter experiences before us yet which we hardly anticipated. The morning after our return to Cathkin was spent in enclosing the powder-casks in envelopes of green ox-hide, in order to strengthen them against the vicissitudes of the rough travel to which they were about to be exposed. This hide, when dry, becomes as hard and stiff as board, and is besides thoroughly impervious to wet.

About midday we marched, starting at first back upon our old tracks over the already twice-trodden ground, and crossing the Sterkspruit again, but then striking off upon a fresh line of march, by which we were to reach the Draakensberg at a point many miles beyond the scene of our late labours.

Once upon the new track we felt that we had really made a fresh start, and hoped to make a good first day's march. That, however, was not to be, for, a mile or two farther on, our second waggon was upset in a 'mud-hole,' and the catastrophe gave us all full employment for at least two hours, in rescuing the contents and getting the waggon out.

The delay was not inspiriting, and somewhat damped the ardour with which we had set out in the morning; and when we encamped upon an open flat, at the end of the hard day's work which had advanced us so little, we were hardly so cheerful a party as usual. Water was plentiful where we camped, but there was no wood to be had at all. It was fortunate that we carried an ample supply with us, or we should have been fireless that night, than which I can hardly imagine a greater misfortune under the circumstances.

We made an early start next morning (18th) to make up for lost time, and as we were now travelling over a fairly level country, below the great mountain spurs, our march was a tolerably rapid one during the earlier part of the day. It might have continued so until nightfall but for the misbehaviour of one of our drivers, which interfered with our progress in the following manner.

During the afternoon our line of march had lengthened out, owing to the different speed of the horsemen, footmen, and heavy vehicles, but we were all sufficiently in sight of each other to know what was happening from front to rear. The Colonel, as usual, rode some little way ahead with his advance guard and a portion of the pioneers, for the special purpose of inspecting the road over which the waggons must pass, and of repairing such places as were unfit for them to cross in safety.

Accordingly, on reaching a small stream running between very high and steep banks, and flowing right across our track, we found the workmen, superintended by our Chief himself, completing the construction of a good firm causeway of broken stone, with earth and sods beaten down upon them, crossing from bank to bank, and wide enough to give ample passage for the waggons. To make all complete the Colonel had also caused the sides of the causeway to be well defined by poles planted at either edge, with wisps of grass attached to their tops.

The work being completed, and the waggons close at hand, our Chief rode on after leaving strict directions behind him. Each waggon was to be stopped while its driver went forward to examine the place for himself, and see what he had to do. He was then to return to his charge, and drive slowly and carefully over, keeping to the centre of the causeway.

We waited to see the result. Down the steep incline came waggon No. 1, its driver carefully obeying orders, and, crossing in perfect safety, it continued on its way.

Now for No. 2! But the driver of No. 2 is rather a free and independent gentleman, and has more than once earned for himself one of our Chief's quiet but severe reproofs. It was his waggon which delayed us yesterday, and he is always sure to get into difficulties. On this occasion he chooses to disregard his orders altogether, thereby sufficiently proving that he has not long served under his present master. He altogether declined to get down and reconnoitre, or to proceed at a slow pace, but driving recklessly down the incline, came upon one edge of the causeway instead of upon its centre. With a rush and a crash the whole thing went over the side, and fell into the mud and water below, breaking the tilt and shooting all the contents of the waggon into the stream. First a warning cry, and then a general shout from the bystanders announced the event; and then, as the first thing to be done, we sent a mounted man off after the Colonel, to tell him of the catastrophe and to bring him back.

The driver looked foolish enough now, but his face wore a thoroughly alarmed expression when the Colonel galloped back, and inquired into what had taken place. That it was no mere accident, but the result of wilful disobedience and gross carelessness on the part of the man, was plain enough. The Colonel's face grew stern as he listened to the tale. 'Here!' he said, turning to the Basutos, 'you four dismount and seize that man.'

The order was promptly obeyed.

'Now take off his coat and lay him down—and give him a dozen with a stirrup-leather.' And he turned away to superintend the operations for rescuing the fallen waggon.

The Basutos were sturdy fellows, and knew what they were about, and the effect of this well-merited punishment was undoubtedly good. The man who received it drove his waggon with the most exemplary care and attention during the rest of the expedition; and it is possible that the others benefited by his experience, for, with one unavoidable exception, not another waggon was upset from that time until we returned to Pietermaritzburg.

June 19th brought us another early start and fresh delays on the way—not, however, through anyone's misbehaviour this time, but through the necessity of spending a couple of hours in repairing the road at a shockingly bad drift over the Umlambonga, a stream running into the Tugela; which latter important river takes its rise in the mountain range.

While halting here we were met by Nyati, chief of the Zikali tribe, which resides in this part of the country. He had an interview with our Chief, who directed him to send supplies of every description to his camp, promising that there should be a market established there, at which everything should be paid for at once, and at proper rates. The Colonel, I soon observed, was always very particular about enforcing strict honesty towards the natives from all serving under himself; and this, not only for the sake of upholding abstract justice, but in order to teach the natives to place that implicit confidence in the perfect good faith of 'Government' which is so necessary in ruling a savage nation, and which the native population of Natal has lost to a sad extent through bitter experience during a long term of years.

The chief of the Zikali people seemed ready enough to sell, for we had not had time to pitch our tents that evening, near a German mission station, before long strings of women and boys were to be seen approaching from every side, bearing upon their heads loads of firewood, large baskets of mealies, pumpkins, and kafir corn, pots of *tshwala*, milk, eggs, and fowls, etc., which were all welcome articles as a change in diet. The troops, as well as ourselves, were glad to make their purchases after the everlasting rations of fresh beef on which they had lived of late, and our camp soon presented a busy scene. Nearly all the articles offered for sale were disposed of before the merchants departed, evidently half-frightened, half-admiring, but wholly wondering at the sight of so many white faces, and, still more, so many scarlet coats.

Our poor pioneers were not forgotten, for, although they had no money to spend, yet the free natives, with the liberality common amongst the kafirs, presented them with huge messes of mealie meal and kafir corn mixed with pumpkin, prepared according to the native taste. They called the mixture *isijingi*, and appeared to enjoy it immensely.

We did not march next day, but spent it in making preparations for the ascent of the Amaponjwana Pass, which was situated about eighteen miles from our present camp. This day's routine was diversified by a visit which we, or rather I should say, which the Colonel received, from a lady of distinction in this part of the world, although her fortunes were temporarily in the shade. About sundown, while we were seated round the camp fire waiting for our dinner, our attention was attracted by a considerable commotion in the line of the pioneers. Sounds of rejoicing were borne upon the wind, and a perfect babel of tongues. Presently we observed the men falling into line as they had been taught to do during the last six months by the corporal in charge of them, and a minute later they were marching towards the camp fire, round which the Colonel, Captain ————, I, and others were seated. As they advanced, singing some dirge-like chant of their own, we saw that they were accompanied by several women and old men, strangers to the camp, whom they were evidently conducting to the Colonel's presence. They halted opposite the fire, drew up in order and saluted, crying with one voice '*Bayete!*' a salute properly given to royalty alone by the Zulus, but with which they occasionally greet an *Inkos* whom they are particularly anxious to propitiate.

After paying this mark of respect a dead silence fell upon the party, while one, advancing to the front, accompanied by the strangers, presented to the Colonel the chief personage of the newly arrived party.

She—for it was a lady—was a slight, good-looking young woman, attired in the ordinary costume of the Zulu matron, yet with a singularly prepossessing and dignified bearing, and possessing that charm in woman, a soft voice. Of course she did not know a word of English, nor could we address her in her own language. But amongst the pioneers was one who had once been taken to England by a former master, and who spoke English fairly well. This man came forward as interpreter, and informed our Chief that this lady was Umkosaza, the widow of the late chief of the Putini tribe, to which they all belonged, and with her little son, a child of about two years of age, was at present living under the protection of her brother Nyati, chief of the Zikali tribe. She had now brought her little boy to see and be seen by these captive members of the tribe to the chieftainship of which he was heir.

Umkosaza, explained the interpreter, now desired to pay her respects to the Colonel, and to implore his protection for herself and her young son; and then the little fellow was brought forward, carried upon the hip of Umkosaza's female attendant. As far as one could judge from tone and gesture, and from the interpreter's version of her words, the exiled lady expressed herself in the most becoming manner, and altogether she impressed us all with her self-possessed and well-bred demeanour.

When she appeared to have uttered all she wished to say, the Colonel offered her and her attendants refreshment in the shape of Cape port, or Pontac, 'the white man's *tshwala*,' as the interpreter explained to them. They gave it as their opinion that it was extremely good, but confined themselves, nevertheless, to tasting the merest sip of it; and I fancy that the biscuits, sugar, and finally the joint of beef which followed were more highly acceptable presents. This last, a truly barbaric but perfectly suitable gift, was not, of course, for immediate consumption, but was handed over to an attendant to be carried away when the party left us.

The Colonel then made a little speech to the pioneers through the interpreter, telling them that he was pleased to see their young chief and his mother, that they must all be very good and obedient to 'Government,' and some day who knew what might not happen? etc. He then dismissed them all to the pioneers' quarters, from whence issued sounds of rejoicing which lasted until the bugle sounded 'Out lights,' when a profound silence and darkness fell upon the whole camp, with the exception only of the head-quarters' tents.

Next morning, before we had made a start, Umkosaza appeared again, attended by her maid, but carrying upon her own head a pot of *tshwala*, which she presented with great respect to the Colonel, thanking him at the same time for his goodness to her people. With his usual kindness he accepted her gift, and then made her another himself, in the shape of a brilliant scarlet blanket, in which he arrayed her and sent her to show herself to her people. I was glad to see great masses of pumpkins and mealies sent over to the pioneers from the kraal where she resided, which showed that she had a heart for 'her own.'*

The Colonel had sent for a fresh supply of pack-oxen the day before, and

---

* I observed that from this time forward the Colonel not infrequently received the royal salute, '*Bayete!*' from his grateful pioneers. He, however, checked the utterance whenever he heard it; and made a point of explaining to them, and to all his other road parties, that that particular salute was due to the governor of the colony alone, and that neither to himself nor to any other official was it ever to be given.

UMKOSAZA AND HER ATTENDANT

some twenty appeared in the course of the morning, each with a rider on his back. Wild-looking riders they were too. They formed part of our line of march for some time. What with white men and Basutos on horseback, soldiers and pioneers on foot, pack-horses and oxen with their burdens, and the newly arrived animals with their savage riders, our party looked a very mixed one indeed.

We started again at about 11 A.M. upon the 21st, the day of Umkosaza's second visit. Leaving the waggons behind us, and our tents standing, we marched up the fertile valley inhabited by the Zikali tribe. It is thickly populated, with kraals on every rising ground, and large mealie and *amabele* (kafir corn) gardens lying in every direction. The day's march was uneventful, and we camped for the night close under some high cliffs in a beautiful spot covered with 'sugarbush' of a large growth.

At ten o'clock that night, when all were asleep in camp, the sentry gave the alarm of fire. The whole camp was instantly alive; and, hurrying into our clothes, we all turned out to find a tremendous grass fire rapidly approaching. As I left my tent the high ground right above us seemed suddenly to burst into one roaring sheet of flame, which extended for a considerable distance. The sight was indeed a terrible one. The wall of fire was close above us, sending up heavy volumes of smoke into the black night, both flame and smoke caught and tossed away into the darkness by the gusts of a violent gale of wind which was blowing at the time. A lurid light shone down upon us, making all as distinct as by day, but with a redder, more unnatural glow. Our greatest danger was from the violence of the wind. Should some of the patches of flame, which were driven off from the cliff and scattered far and wide, fall amongst our tents, we should save but little from the conflagration that would ensue. Every now and then the wind fell a little, and, as its howl died away, the loud and steady roar of the flames above took its place, and filled the night with sound, until its terrible voice was once more drowned in the renewed fury of the storm.

I had not much time given me to receive my impressions of the scene, for our Chief was amongst us instantly, and no man might be idle long. His orders were given with promptness and decision, and obeyed by us with equal alacrity. In another minute every man had a green branch in his hand, and the next they were all along the edge of the fire, beating it out with the boughs they held. A few men were posted below to extinguish in the same manner any flame that might be blown amongst the tents, and I was selected to superintend this party. There was not much for us to do, and I had ample leisure to continue my observation of the picturesque scene before, or rather above me. It was a doubly strange one now, for the two hundred figures, black against the flames, and all working vigorously at beating them down, had no small resemblance to Dante's demons dancing round their unhallowed fires, and thrusting their struggling victims back with forks.

An hour's hard work, however, thoroughly conquered the fire, and all returned to camp, very smoked and grimy, and glad enough to get back to the beds which had been left upon the first alarm, and which had had so narrow an escape of being more smoked and grimy even than their owners.

CHAPTER XI

AMAPONJWANA PASS AND MABUDHLE

Two days later found us encamped under the Amaponjwana Pass, and at work again, in spite of falling snow and hard frost. We had got into wintry regions indeed, although we had still worse before us.

Immediately upon our arrival the Colonel had started up the mountain to see how the land lay, accompanied by myself and a guide. A two hours' climb took us on to the mountain top, passing through a narrow rocky gorge, about ten yards wide and two-hundred yards from the mountain crest. In this gorge the sun never shines. The cold was most intense, and our only road lay over masses of ice and boulders intermixed and frozen together. The numerous frozen waterfalls, which this pass contained, formed huge ice-columns at frequent intervals, and the scene was as bleak and dreary as could well be imagined. The mountain top itself at this point is undulating, covered with a short dense grass, and watered by innumerable streams, which rise immediately on the mountain crest, those bound for Natal running towards the rising, and the others towards the setting sun. The water was deliciously cold and pure, the streams under the mountain running over beds of rock and forming frequent cascades of various dimensions, the banks being clothed with shrubs of kinds unknown to me.

During this climb up the Amaponjwana Pass we experienced the extremes of both heat and cold. The severe exertions which we were making threw us into such a heat that we had not a dry thread left upon us, and were glad to throw off greatcoat and patrol-jacket, and hand them over to be carried by our attendants until we reached the top, where we were equally glad to put them on again. At the same time the air was so cold that it froze our breath as it left us, gradually forming icicles upon the moustache and beard.

At this place we worked for two days. The pass was about thirty-eight feet wide at the point where we were engaged, and ran between high perpendicular walls of rock. Across it we built a barrier, at an average height of twelve feet, of the boulders which lay about in every direction—which we banked in securely, and formed into a solid wall with broken stone and turf. This labour was performed under considerable difficulties. We were working in a narrow gorge, whose walls of rock and ice towered above us, shutting out the sunlight, and making the spot like an ice-house. The cold was so excessive in this sunless spot that it would have been unendurable without artificial warmth. Half-an-hour's exposure to it would have numbed and stupefied our half-clad pioneers. Accordingly our Chief caused great fires to be made within the pass, and the men to be divided into two companies, one of which relieved the other every ten minutes, returning to the fires when again off duty. Never before surely had such a scene been witnessed in this frozen rift of the Khahlamba range!

Upon the second day there was no more sunshine without the pass than within it. The weather appeared threatening, and the snow-sprinkled rocks and cloud-covered sky made up a wintry scene indeed. We did not get down to our camp till dark, and this was the severest day that we had yet encountered.

The pioneers, poor fellows! suffered a good deal, although they were very cheerful on the whole, inspirited doubtless by their hopes of freedom.

One could not but admire the willing zeal and cheerfulness with which these men went through the labours to which they were unaccustomed and the hardships to which they were not inured. The natural life of the wild man in South Africa is not one of hard work; his wants are simple and easily supplied; his garden and his cattle are all he needs; his women till the one—in which nature with but little assistance produces abundant crops—his children herd the other. With such a climate as that in which he dwells, why should he bestir himself to unnecessary exertions? What wonder that he prefers to pass the long summer days in peaceful idleness, instead of spending it in labour, the only object of which is to supply himself with the luxuries of civilisation which he does not require and half despises! The South African undoubtedly has not the physical strength and endurance of his European brethren, who, however, it must be confessed, soon lose all inclination to exert the same in a country where the poorest labourer soon rides his horse and commands his kafir, where the journeyman carpenter disdains to carry his own tools, or the kitchenmaid to clean her own pans.

We finished our work at the Amaponjwana Pass, and got back to the German mission station, near which we had left our standing camp with the waggons and oxen, by the 25th. Glad enough were we to leave the frozen mountain tops, and to descend into the more temperate atmosphere of the valley beneath, which we had thought excessively cold on first arriving from yet warmer regions, but now felt to be delightfully mild. But we found at the camp men standing who had even greater reason than we to rejoice at reaching it, namely, Mr. G. Mansel, of the Natal Mounted Police, with half-a-dozen of his men. They had followed the track of our patrol between Khahlamba and the Little

Berg, but had descended into the Zikali valley by a most precipitous break-neck way of their own finding, down which they had had the utmost difficulty in leading their horses. They had also endured considerable privations during their patrol, having been unable to procure food in the uninhabited country between the mountains. Indeed, even when they reached the Zikali valley they could not at first obtain any assistance. The people plainly distrusted them. Knowing nothing of them, except that they were not '*Amasoja*' [soldiers—regulars], they put them down as '*Campkettles*' [volunteers], whom they neither feared nor trusted. Possibly they were too much accustomed to being cheated by the few traders and others who had come amongst them to care to deal with them. They would have met with fair dealing from Mr. Mansel, but that they did not know; and consequently the little body of Mounted Police were nearly starving when at last they reached our camp. There, of course, their wants were immediately supplied by the men left in charge, and we found them already quite at home. Mr. Mansel had paid us several previous visits, one on the 1st of June, when we camped near the Sterkspruit, and once again on the 15th at our old camping ground under the Little Berg, but had remained with us each time for one night only. Now, he and his men formed part of our column of route, and kept with us for ten or twelve days.

Mr. Mansel was, I knew, a favourite with my Chief. I had often heard him speak of him as 'a right good man for his work,' 'full of energy,' 'no day too long for him,' and 'always ready.' He was a good-looking fellow, with an upright, well-made figure, and rode as though he had lived in the saddle all his life. He was besides a capital companion, full of quaint humour, and with a never-failing flow of conversation, jokes, and anecdotes.

Nevertheless, though I should like to have made a companion of a man of my own age and standing—one with whom I was disposed to fraternise, and whom my Chief commended—yet I kept aloof from him from first to last, and avoided all chances of making his further acquaintance. Why I did so I can hardly say, except that I had sometimes still my sombre and *farouche* fits of regret for the place I had lost in the world.

Upon the 27th June we found ourselves once more at Cathkin, where we were received with enthusiasm by old Mr. Gray. The sentiments of this worthy gentleman appeared to have undergone a considerable change since we saw him first. Then he was certainly all that could be desired so far as hospitality was concerned; but he evidently had not the slightest faith in us, and was firmly convinced that the Putini men would desert, and ravage the country as bands of marauders. Now, learning his mistake by experience, and appreciating at last what must have been the influence of the unwonted presence of the soldiery in these secluded districts, he changed from grim distrust to enthusiastic partisanship of our Chief. He greeted us most warmly, and, hastening up to the Colonel, stood beside his horse's head with his hand upon the mane, saying in his broad Scotch accent, 'Colonel, I had heard a great deal about you before I saw you, and when you first came I did not believe in you. But now! by G———, I see you're just a man, and I'll stand by you through thick and thin.'

Our Chief received the acknowledgment in his usual quiet manner, but I suspect that he was not more above taking pleasure in the simple tribute of respect paid him by the blunt sturdy Scotchman than others would have been in his place.

At Cathkin we remained for a day or two awaiting the arrival of fresh pack-oxen and slaughter-cattle, for which the Colonel had sent to Zikali. Some of these duly arrived, but not the whole number of pack-oxen ordered, which the chief found himself unable to supply. Those that we received were accompanied by a messenger, bearing humble apologies from his chief that his supply fell short of the Colonel's demand. With him came a small troop of cattle *as a present*—'smart money,' in short—to turn away the supposed wrath of our Chief! The ambassador was excessively surprised when he found his excuses quietly accepted, and the 'present' returned as quite unnecessary. What effect must not the late reign of terror have had upon the native mind when they think it necessary to come in fear and trembling to *buy off* the anger of a white *Inkos* because they cannot sell him what they have not got!

I saw much during our expedition which showed me that it will take many years, nay, a lifetime, to restore things to their old footing in this country; and even then the memory of cruelty and injustice will remain, causing distrust and hatred to the British name.

Amongst the purchases which we made from the natives of Zikali's tribe there were, as I have previously mentioned, many fowls. Of these some were daily killed and eaten, the gradually decreasing stock following us with our other provisions wherever we went. When we were on the march I am afraid that our feathered companions had no very easy time of it, as we could procure no baskets for their transport, and they were therefore obliged to perform their journey tied together by the legs and put upon a pack-horse. At night they were set loose and well fed; but, poor things! they were generally too fatigued by the shakings and joltings they had received during the day to be very lively or active. There was, however, one exception to the general langour that prevailed amongst our fowls in the person of a fine red cock whose spirit appeared indomitable. Every night, the moment he was released, he sprang to his feet, shook himself, and crowed with as much vigour as though he stood upon his own dunghill! Nothing would induce him to show the slightest sign of fatigue, and whenever fresh fowls were purchased he made a point of seizing the earliest opportunity of asserting his supremacy by beating all the cocks of the party in turn. In fact his conduct was so plucky and singular that general attention was drawn to his superiority, and the Colonel gave orders that he should on no account be put to death and eaten. He was at once raised to the post of favourite, and received a name, being called by the Colonel 'Mabudhle,' after the *Induna* who had commanded Langalibalele's men at the Bushman's River Pass, whom the Colonel looks upon as a brave man and one worthy of his steel. From this time forth Mabudhle, the cock, performed his travels mounted upon his own pack-horse, no longer dangling helplessly by the feet from its back, but perched upon it in his natural position, and merely attached by a loose cord to one claw. In this manner he accompanied us through the rest of our expedition, either proudly sitting his steed, or, when the waggons were with us, perched upon one of them. He took kindly to his position of favourite, would soon feed out of our hands, and, when we were encamped, was usually to be found pecking round our kitchen fire, as much at home as any one of us. Mabudhle will probably end his days in peace and contentment, for, upon our return to Pietermaritzburg, the Colonel gave him to some friends of his in the country, with strict injuctions that he was to be allowed to die a natural death, and was to be well cared for in the meantime.

CHAPTER XII

A SNOW STORM

On the morning of the 29th we started once more upon our travels towards what was to be the scene of our last and most arduous mountain labours—namely, the Bushman's River Pass.

I was particularly anxious to see with my own eyes the spot where my Chief had fought the year before, and over which so many bloodless battles of words had since been waged. Of course I took myself the only view of the matter which I had ever heard propounded by men of my own cloth who had seen the ground—namely, that the position taken up by the Colonel was clearly defensible, and could have been held long enough to serve all requisite purposes had he been followed by twenty regulars who knew what is meant by discipline and obedience, two qualities quite as necessary to the making of a good soldier as the mere courage which we are all supposed to possess. My knowledge of my Chief was all that was necessary to convince me that even his valour had not outstripped his judgment, as pretended by those whose interest it was to throw the blame of the failure upon one who, according to the rules of the Service, could not speak in his own defence. Nevertheless, I wanted to see the place with my own eyes, and to be able to say that I had done so. Consequently I set forth with renewed energy, although but for this special subject of interest I might have begun to feel that I had had about enough of frozen passes, rugged mountains, and perpetual climbing, with the monotonous round of newly discovered passes, scarped works, and boulder walls.

It is curious how very little the number and nature of these mountain passes is known to those whose interest, nay, whose duty it is to keep them in mind. Not half of them are set down in any map, or have any names save those given by us while working their destruction. Determined to do thoroughly the work entrusted to him, the Colonel gave rewards to the finders of new passes, and the result was excellent for the object we had in view at the time. To give one instance only: everyone who knows anything about Natal knows also that there is a 'Bushman's Pass' in the Draakensberg range, and some few may likewise be aware that there are two, the 'Old Bushman's Pass' and the 'Bushman's

River Pass,' some fifty miles apart. But how many Natal Government officials —how many Natalians—are aware that round about the Bushman's River Pass alone there are six several smaller ones, all of which we destroyed as thoroughly as the only one upon our original list?

After leaving Cathkin we soon found ourselves in the deserted location of the unfortunate Putini tribe. A fertile valley, well watered by the Little Tugela river, which takes its rise in the Khahlamba range, lay before us. But nine months ago, this pleasant spot had been the happy tranquil home of the then well-to-do tribe, numbering some five-thousand souls. Here they had spent many peaceful years, cultivating their land, and bringing up their children to be, like their fathers, simple and honest, though untaught, savages. And here, while so unsuspicious of approaching evil that not a man had taken up arms nor a woman fled, they were surprised by the Government forces. Their habitations were pillaged and burnt, their cattle seized, and themselves carried off prisoners, with no knowledge on the part of the victims as to what their offence might be. It was said indeed that some women of their tribe, who had married amongst Langalibalele's people, had taken refuge in the huts of their fathers and brothers from the assegais of the murderous loyal native force. The women were not turned out by these near relatives to meet a bloody death, or, still worse, a dishonourable captivity; and the Government forces promptly taught the whole tribe that family affection and common humanity may be accounted as crimes; or, shall we rather say, that it is dangerous for a well-to-do and prosperous little community to lie right in the path of an armed, rapacious, and disappointed mob?

A little later the authorities themselves acknowledged that the capture of the Putini tribe, and confiscation of its property, was a complete mistake. Nevertheless, at the time of which I write, eight months after the affair, the Putini women were still living under strict surveillance, the men still working as convicts upon the roads. The only improvement in their condition was the hope of regaining their freedom through my Chief's energetic interference on their behalf, and by their own painful labour and perilous exposure. Nothing but the childlike trust and confidence which these poor creatures plainly put in the master under whom they served, and who shared their perils and sufferings to the full, could have carried them through their work.

We had marched over much savage country, through wild and uninhabited districts, but in all our travels we had never reached a spot which struck me with such a sense of desolation as did this smiling fruitful valley. On every gentle slope and every rounded knoll were to be seen the charred and blackened remains of ruined kraals, strewed round with broken utensils of native manufacture. A silence as of the grave reigned over the deserted land. No voice of child nor low of cattle could be heard, but only the long sigh of the wind amongst the neglected gardens, as the feathery heads of the stately maize waved slowly in the breeze, and the sharp trickling sound of the brooks that fed the Little Tugela river, distinctly audible through the clear atmosphere and the perfect stillness of the vale.

The mealie and *amabele* gardens which lay on every side were green and young when fire and steel swept through the land in the spring time of the year. Their soft green blades, if crushed down and trampled upon for a while, had risen again with the elasticity possessed by all young things, and the grain was now ripe and ready to gather. There were none, however, to reap the crops, save the wild deer or 'bucks' as I learnt to call them in Natal, and the many thousand birds which perched on every stem and took flight in clouds as we passed by. The little feathered rascals, indeed, were enjoying an unwonted feast, undisturbed by the children whose business it should have been to sit all day long upon little wattle stages or scaffolds, shouting to each other and to the winged robbers, much as country lads are set to do at home in England. Our horses and cattle, too, enjoyed a meal of their favourite food, these deserted gardens furnishing excellent provender for them.

I could not help wondering, as we marched through this valley, what might be the sentiments of our poor pioneers, the rightful dwellers upon the soil. Did the joy with which the hope—certainly unlooked for—of a return to their old homes ere long predominate, or did their souls rise indignantly against the cruel injustice which had dragged them away; and did they wonder why they should not be allowed to return at once, now, while their crops were still safe and whole, instead of being forced to leave them to be carried off by anyone who chose to take possession of them? The crops were gone to the last grain before they returned as free men once more; nor, but for the strenuous exertions and determination of my Chief, would they then have reached their homes in time to plant their next year's crop.

On the 30th June, after a fatiguing march over a very broken country, we camped in a valley near a stream of beautiful cold water. The march had been so severe that there were many stragglers from our lines, some of whom, as night fell, lost our track, and had considerable difficulty in finding their way to camp. Indeed they might have slept in the veldt that night, a recreation for which the weather was far too cold, had not Mr. Mansel ridden back some miles to find them.

Next day we reached the Bushman's River Valley, and having formed a general depôt in a most picturesque and well-wooded spot, with the Bushman's

River flowing close by, we followed the course of the stream towards its source, and encamped late that afternoon about a mile from the foot of the pass.

About sunset we all prophesied snow, from the appearance of the sky; but later on the night cleared, and when we turned in we had good hopes of a fine morrow. It was a lovely night; a great big moon, like a harvest moon at home, rose splendidly into a cloudless sky, lighting up the Berg above us, and performing for us the meaner functions of many lamps, whereby we greatly profited, avoiding tumbles over tent-lines and such like impedimenta.

Our hopes, however, proved to be delusive. Waking up, about three o'clock next morning, I became aware that snow was falling fast, mixed with little lumps of ice, which pattered on my tent like hail, although hail it was not. It was deadly cold, and further sleep was out of the question in such an atmosphere. I lay and shivered beneath the blankets through the long hours that yet remained before the tardy winter's dawn, and was glad enough when at last it broke, enabling me to get up and try what moving about and then crouching by the first-lit fire would do towards thawing my frozen blood.

On comparing notes at breakfast time I learnt that one or two of our party had been wise enough to carry off hot stones to bed with them as foot-warmers, and had thus been able to defy the intense cold of the past night. Their experience was so satisfactory as compared with ours that for the future hot stones became the order of the day, or rather night. Our breakfast party presented an odd enough appearance upon that snowy morning. A bleak hill-side surrounded by other hills as bleak, and the Berg frowning above, the whole white with snow —such was the background to the scene. For foreground objects we had our fire enclosed by a sod-wall tipped with heather, with figures seated round it wrapped to the eyes. Upon the fire were sundry pots and kettles, and busy over them a British soldier, with a scarlet nightcap on his head, as ministering angel to our wants, which indeed he supplied luxuriously with partridge curry, mutton-chops, coffee, bread and butter, so that we could hardly complain of starvation in addition to the cold. Snow fell fast the while into the plates and cups, so that we ate as quickly as possible, and then huddled over the fire to talk, getting up occasionally to shake the accumulating snow from off our backs, and sitting down again as speedily as possible to keep our camp stools dry.

We discussed our present prospects, and rather shook our heads over them. Should there be any truth in the saying that bad weather once set in lasts with the waning moon, it was rather a bad look-out for us. No work was possible for that day save the erection of certain turf-walls around the principal tents, as a shelter from the biting wind—a wise precaution seeing that we might be detained for some days by the fall of snow, which, should it block the pass, would entirely prevent our work for the present. Meanwhile, every man who could do so remained in his tent and in his blanket. The British soldier is but a helpless creature when thus exposed to hardships, and seems to be too idle to make himself a shelter under which he can eat in warmth and comfort. He prefers to lie about under shelter and be cold. Upon this occasion, too, our native force seemed rather inclined to follow the example of the white, and no man in camp was to be seen beyond his tent, except those on duty at the time.

About noon Mr. Mansel and his mounted policemen took their departure, in spite of driving snow and wind, for their return to their own camp, having been ordered into Estcourt. Their commander evidently left us with extreme unwillingness, liking the life we led in the wilds far better than his camp at Estcourt; but his sense of duty took him away without delay. Poor Shot, too, his favourite spaniel dog, who invariably accompanied his master on patrol, looked very melancholy at having to leave a camp on such a day. He had been enjoying himself immensely, alternately lying in the warmth of our fire and dashing out to have a game with the snow, which was a novel, and apparently a welcome, playfellow for him. There was no fear of starvation for the party this time, for we sent them off well-provisioned for some days to come.

It was by no means a cheerful day upon the whole. The Colonel sat in his tent writing letters and despatches, busy as usual; but the rest of us did not do much besides talk and smoke and endeavour to keep ourselves warm. At four o'clock a slight distraction occurred in the arrival of fresh supplies of pumpkins, mealies, and wood from the depôt below. The snow still fell fast, and the long string of horses and oxen, with packs upon their backs, looked like a train of ghosts as they approached, winding round the hills, and white with the snow which filled the air so thickly that all objects at a little distance became dim and indistinct to view.

At sundown, however, the weather cleared again. We trusted that the snow was over, and made all our arrangements for work upon the following day before we went to bed.

What was my dismay, on awaking at about two o'clock, at hearing once more the soft sound of fast-falling snow and the howl of the rising wind! 'No work today!' thought I, and turned to sleep again. Useless attempt! The wind howled louder and louder, while the cold grew ever more intense. In another hour a perfect hurricane was blowing, which drove the snow, or rather frozen dust, right through the tents, which were made of cotton stuff instead of canvas, as well as under their walls. Soon the tents were full of snow, and the sleepers covered with a frozen winding-sheet of the same. It beat in at the tent doors, and there froze into a mass of ice. We might almost as well have been lying in the open air; it was indeed a bitter night for us all.

When daylight appeared I went out to see how matters stood, and found the Colonel out before me, looking at a couple of tents which had been blown down, the occupants of which were huddled round a fire. They had a screen-wall round them, without which they could not have kept their fire alight, and very miserable indeed they looked.

I saluted my Chief, and asked for orders; but the wind blew so strong that we could scarcely stand against it, and forced the icy dust into our faces until it was difficult to draw breath. The ice morsels froze upon one's hair, one's coat, and beard, until one had all the appearance of a snow-man. They collected at the back of one's head, beneath the forage-caps which we all wore, and froze there into a solid mass, which we were obliged to submit to the influence of the fire before we could get rid of it. Such a bitter day I never experienced before or since. Even the Colonel looked grave and anxious over our plight; although his resolute courage and endurance carried him—in spite of the exhaustion consequent upon long ill-health and yet unhealed wounds—through what tried the fortitude of the strongest man amongst us.

The pioneers lay in their tents, covered with snow, and nothing would induce them to stir. They utterly refused to get up, to light their fires and cook their food, to do anything, in short—begging only to be allowed to die where they were. There was no doing anything with them, even for their own comfort. Nor were the Basutos and white men in a much better condition. We endured this state of things until noon, hoping for a change in weather; but the only change was from bad to worse, for by twelve o'clock the snow was driving in such clouds that we could not see a yard in any direction. The Basutos now became terribly alarmed, fearing that we should be snowed up altogether. So, yielding to dire necessity only, the Colonel decided to beat a retreat from the elements.

Accordingly he directed the Basutos to go down into the valley where we had left our horses and cattle, and to send up all the men and horses there to help us shift the camp equipage as speedily as possible. Off started the Basutos, in such a hurry that they left their tents standing; and the Colonel turned his attention towards the Putini young men, over whose heads he had to have the tents pulled down, in order to induce them to stir. Even then they did not move, but lay under their fallen tents, crying, 'Let us die, 'Nkos; only let us die!'

That not being his object, however, he proceeded next to pull them out. They were perfectly helpless, paralysed, their brown skins *white* with cold. Finally, with the greatest difficulty they were started off down the mountain in the tracks of the Basutos. Once fairly off, they made no delay, until they reached the warm valley beneath, and hid themselves in the old Bushmen's lairs with which the place abounds. The South African is certainly unable to endure severe cold, and these men would have died had they been kept upon the mountains, or allowed to remain stupefied in their tents.

Meanwhile the Colonel waited with the ——th and with ourselves for the pack-animals. It was getting late before these began to arrive. A Basuto boy, whom the Colonel had taken for an after-rider, was the first to appear, driving seven pack-horses before him. These animals were immediately loaded up and sent off again, and then, as each horse or ox appeared, he was taken and loaded by white men—for the native drivers were helpless and could only cower over the fire. At last the work was done, our last tent struck, and the last animal loaded. Nothing remained upon the ground save the tents of the pioneers and Basutos and our frozen selves, and we made the best of our way down the mountain side.

I had been wishing all day that the Colonel would leave us, for I feared the effect of the intense cold upon him; but, after all, it is mental rather than physical strength which 'carries men through.' He was as active and energetic as usual throughout that trying day, and no power on earth would have taken him away until all was finished, and till he could follow the last man down to the valley below.

Glad enough were we all to escape, more especially from the dreadful wind, which seemed to penetrate to the very bone, rendering some even of the white men quite helpless. We could not have stayed, and, much as our leader disliked being beaten, there was no help for it. He sent a mounted man down before us to see how far the snow extended, and we found that it lay for miles beneath us. In the valley about four miles from the foot of the pass it was knee-deep, but this only in the morning; for the sun, which shone out there, soon melted it. Drifts formed in many places, deep enough to swallow us had we fallen into them, and on the mountain side they froze hard.

CHAPTER XIII

BUSHMEN'S CAVES

The change in temperature from the mountain heights to the valley beneath was wonderful, and the following day was sunny, which made us all alive again. Yet the night had been cold enough to freeze a can of water standing in the Colonel's tent.

Our camp next morning presented a more cheerful scene than the one which we had left behind us in the snow. It was a lovely day, with a bright sun shining from a clear blue sky. The berg was clad in white right down to the valley, and the passes were so completely blocked that we were forced to wait for a thaw before we could commence our labours. Meanwhile all hands were at work erecting shelter by the orders of our Chief, who himself sat writing despatches in the midst of a busy scene. The tents were all down, in order that the ground might dry in the hot sun. Some of the men were cutting timber, some carrying it, and others putting up screens for tents and fires. One party groomed the horses, while another prepared a train of oxen for a foraging party. The latter were to bring in loads of pumpkins, mealies and kafir corn from the deserted gardens of which the valley was full, as it formed part of the location from which Langalibalele and his tribe had lately been driven out. The troops, meanwhile, were engaged in cleaning their rifles, etc., their Captain in reading a newspaper, and our Colonel, as mentioned before, in writing, all under an Italian sky and a brilliant sun. In his capacity of Colonial Engineer, the Colonel had continually to answer letters and to send written directions to every part of the colony, and he always kept a post running to Estcourt from wherever we might happen to be camped at the time.

Not twenty yards from our camp flowed the Bushman's River, a rapid stream of clear water, which would be charming for bathing in summer time, but was quite too cold to be pleasant while we were there, although some of us made constant use of it.

That afternoon we explored the Bushmen's caves—huge caverns rather—situated in the precipices which tower above the Bushman's River, and in which our pioneers had found temporary shelter. They had made themselves very comfortable, having built screen-walls of stones across the entrances to the caves, to be a shelter from the cold winds. They had also constructed their bed places in the various recesses and ramifications within, while the mouth of the cave formed a general dining place, in which, while we were camped there, huge fires were kept burning by those whose duty it was to prepare the food for the whole party.

These caves are full of coloured drawings by the Bushman, hideous representations of eland hunts, cattle raids, or fights with kafirs, whose figures are distinguished by being painted much larger and of a lighter colour than those intended for their small opponents. Some of the drawings are very clear and distinct, the colouring as brilliant as though just put on; others are less so; but each one is more ugly than its neighbour. We found also in the caves a good many poisoned arrows left by these Bushmen. They were very small, looking more like toys than weapons of war, but were doubtless deadly enough, with their venomed tips, and shafts of mountain reeds.

But there were other caves not very far from this valley which had a later and a deeper interest than any connected with the Bushmen. Here was the scene of one of those tragedies with which, alas! the history of Natal for the year 1873–74 abounds; for here certain fugitives of the Hlubi tribe had been smoked to death by a party of loyal natives under the command of a white man. The caves are situated in a tributary valley to the great Bushman's River Valley, and are formed by masses of rock, resting one against the other, and having three openings or entrances. The story, as far as I could gather, is as follows: a party of 'loyal' natives, while patrolling the valley after the main disturbances were over and the troops had returned to head-quarters, observed a track leading up from the stream to some fissures in the rocks. Following up this track, and seeing evident signs of occupation about the rocks, they called upon the fugitives to come out and surrender themselves, informing them at the same time that their chief Langalibalele had been captured, and was in prison.

There were women and children in the cave as well as men, and, after some parley, the former are said to have come out and to have been taken prisoners. But the men refused, saying that, if their chief was a captive, he was indeed a dead man and they themselves would die where they were. And, perhaps, they had no great belief that their lives would be spared, even although they should give themselves up, knowing that prisoners had frequently been put to death, and sometimes even tortured in a most cruel manner, by the native forces— possibly being also aware that the presence of white men had sometimes been no safeguard against such cruelties.

However this might be, whether it was devotion to their chief, whom they did not care to outlive, or whether, despairing of life at the hands of the enemy, they preferred to die fighting, the men refused to surrender. No further attempt was made by the attacking force to get them out. But, they piled heaps of brushwood against the apertures of the cave, and set fire to it. Then they sat down to wait until their victims should be smothered by the smoke, or burnt to death should they attempt to force a passage out. This too, reader, was done under the orders of a white leader—though not one, thank Heaven! in H.M.'s Service—the only crime of the victims being that of having run away and hidden themselves in fear of death! It appears that one or two of them escaped after the fires were lit, passing along a narrow rift between two huge rocks, the mouth of which was concealed by underwood from the observation of the besiegers. Seven are supposed to have perished; but, if there really were so many, the remains of some of them must have been removed, as, although we made a searching examination of the whole place, we could only find the skeletons of two. After the lapse of so many months that fact, however, is hardly a proof that more men were not killed at the time.

That the caves—if such they can be rightly called—had been well supplied with food was evident from numerous bones of goats, remains of mealies and kafir corn, etc., which lay about on every side. Comfortable bed places, too, had been constructed in various recesses, and a tiny rill of pure water ran through the rocks within the caves. On the ground outside, and near the entrance, could still be seen the remains of the bivouacs of the attacking force which had camped there for one night. One almost regrets that the besieged did not surprise the 'Government devils'—black and white—asleep, and put an end to the lot, only that such an attack, however much in self-defence, would have been another crime to be charged against the unlucky tribe.

In connection with this story I may as well mention here a little judicial circumstance which came to my knowledge while in Natal, and which perhaps some of my readers, learned in the law, may be better able to understand than I, a plain soldier, can be expected to do. It appears that during the 'Rebellion' of 1873 a party of men on the Government side were attacking some fugitives at bay amongst the rocks. Two of the latter had guns, and used them in defence of themselves and the women and children who were with them, one of them killing his man (a 'loyal native'). Finally the fugitives were captured, and carried off to Pietermaritzburg. At the famous 'trial' which took place there, they told, of their own accord, exactly what had taken place, without which free confession, by-the-way, no one would have known that they were the two who had held firearms. The sentence upon the party was as follows: those who had no guns, and therefore did not fire, received imprisonment with hard labour; the man who fired and missed was condemned to seven years; and Sibanyana, the man who hit one of the attacking party, to twenty years' imprisonment with hard labour!

But this is a digression from which we will return to the Bushmen's caves, in order to mention a native snuff box and assegai-head, differing from the poisoned arrows described before, and a kind of needle used by the kafirs to pick thorns out of their feet, which we found and carried away as relics of the place.

The Colonel sent a patrol up the mountain during the day to ascertain the actual depth of the snow, and, if possible, to bring away the Basutos' and pioneers' tents left behind in their hurried retreat from the weather. On reaching the spot where our camp had stood the men beheld eight eland busily engaged in discussing our stock of pumpkins and mealies, which were buried in the snow, but which their sagacity had discovered, while hunger had so far overcome their natural timidity that the traces of the recent presence of man had not been sufficient to scare them away. Of course they fled at the approach of the patrol, and, though the corporal in charge of the party had several shots at them before they got out of range, he failed to bring any down, for his fingers were so numbed by the cold that he could hardly handle his rifle.

Meanwhile all hands were turned out on a general camp fatigue. The Colonel had decided that, owing to the season of the year, it would be safer for us to camp in the valley than higher up, in a position from which we might at any time be driven by another fall of snow, and where we might even find ourselves snowed up altogether. Accordingly, he set us all to work, and we finally made ourselves very comfortable, considering our materials and the capabilities of the locality.

The head-quarters' tents were pitched between the Bushman's River, which flowed, close by, over a rocky or pebbly bed, and an enormous cubical mass of rock, about thirty feet of a side, which stood alone at this point in the valley; while the troops' tents were placed at some little distance, on the right bank of a tributary stream to the Bushman's River, all being sheltered by strong fences of sugarbush, quantities of which grew close by. The fires for cooking purposes were built against the aforementioned mass of rock, and were also sheltered by thick bush screens; whilst a rude shanty was put up, made of poles and brushwood, with window, shutters, and door of basket-work, and a roof thatched with grass. This shanty was our dining and sitting room henceforward, and possessed one important advantage, of the ingenuity of which we were very proud. It boasted of a noble chimney, which our Chief himself designed, of oxhide stretched while green upon a frame of timber, something after the

CAMP AT BUSHMAN'S RIVER PASS

fashion of the chimney of a blacksmith's forge. Fixed chairs, couch, and table of rustic workmanship completed our dining hall, which we regarded as an immense success, and which was a palace to us, although in reality but a mere shed.

A guard hut and powder magazine, of brushwood also, were constructed in front of the troops' lines, the latter containing our store of powder, which was thus placed under the immediate eye of the sentry. An oven was next built near the troops' kitchen, from which our soldier-baker turned us out most excellent bread; whilst the blacksmith's forge, in constant requisition for sharpening and repairing the pioneers' tools, was placed in a convenient position hard by. Our horses had no stables, indeed, and lived in the open; but we put up rough timber horse-lines, to which they were taken twice a day to be groomed and fed with mealies, and they were allowed to graze at will upon the mountain slopes. Finally we threw a substantial bridge across the tributary to the Bushman's River, immediately in front of our camp, as it ran right between us and our work, besides separating us from the pioneers lodged in the caves.

The Basuto camp, upon rather higher ground at a distance of some hundred yards to the rear, completed our establishment. Thanks to the forethought and ingenuity with which the work was directed, and the alacrity and attention with which it was carried out, it was as comfortable a bivouac as we could have contrived under the circumstances.

These more permanent arrangements for our comfort and safety were the more necessary, as, in addition to the increasing severity of the season, the works upon which we were now about to commence operations were by far the most extensive that we had yet undertaken, and would detain us at our present camp for some weeks, whereas none of the other passes had occupied us for more than a few days each. Our present party of pioneers were at work upon the Bushman's River Pass itself, and other smaller ones close by, from July 6th to July 28th, while the working party, who then relieved them, did not finally quit the place until September 25th.

On the return of the patrol with the tents, the corporal in charge reported that although they had with great difficulty succeeded in forcing their way as far as our old camp ground, yet that it was impossible to get higher up the mountain. 'Impossible' was a word which we were hardly allowed to admit into our dictionaries during this expedition; and the Colonel determined to go and see for himself what the state of things might be. Accordingly, next day, taking with him his more immediate followers and attendants—his faithful henchman Campbell, the trusty Basutos, and myself—he started up the mountain. I am sure that throughout this expedition (I might say with equal truth throughout his life in Natal) my Chief was pitiless to himself, forcing himself to exertions and to an endurance for which he was physically unfit, and which he himself would never have imposed upon any but strong healthy men. He had never spared himself, nor taken a week's rest since he received his wound and other severe injuries eight months before; nor can it be imagined that, with that still open wound and weakened frame, he could have gone through the severe exertions and hardships which I am now recounting, without suffering seriously in consequence—perhaps for the remainder of his life, certainly for many years.

Upon this occasion we found it comparatively easy work getting as far as the old camp, where much of the snow had melted; but beyond that point it was still very deep, and it took much time and trouble for us to reach the site of my Colonel's camp when on patrol in 1873, after the affair of the 4th November. Here he pointed out to me the long line of the strong sod-wall which had been thrown up to protect from the violent winds the patrol-tents of the small force encamped for some time upon this bleak ill-omened spot. I saw also some small musketry parapets constructed for outlying pickets in situations commanding access to the pass. All showed that, however futile and needless was the errand upon which my Chief was sent by those in command, he had done his duty as a soldier. The arrangements still existing made it plain enough that no point for defence or attack had been overlooked by him.

We halted here for a little while to recruit ourselves after our exertions in struggling through the deep snow, and then advanced along the side of a steep incline, testing each step with our long kafir sticks. It was indeed a service of some difficulty and danger, as in many places the snow was waist-deep, and a false step would have preciptiated one into the rocky river bed beneath.

We got as far as where the Bushman's River crossed our path as a tiny stream, springing from near the mountain crest, and then the Colonel, having decided that, with the aid of the pioneers, the pass was practicable, we retraced our steps, and after a toilsome return journey were glad enough to find ourselves once more beside a blazing fire, at our camp in the more sheltered valley, some five miles down.

CHAPTER XIV

THE TOP OF THE PASS

Next day we took our pioneers up the mountain and set them to work at clearing away the deep snow, and forming a track to the foot of the pass. From this point our course lay up the left bank of the Bushman's River for a considerable distance; then we crossed it, and had to scramble up a steep hillside over rocks and loose stones, which at times afforded but a precarious footing.

The snow did not lie so deeply here as we had expected; yet in places the pioneers were working mid-leg deep. Although the Putini lands lay near the Draakensberg, it is probable that these men had seldom handled snow, for the natives shrink from cold, and remain much in their warm huts during the bitter days of July and August. Consequently our pioneers were praiseworthy in a double degree for the energy with which they worked through such cold as they may never hitherto have experienced.

Before we returned to camp upon that first day a practicable track had been formed to the spot selected by the Colonel as the most suitable for the formation of a line of scarp; and for the next two-and-twenty days the work steadily progressed, with the occasional interruption of a day unfit for outdoor labour, when a fall of snow, or a violent gale which neither white nor black could face, drove us down the mountain and compelled us to take refuge in our camp below. Our life was too regular and monotonous to admit of my giving a detailed account of its daily incidents, and the whole may be summed up in a few words. To march at daylight (about 7 A.M.), reaching the pass and commencing work by 10 A.M., to scarp rocks and build walls, to bore and blast where necessary for our purpose, and then to return to camp by sunset—such was the routine of our daily life.

As time went on the unusual exposure and hardships which our working party underwent began to tell upon them greatly. The hard thick soles of their unshod feet began in many cases to crack and split, making marching difficult and painful. Coughs and colds abounded, and some few fell ill with inflammation of the lungs, and other serious complaints. We had no medical man amongst us, but our Chief successfully performed the functions of one. In the course of a very varied experience he had picked up a good deal of practical knowledge, both medical and surgical, and had been careful to provide himself with a plentiful supply of simple drugs, etc., for the use of the expedition. His medicine chest contained chlorodyne, quinine, carbolic acid, castor-oil, tartar-emetic, turpentine, etc. etc., not to mention lint, plaster, bandages, and splints, in case of accidents.

Upon the first appearance of sickness in the camp the Colonel established a standing soup-kitchen, at which the strongest beef tea was kept going in large quantities the whole day long. Every morning he had a sick-parade, at which I assisted, while the Colonel's two native servants attended to carry out his directions. Symptoms were inquired into, medicines dispensed, hot fomentations and mustard applied in cases where such treatment was required, and then the patients were sent off to the kitchen fire. Here the man in charge was directed to supply each sufferer with a basin of hot soup at once, and the same again at midday and evening. This service the soldier who officiated as cook performed with the greatest willingness, taking an evident interest in the progress of the invalids.

Perhaps the practice was not very regular—but it was successful, and the best proof of our Colonel's skill lies in the fact that all his patients recovered. We did not lose one during the whole expedition. The respect in which the people themselves held the *Inkos* had been great before, but it amounted to awe when they discovered what a great *innyanga* [medicine-man] he was. Indeed these simple people have an especial reverence for medical skill, which they seem to regard as something with a touch of the supernatural in it.

Our monotonous existence was varied in my own case by occasional excursions with the Colonel to examine new passes discovered and reported by our Basuto guides.

During one of these he took me, at my request, over the ground of the disaster of the 4th November, 1873, pointing out to me the various positions held by himself and party, and by the enemy; and, as I had expected, I found that I could most thoroughly coincide with those of my own cloth who, having seen the place, asserted that the Colonel had been perfectly right in his estimate of its capabilities, and in his proposed course of action. It moved me strangely to go over the ground with him who had done so well there, and who, but for his faithful Basuto followers, would have been left upon it. Looking upon the great cairn which he had afterwards built above the dead, and which, covered with snow as it was, seemed like part of the mountain, I rejoiced that he stood by my side, alive though not uninjured, instead of lying there beneath the cold gray monument upon that bleak and desolate hill side. And yet I thought that, had it been my lot to follow him, and to die upon that day, I would rather have had the soldier's burial which he gave them himself, in the lonely spot on which they fell, with the eternal peace and majesty of the great hills around them, than have been disturbed from my quiet rest, and carried away to the dusty cemetery of Pietermaritzburg. The citizens of that town have erected in their market-square a monument to those who were killed at the Bushman's River Pass, which is a flimsy trifle compared to the grand hills that here 'keep record of their names,' where 'never can a touch of shame sully the buried brow.'

My Colonel, when he raised that mound above them, had planted it with a great mass of beautiful white everlastings, which grew all around, some flowers of which, with locks of hair which he cut from the heads of the dead, he sent to their relatives on his return. The snow covered all when I was there, making the spot doubly melancholy, and I was glad to follow my Chief away from what was no cheerful place to either of us. Before we left he pointed out, at my request, the little stream, now frozen to a block of ice, where he so nearly lost his life—also the place, some four hundred yards in advance of his position, to which he rode to parley with the advance-guard of the flying tribe. He was accompanied by his interpreter only, who was without weapons, while he himself was unarmed to all intents and purposes; since with his injured shoulder, put out by a fall the day before, his sword was useless to him, and was carried throughout the day by the Basuto, Hlubi; while, although he had a revolver slung round his neck, it was no easy task to use it and to manage his horse with his one hand. I heard (though not from him) how, when the interpreter, Elijah, was wounded, and his horse shot, my Chief rode in and endeavoured to save the man, who then was killed by his side, he himself surrounded, and his horse's bridle seized. Dropping the reins, he used his revolver. This and his good horse saved him; and, after running the gauntlet, amidst cries of 'Shoot the Chief!' he escaped with only one serious wound, an assegai having passed through his left arm. He also received one or two slight wounds, and his patrol-jacket was cut in many places.

Naturally I took the most vivid interest in all that I could learn from my Chief on the subject. But I could never gather more than the barest facts from himself; and it was from the Basutos that I got the fuller account which I desired of what he did and endured upon that bitter day. Of himself he never spoke at all, and, great as appears to be the grudge borne against him by the friends of the volunteers who left him and fled that day, I never heard him say a word against them. As far as I could learn, he has never uttered a word of reproach or accusation against them beyond his most moderate and mercifully worded report to the commander of the field force, which was published at the time.

Upon another occasion we went over the mountain to inspect the Giant's Castle Pass. This was the place where my Chief and his followers passed the night of the 3rd November, 1873, on their way to the Bushman's River Pass, and after the Colonel had had the fall which so severely injured him, but which yet did not arrest him in his course.

The way up the Giant's Castle is very narrow, and excessively steep, passing near the top between two great walls of rock, and over a mass of loose stones and huge boulders. We climbed down the pass for a considerable distance, as the Colonel wished to see again the rock under which he had lain from shortly before sunset on the evening of the third, until nearly midnight. We easily found the place where still remained the line of stones which had been piled beneath the overhanging rock to prevent his rolling down the steep side of the pass from the place in which his helpless body had been laid. There was still visible the long grass that had been collected and packed within the line of stones, to form a bed for their injured commander, by the hands of the devoted few who had stayed with him, one half of whom lay dead on the mountain top before the sun was high on the following day. From this spot a most wonderful view presented itself. The country beneath appeared like the waves of the sea running mountains high, and then petrified before they fell. Their crests rose so tumultuously one above another in all directions that it seemed as though nature had exhausted her wildest fancies in flinging the great hills into forms which should have no leading or consecutive line amongst them, and which should appear to be in utter defiance of all law and order. Such was my fancy as I looked down upon that amazing scene, though no doubt a better geologist than I would have traced a rigid obedience to law, even there, where my eyes could discern nothing but chaos.

My eyes only were long chained by the view beneath me, for my imagination was soon busy with a scene which a few quiet words from my Chief summoned up before me. The same frozen sea of hills, but glowing in the last rays of the setting summer sun, was visible to my mind's eye. But I thought of the rough hard resting place beneath the overhanging rock as occupied by a bruised and shattered figure, whose weary eyes rest upon those burning hills as they changed rapidly from fiery red to deep rose, and through pale pink to pearly grey. The injured exhausted man wonders as the last ray vanishes whether he will ever see the sun again; for he and his few brave attendants are alone in this wild spot; their comrades have gone on ahead, and a numerous armed foe is supposed to be close at hand. But with the fading light the tired eyes close in a quiet sleep, which strengthens mind and body for the exertions yet to come.

We retraced our steps to the top of the pass, and found it a severe climb indeed. It was much like going up a gigantic staircase, all the steps of which were broken down, and the ascent required efforts that tried the soundest lungs and the strongest limbs.

A few days later I got the whole story of the Colonel's first ascent of this place (in 1873) from one of the Basutos who assisted him on that occasion. The man told me that when my Chief awoke after his sleep beneath the rock just described, he immediately insisted upon going forwards; but, in consequence of his injuries, the men who were with him took three hours to get him up a place which he ascended in fifteen minutes at this time, nine months later. At first, it appears, they carried him in a blanket, but, after a while, it became impossible to advance any farther in this manner, on account of the intense pain which this mode of progression inflicted upon his dislocated shoulder and shattered frame, as well as because the strength of the bearers was failing, owing to the excessive steepness of the pass. None could have blamed him had he given up his purpose, and ordered himself to be conveyed back to the camp. But no amount of personal suffering would induce him to relinquish the work entrusted to him while it was possible for a brave determined spirit to conquer and control the body's pain. What he had to do was to take his men to the top of the Bushman's River Pass as speedily as possible, and there he and they should be if he preserved breath enough to give his orders, and consciousness to know that they were being carried out.

He got over the rest of the way on foot, by means of a blanket passed round his body, with two men holding on to either end, and slowly pulling forwards, whilst two others supported him from behind as well as they could. They were obliged to halt every two or three steps, and lay him down upon the ground to give him rest, yet his spirit was undaunted to the last. His first order, upon reaching the mountain top after this terrible ascent, was to up-saddle the horses; but then he sank to the ground, utterly exhausted and overcome. Yet half-an-hour's rest was all that was necessary to restore his resolute spirit to the mastery; and when the horses were brought up to where he lay, he made his men lift him on to his gray Basuto horse, and led the advance himself, over a rough and broken country, as energetically as if he had been in his usual state of health and strength. After riding for a few miles, the gray horse fell lame, and the Colonel then caused himself to be lifted from its back, and placed upon that of his favourite, Chieftain, who bore him safely through all the dangers of the rest of that eventful day.

I have told this incident simply as it was told to me by Jabez, without any unnecessary flourishes of description or admiration. Yet I venture to say that few will realise the facts of the case without appreciating the indomitable courage and perseverance with which my Chief pushed on to his assigned post, regardless of himself, of his own severe suffering and extreme exhaustion. He cared only for his duty, and did that with a noble fortitude which should be an example to all. In setting such an example he has done the state a service which should not be overlooked; and, if ever man deserved honour from his fellows, my Chief has earned it in two instances which stand prominently forward—not to mention his admirable conduct at the Bushman's River Pass; first, for the fortitude and determination which I have just recorded; and, secondly, for that which took place immediately on his return, wounded and nearly exhausted, to the head-quarter camp at Meshlyn next day. Captain ———— and his detachment had, it appears, been sent to support my Chief by holding the Giant's Castle Pass until his arrival there from the Bushman's River Pass. This detachment, however, entirely lost its way upon the mountains, and never approached the pass at all; and upon the Colonel's return to camp he heard that the party was supposed to be lost and to be in great danger from the enemy. Fearing that this might indeed be the case if Captain ———— should reach the Giant's Castle Pass, meeting there in all probability a large and triumphant force of Langalibalele's men, he at once volunteered to lead a party to the rescue. He started upon the quest within a few hours of his return to camp, and found the missing men next day, after marching all night in search of them.

The appreciation of the troops for this act of devotion on my Colonel's part, was plainly shown by their turning out en masse, and giving him three cheers, after he had been lifted upon his horse, and was about to take his place at the head of the relieving force.

We met with a good deal of severe climbing work during our excursions to new passes, sometimes riding, sometimes walking and dragging our horses after us over places where one would have thought that nothing four-legged save a goat could have kept its feet. Upon one of these latter occasions the Colonel very nearly lost his horse altogether. He and I were climbing up a steep bit of hill, our horses following us, led by the more practised Basutos, when a scuffle and a shout made us look round just in time to see a confused heap of legs and tail disappear down the side of the hill. The Colonel's horse, Chestnut, had slipped up and rolled over and over again down some fifty yards before he was brought up, immediately above the bed of a rocky stream, by a tree into which he plunged, and there hung, to all appearance dead. We scrambled down to him with all the speed we could, the Colonel being the first to reach the tree, when Chestnut proved himself to be alive by greeting his master with a joyful neigh. To our no small surprise and relief, when he was extricated from his unpleasant position, and set upon his legs again, he proved to be absolutely uninjured by what might have proved an uncommonly awkward fall but for the long heather and brushwood with which the sides of the hill were thickly clothed.

It was about this time that we were much annoyed in camp by the marauding propensities of some huge dogs, which, left masterless by the dispersion of the Hlubi tribe, had become perfectly wild, and would, indeed, have proved formidable antagonists to an unarmed man. They lived in the rocks hard by, and, coming out at night, wandered about the camp, attracted, probably, by the smell of freshly-killed meat.

The Colonel had a fancy to possess himself of one of them, a noble-looking fellow, whom we had seen several times at a distance, thinking that he would make an excellent companion could he be caught alive and tamed by kindness. Accordingly, one night—it was the evening of the day on which Chestnut had taken his perilous roll—a trap was set, baited with fresh meat, and so contrived that it would catch any animal that entered it, alive and uninjured. We retired to rest, confident of findng a foolish-looking prisoner in the morning. But the camp had not long been silent before we were roused by a tremendous disturbance, and some of us, rushing out, were just in time to see escape two great dogs who had entered the trap together, and, by their united efforts to get out, had completely smashed it. Next day we determined upon another plan. We cut a hole in the side of a bank, in which hole was placed a large piece of meat for bait. We then bent a sapling which grew opposite our hole, so that a noose attached to the end of it hung down exactly over the hole. The arrangement was such that when the dog seized the bait he would release a catch, the sapling would fly up, and the animal, having his head in the hole, would be caught by the noose round the neck, and swung off the ground in a manner perilous to his neck should he not be immediately released. Captain ———'s soldier-servant, who took the greatest interest in the dog-catching, willingly undertook the post of watch, in order to prevent any captive being hung outright. The rest of us, after visiting the trap, and seeing that all was quiet (although we were aware that the dogs were prowling about at no great distance), went to bed, and most of us soon fell asleep. But, as upon the previous night, we were shortly aroused by a most frightful uproar, to which the former disturbance bore no comparison whatever. Shouts of 'Sentry! Sentry! Come here! Come here!' and then the sentry's cry of 'Turn out the guard!' repeated twice, made us all jump out of bed and hasten to the spot.

A bright moon was shining, and by its rays we beheld Captain ———'s servant, holding on with all his might to the bushy tail of an enormous yellow dog, which he was swinging round and round to avoid its teeth. He was shouting vigorously, meanwhile, to the guard for assistance, while they stood helplessly looking on at the struggle between man and beast. Just as we ran up to the place, the poor fellow, who was quite exhausted by his exertions, let go at last, and the dog made off as fast as he could run.

The man was greatly chagrined at his failure, having set his heart upon carrying out the Colonel's wishes. He was also somewhat inclined to grumble at the guard, who, however, very naturally did not see the point of seizing the huge brute with their naked hands; for, while it was all very well for the man who held the tail, there was no second tail to hold by, and there was a very formidable array of teeth. It appeared that hearing the trap spring, the soldier had rushed out, and found that two dogs had been hunting together again, for there were two caught in the noose. The moment they found themselves captured they fell to fighting and tearing each other, the smaller of the two struggling out of the noose and bolting as the man approached. He had only just time to catch the other by the tail before he was clear as well, and then ensued the comic performance, the finale of which we witnessed.

'Well!' said the Colonel, 'the dogs show excellent good sense. We shall never catch one if they persist in hunting in couples.'

Our chances were over for the night, so we turned in again, after a hearty laugh, and a stiff glass of grog all round. The latter was a highly desirable precaution, for it was freezing hard, and our attire was of the most airy description.

After this all our efforts in setting traps proved futile, for the dogs had learnt a lesson, and would not approach them again. Nevertheless they continued their nightly visits to the camp, attracted, doubtless, by the joints of beef and mutton which hung upon a framework of poles some height above the ground. Beneath this they ran, and sat, and jumped, until the ground was beaten hard and smooth by the constant action of their paws. Not that they seemed starving; from the occasional glimpses that we caught of them, they appeared to be in very good case; but I suppose beef was a luxury which they seldom enjoyed.

Although we were unfortunate in our attempts upon the full-grown dogs, we managed to secure some of the breed. To our great satisfaction we found a litter of pups amongst the rocks, which, after watching for some weeks, we took into the camp, where we brought them up, and where their mother visited them at night, but resisted all our attempts at enticing her into sharing their comfortable captivity. By the time the camp finally broke up these pups were able to march with the men, and went with them to Pietermaritzburg. But they never attained the fine proportions and noble bearing of those that escaped us, and were always unmistakably the regular 'kafir-dog.' Strange to say, although brought up by us, and treated with the utmost kindness, they never reconciled themselves to our white skins; and while they were on excellent terms with all the natives, they would never allow a white man to approach them. One of them was taken by my Chief, and kept at his quarters. It was many months before he succeeded in making friends with *Kwibi*, as the dog was called by the grooms. After that I believe his devotion to the Colonel was excessive, but he would never look at any other white man.

CHAPTER XV

HLUBI AND HIS HOUSEHOLD

By the end of July, hardships and fatigue had greatly told upon our pioneers. The poor fellows were gaunt and worn-looking, suffering much from chest complaints, and from the effects of the frost and snow upon their feet, large portions of the soles of which had begun in many cases to come away. My Chief decided to replace them by a fresh working party, and to start with them at once for Pietermaritzburg, in order to obtain for them there in person that promised reward of freedom which he considered they had fairly earned. He hoped also to procure the release of the whole of this innocent and ill-used tribe. But, although he would not for a moment allow that there was any fear of his failing in this latter object, yet I could tell that he was anxious, and especially that he was annoyed by the apparent impossibility of extracting from Government any definite answer to his despatches on the subject in question. Now, however, he considered that the time had arrived for putting an end to all doubts and delays; and with this view he ordered up two parties of men who had been employed for some time under civilian overseers upon Colonial road works, and who arrived in camp on the 27th July. The white men in charge of them had been directed to see that they joined us fully equipped in every respect. Nevertheless, when they made their appearance, they were practically deficient in everything, and had to be supplied with necessaries by us. However, their strong and healthy appearance was undeniable, and in that respect the contrast between them and our trusty pioneers was painfully marked.

We found one of the fresh road parties at our camp when we returned to it on the evening of the 27th; and the Colonel, having received the overseer's report, directed him to turn out the cooks of his party at 5 A.M. next morning, and to see that their breakfast was ready by six, and that the whole body of men marched at seven for the pass, such being our own daily custom.

The overseer stared on receiving these orders, but said nothing in reply, and retired with a salute. But a little later on that evening I happened to be standing before our kitchen fire with my Chief, when the man approached again and addressed the latter. He said that he desired to inform the Colonel that it would be utterly impossible for him to get the cooks of his party up, or to make the men eat their breakfast at that early hour. Also that none of them would go up the mountain at all unless they got extra pay, while as for himself, he thought he might manage to get up once a week, but not oftener, as he did not think his health would allow of it.

Upon hearing this audacious speech I felt much the same inclination to run away as I experienced in the Pinetown stables upon my first visit to them. Curiosity prevailing, however, I stood my ground and waited for the result.

My Chief looked at the overseer steadily but calmly, as though the man who could venture to dispute his orders to his face for self and party were a natural curiosity worth observing. He then simply repeated his former orders in a quiet tone of voice, adding these words, 'Go back to your party, and tell your people that I will flog the first man, be he black or be he white, who disobeys orders. You yourself will also parade at seven o'clock with your horse saddled and bridled, when you will leave the camp, and proceed to your own residence, where you will remain until the work upon which these people are employed is finished, as you are perfectly useless here. I should dismiss you from the service of the Government were it not that you have been employed for so many years that I am disposed to overlook your shortcomings for this time.'

The worthy man looked somewhat astonished, but did not attempt to remonstrate, and my Colonel, turning to me, remarked, 'It is better that that man should live in idleness and away from here for the next two months, than that he should remain here, where his example is sufficient to corrupt the natives who would work under his directions. He is morally and physically unfit for the work, and would be perfectly useless; that is quite clear.'

The morning of our departure—for I, of course, was to follow my Chief—broke bright and clear, and as the sun rose higher in the cloudless sky, the very sight of its brilliancy seemed to impart that sensation of warmth which, in very truth, his rays had little power to produce, even at midday, amongst those ice-bound, snow-clad hills. Our gaunt and toil-worn pioneers were early paraded for their return march to Pietermaritzburg, only one of the party being unable to make the journey on foot. He, by the Colonel's orders, was mounted upon a spare pack-horse, to the sufferer's own great satisfaction.

All the men, the soles of whose feet had been cracked by the frost, were provided with sandals of ox-hide, which had been fitted to them under the supervision of our excellent soldier-cook, to whose strong broth no doubt many of these unfortunates owed their lives. Every man of the party had provided himself with a long walking-staff cut from the mountain bush, without which no native seems to consider himself fully equipped for a journey. The cortège

started, led by the corporal of infantry, who had been in charge of them ever
since they had been employed under my Chief, and who, by his kindness,
firmness, and strict justice combined, had gained their entire confidence. I was
glad to see the hearty manner in which the few soldiers left in camp gave them
their parting good wishes, as it showed that a kindly feeling had resulted from
their intimate companionship of the last few months, and that our red-coats, to
whom naturally I am partial, had good hearts amongst them.

As soon as the pioneers had left, with the corporal at their head, upon his
stubborn Basuto pony which no one but himself could ride, we returned to
camp, to make arrangements for our own departure. A few hours later my Chief,
attended by myself and a small party of Basuto horsemen, started in our turn for
Pietermaritzburg, which, if the pioneers made good marches, we hoped to reach
in three days' time.

Our way led us through a new country, and the Basutos were our proper
guides, for we were to spend our first night at Hlubi's house, and our second at
that of Jabez, to the solemn delight of these strange, undemonstrative,
independent people, who certainly showed their devotion to the Colonel by
deeds rather than by words. The Basutos were always very friendly to me, and I
think that they took me for some relative of the Colonel's, especially after they
discovered that he commonly addressed me by my christian name, which they
evidently looked upon as a mark of relationship amongst Europeans, although
using no such distinctions themselves.

The morning had been brilliantly fine, though cold; but towards noon the
clouds rose and began to bank up with every appearance of a heavy snow-storm
impending. We escaped, indeed, with but a slight sprinkling of snow, but came
in for what was far more unpleasant, namely, a severe hail-storm, which,
beating in our faces, left painful effects for some days after.

Late in the afternoon, after a twenty-four miles' ride, we reached the village
over which presided Hlubi, the chief of this small section of the Basuto nation,
who possessed land of his own in this part of Natal. Hlubi had sent word to his
people beforehand of the honour which was to be done them by his white Chief,
and we were received upon our arrival with the utmost hospitality. Two sheep
and an ox were presented to the Colonel, according to the custom amongst these
people upon the reception of honoured guests. That is to say, the animals,
having been accepted, were there and then returned to the donors to be
slaughtered and eaten by the retainers of the guest and the hosts themselves,
who in our case were one and the same party.

We were at once shown into our lodgings for the night, namely, the young
chief's own dwelling-house. This was a square two-roomed building, sur-

rounded by a verandah. It had a thatched roof, and doors and windows upon the European pattern; in fact it was quite a civilised habitation, and all as clean as a new pin. The furniture was certainly not abundant, but the substantial table and form of which it consisted were as white as scrubbing could make them. The table was covered with a clean white cloth, upon which was speedily placed an excellent repast. Tea, eggs, a pair of capital fowls, and some good bread, flanked by a bottle of brandy and another of gin, showed the ideas of our coloured friends upon the tastes of white men. As we had now had a long fast and an equally long ride, we were quite ready to do justice to the provisions set before us.

When our meal was over we received a visit from Hlubi's wives, who came to pay their respects. They were three in number, each living in a house of her own; but one was the favourite, and decidedly the best looking. She led by the hand a boy of about eighteen months old, the most precocious infant I ever saw, and evidently the pride and delight of both parents.

Our lady visitors did not attempt to enter the house. They sat upon their heels, with their knees also touching the ground, outside, where my Chief received them and conversed with them. Amongst the natives of South Africa the sitting posture is that of an inferior, and denotes respect. In the presence of their king, for instance, no Zulu would dare to stand without express permission; and the wild native invariably sits, or rather crouches down, the moment he comes into the presence of a superior.

These women were dressed alike, in leather petticoats, embroidered or studded in pretty patterns with what had the appearance of brass-headed nails without the spikes, and had their shoulders covered with shawls or gaudy-coloured blankets. Round their necks they wore heavy necklaces of brass, medallions made in the shape of quoits; bracelets of brass upon the arms, and a bright handkerchief upon the head completed a decidedly picturesque costume.

The precocious infant soon attracted general attention, and we were much amused by his proceedings. At one moment he was clinging to his father's knee, and sharing with him a bowl of *tshwala*; at the next, running to his mother, who remained seated upon her heels, he applied to her for his natural nourishment, with which, indeed, she supplied him without appearing at all disconcerted by our presence.

'Have you any more children, Hlubi?' inquired my Chief.

'No, *Amarail*, only this one,' replied Hlubi.

'He is a fine boy. What is his name? asked the Colonel.

Hlubi hesitated a little before replying that the child's name was Major, and explained that he had been so called because he had received his name while his father was following the Colonel—then Major—to the wars.

A long story followed of how Hlubi had had the honour of some talk, during the expedition of 1873, with the Head of the Native Department, who had been graciously pleased to inquire after Hlubi's family. Upon hearing that he had a son and heir who had not yet received a name, he had himself proposed to bestow upon him that of Benjamin Shepstone, in honour of the two great chiefs of the colony, one the ruler of the whites, and the other of the blacks. So Hlubi brought the news of the great man's condescension home to his wife. But, as usual, there was no counting upon a woman's fancy. Mrs. Hlubi would have nothing whatever to say to Benjamin Shepstone. She knew nothing of those two names, nor of the chiefs who bore them, and they were not pretty names. *One* white chief she had seen, and he was a leader of soldiers, whose look made bad men and cowards afraid, but warriors and women rejoice. Had not her people, when they returned from the fight, told her that he was not a man like other men, but one made of steel? Yet had he not spoken kindly to her and some other women when he passed through their land before? His name was Major, so she understood; and Major her child should be, or he should not have a name at all. There was nothing more for Hlubi to say, as he was evidently a little under petticoat government to this favourite wife; so Major the child was called, and Major he remained.

After this explanation, the Colonel evidently felt bound to look upon the boy in the light of a godson, and asked the mother to say what present he should send him from Pietermaritzburg. After some consideration, she decided upon a little suit of clothes, in order, she said, that the boy might look like his father. She would like him to have a little coat, trousers, and waistcoat, and particularly she desired that he should have a cap with a tassel to it. Of this she made a great point.

The aged grandmother now appeared upon the scene, bearing upon her head a pot of special *tshwala*, which she placed at the feet of the 'Major,' by which title the Colonel was still universally known amongst the natives. The old lady signified to him that she begged his acceptance of her gift, which he received with his accustomed courtesy. I have since observed that it is a special mark of respect for the grandmother, the old woman of the tribe, to present this pot of *tshwala*; but I am not sufficiently acquainted with the habits and customs of the natives to explain the origin or meaning of the ceremony.

By this time it was quite dark and becoming uncommonly cold, yet none of our pioneers had arrived. We had taken a different line across country from theirs, and had seen nothing of them since they started in the morning, and we now began to feel a little anxious on their account. At the Colonel's request, a couple of mounted men were despatched from the village to look for them, and to guide them by the shortest way in. Meanwhile, great preparations were made by the Basutos for the entertainment of the weary travellers. Fires were lit in all directions, large masses of *isijingi* [mealie meal and pumpkin boiled together] were prepared, and an ox was killed for their consumption. At the same time the occupants of the different houses arranged amongst themselves how the pioneers should be billeted among them for the night; and all was ready for them by the time the corporal reported the safe arrival of himself and party.

Very shortly all were seated round the blazing fires, and, encouraged and assisted by their Basuto hosts, were soon enjoying their meal of *isijingi* and meat, the latter just warmed through—I cannot call the process cooking—according to the native taste.

When my Chief was thoroughly satisfied that all was well with his men, he retired with me to the house set apart for our use, where he was attended by Hlubi and all the heads of families in the village. They sat down upon the ground around us, while we placed ourselves upon the form, quite prepared for what was sure to ensue, the inevitable *indaba* or 'talk.' Under our present relations of guests and hosts the Colonel not only permitted but encouraged the good people to talk; and, knowing how dear to the heart of the native is a palaver, he indulged them in a lengthy one. At last, however, they departed to join in the festivities going on without, and we were glad to prepare our beds for the night, consisting simply of blankets laid upon the smooth clay floor. The floor of a house is by no means so comfortable a sleeping place as the open field, for in the latter a man who knows what a bivouac should be never fails to put himself into an easy position by scratching hollows for both hip and shoulder.

However, we were too much fatigued by our long ride to cavil at any warm resting place. Even I, strong and healthy though I was, felt excessively tired. And my Chief, upon whom the two months' hardships had greatly told—although when questioned about himself he always gave the same cheerful answer that he was 'all right'—had the unmistakable look upon his face of deadly weariness which even he could not entirely conceal. For my own part I slept soundly, and woke next morning thoroughly refreshed, and quite ready for another long day's journey.

CHAPTER XVI

THE TRIBE IS PARDONED

After an early breakfast of coffee, eggs, and bread, we started for Jabez's residence, a distance of forty-five miles over a fairly open country, reaching our destination about dusk.

The hamlet was composed of some dozen houses in all, but Jabez was evidently the chief man of the place. He was not, indeed, so great a man as his own chief Hlubi, but he was a much more civilised one, as evinced by the style of his habitation. The house itself was built upon much the same plan as that of Hlubi, but furnished with considerably greater attention to comfort. Besides which, Mrs. Jabez—and there was only one—was a Christian native, and talked English perfectly well. She may or may not have been the better for this fact; I did not see enough of her to judge. But my experience amongst the natives leads me to believe that the wilder and more untaught they are, the greater is their honesty and respectability. Probably this is owing to the fact that a little civilisation immediately brings them into contact with the lowest dregs of the white population.

However, I have not a word to say against Mrs. Jabez, except that she was a 'Christian'—that much ill-used title, alas! being quite one of contempt in Natal when applied to a native. She was a stout pleasant-looking body, who received us with the most respectful cordiality, and took a larger share in our entertainment than did the three savage wives of Hlubi.

The principal room of Jabez's house was entirely papered with pictures from *The Illustrated London News*, the furniture consisting of two couches or settles, a table, a washing-stand, with jug and basin, and a dressing-table, with a looking-glass upon it. Jabez's saddles and bridles hung in order upon racks suitably placed, and a great cupboard, or armoire, stood in one corner of the apartment.

This was the sitting room, in spite of its oddly mixed furniture; for the other chamber, which was next thrown open for our inspection, contained a four-post bedstead, with mattress and pillows complete, a couple of chairs, and a great chest. Mrs. Jabez was evidently very proud of this apartment, and pointed out

THE TRIBE IS PARDONED

the bed in which the Colonel was expected to pass the night. He did not wound the good people's feelings by refusing in words, but nevertheless he did not make the experiment, but slept upon one of the sitting room settles, while I occupied the other.

Much the same entertainment was prepared for us here as at Hlubi's, as notice of our approach had been sent before us. For the pioneers another ox was slaughtered, more fires kindled and *isijingi* made, and sleeping arrangements agreed upon. The same gathering of the heads of families and the same ceremony of 'talk' followed the excellent repast set upon the table for us. Again the bottles of gin and brandy accompanied the more solid refreshment, and again the aged grandmother appeared with her special pot of *tshwala*. There was even a little Jabez to be brought forward for approval, and his mother likewise received the promise of a suit of clothes for him, to be sent from Pietermaritzburg on our arrival there.

It was fully ten o'clock before our tired pioneers arrived after their long day's march. They had been compelled to leave about a dozen of their number behind them at a kafir kraal some few miles back. A mounted native, who called at Jabez's house a little after dark, reported that he had passed the party on the road, apparently very much fatigued; but that, when he asked them why they did not halt for the night at a kraal, their reply was, 'Our Chief has gone on, and we must follow.'

The poor fellows were well fed and cared for; and so anxious were they all to keep tgether and with the Colonel, that those left behind rejoined us before we started upon the following morning.

Our third day's march was but a short one, as Jabez's home is not more than fifteen miles from Pietermaritzburg. Leaving the pioneers barracked at their old dwelling place above the town, we rode on to the Colonel's quarters at Fort Napier, where he was kind enough to make me quite at home for the week during which I remained there.

The 30th of July, the day on which we returned to more civilised life, after our two month's experience of the mountains, was a cold, raw, drizzly day. The roads were slippery with the wet, and our horses slid about a good deal, while I began to think that dry frost and snow were infinitely preferable to damp and mud. We rode through the back streets of the town on our way to the Fort, for our cortège was a somewhat conspicuous one, the armed and mounted Basutos, and the pack and led horses, making quite a little procession.

The Colonel talked to me a good deal that day about his intentions with regard to these men; and naturally enough my own enthusiasm took fire from his, and I felt the keenest interest in his complete success.

The first thing to do was, evidently, to claim from the Governor the freedom promised to the ninety, and then to persuade him to extend his clemency to the whole tribe. But what next? When they were free what was to become of them without homes, without cattle, food, or clothing, and with no means of procuring such, having in fact been stripped of all their worldly possessions by the Government forces? I put the question to my Chief, and he replied as follows:

'As far as my ninety young men are concerned, I intend to pay them for the work they have done at the usual rate of wages paid to native labourers upon the roads. I consider that justice demands that they should be so treated; and I am willing to accept the responsibility myself of my action in this matter. As for the rest of the tribe, I trust that I shall be able to induce his Excellency to see that it is only right, and the bounden duty of Government, to supply the more immediate wants of these unfortunate and innocent people, until they have had time to build new huts for themselves, and to raise fresh crops upon their devastated land. I hope, indeed, that in due time complete restitution may be made to them for all the cattle—some eight-thousand head—which were taken from the tribe last year and sold by Government. But that will certainly not be done at once.'

Whether or no the Colonel felt as anxious and excited about the results of his first interview with his Excellency as I did, I cannot tell. His manner was as calm and quiet as usual, and, except that he was evidently thinking incessantly upon the subject, no one would have imagined that the result of his last few months' incessant labour of head and hand, the success or failure of his most cherished plans and hopes for the year, hung on the balance of an undecided mind, and depended upon the comparative influence of those about his Excellency.

Upon the following morning the Colonel went to Government House, and saw his Excellency, reporting his return, and claiming the promised freedom of the pioneers.

For my knowledge of what passed between them I am indebted to the brief account given me by my Chief upon his return to his quarters after a lengthened interview. It appears that, having spoken of the ninety young men, and their excellent behaviour under trying circumstances, he proceeded to set before the Governor the grounds upon which he desired to obtain the release of the whole tribe. Recapitulated shortly, these were as follows: there was no evidence whatever that the Putini tribe were 'in complicity' with that of Langalibalele. They had done absolutely nothing, with the exception of receiving some of their own women, who had married into the other tribe, and who, upon its dispersion, naturally returned to their old homes. On the contrary, the Regent of the tribe, during the minority of the young chief—the little son of Umkosaza—had been in close communication with the Magistrate of his County upon this very point. He had asked the advice of the Magistrate as to what line of action he had better adopt, since he saw plainly that trouble was impending for the neighbouring tribe. The Magistrate's advice was that all the people should remain quiet, cultivating their gardens as usual, and taking no part with Langalibalele— which counsel was carefully followed.

But, to the Regent's great astonishment, he suddenly received a demand from the Magistrate of another County to supply his white and black contingent with cattle upon the shortest notice. This demand was at once complied with to the best of his ability, although not, apparently, to the satisfaction of the Magistrate. According to native custom, when cattle is orderd to be supplied to a force, the acting chief sent round to collect animals from the different kraals or families under his rule, according to their various abilities. It is not difficult to understand that, as the people expected no payment for their cattle, they did not give up the best of their herds to the spoiler. The immediate result of this—as though the object of Government had been but to pick a quarrel, and to gain an excuse for attacking the tribe—was an increased demand, or rather a heavy fine, imposed in cattle. The excuse made for this action was that any unwillingness to supply food for the Government forces betrayed a rebellious inclination. The distressed Regent, I believe, did all in his power to meet the renewed demand. But the natives are not a prompt people, and are prone to delays and discussions at all times; and, a very limited time being granted him, he failed to make up the number of cattle required of him. What clearer proof could there be of disaffection than this?

The result was simple. The tribe suddenly found themselves surrounded by the Government forces; their stock—consisting of cattle, horses, sheep, and goats—swept off; their stores of grain annexed, and either wasted or sold; their huts burnt down; and themselves—men, women, and children—stripped of all they possessed, down to their blankets, skin petticoats, and sleeping mats, and carried off into captivity.

It seems that antagonistic influences had been at work during the Colonel's absence, for he could not at first induce the Governor to adopt his views. But, although anxious and disappointed, he did not despair, and was determined to do his utmost to bring his Excellency to a sense of what justice demanded at his hands. For five days my Chief went daily backwards and forwards between Fort Napier and Government House, urging, exhorting, warning, and explaining— leaving the Governor converted to his opinion, and promising him all he wished

—returning to find that some adverse influence had been at work again, and that he must commence his task once more. Up to the last he knew not what to expect, and the irritating suspense seemed to harass him more than all that had gone before.

How statesmanlike the Colonel's views were, and how true his warnings, was proved a few months later by the arrival of a despatch from the Earl of Carnarvon to the Lieutenant-Governor of Natal. I was then no longer in the colony. I copy, however, an extract from the despatch in question.

> With respect to the Putini tribe, I have in their case also expressed my opinion that no sufficient cause has been shown for removing them from their location. I can discover no indication of their conspiracy or combination with Langalibalele, beyond the vague and uncorroborated apprehension of some possible movement on their part in connection with the supposed tendencies of his tribe; and therefore I can see no good reason for any punishment on this ground. Indeed, on the facts before me, I am bound to express a grave doubt whether the heavy losses and confiscations to which the tribe has been subjected were warranted by their want of readiness to afford assistance to the colonial forces. Those losses cannot, I fear, now be entirely replaced or repaired; but as far as reparation can be made without lowering the influence and endangering the authority of the local Government, it must be done.
>
> If this tribe has not been already restored, in conformity with the statements contained in your despatch, etc., I have now to direct you to reinstate them without delay, in such manner, and under such precautions as will attract as little as possible the attention of the natives generally to the proceedings, and will be the least calculated to produce any excitement or apprehension on their part.

This despatch (dated December 3rd, 1874) is identical in spirit with the views expressed by the Colonel eight months earlier, and again insisted upon now in his interviews with his Excellency, and needs no further comment of mine, as it must be plain to all that he anticipated the wishes of the Imperial Government by obtaining the freedom of this innocent tribe many months earlier than their release could be effected by the interference of the Secretary of State.

At last, upon the morning of the fifth day, his Excellency appeared to have given in completely, and the Colonel hastened to summon his men that the matter might be clenched before those about the Governor—those whose interest it was to support oppression—had had time to persuade him to change his mind. We had received orders from our Chief, before he left us that morning, to parade our men at a certain hour, to march them down, and to have them drawn up within a short distance of Government House, that they might appear immediately when summoned. We waited some time before we were sent for, and marching our men through the gates, drew them up on the lawn before the house. From thence at last issued forth a company of dignitaries—his Excellency, supported by the Acting Head of the Native Department, various other officials, a few native chiefs, and last, but not least in my eyes, my Chief, in uniform, with the fire of excited determination in his look, but bearing himself with his usual calm self-possession.

The Governor now made an oration to the pioneers, with the Acting Secretary for Native Affairs as interpreter. He told them that he had heard with great satisfaction the report which had been made to him of their excellent conduct, and that he appreciated the services which they had rendered to the Government under circumstances of exceptional hardship, difficulty, and danger, on account of which he now pronounced their pardon—that is to say, the pardon of the ninety pioneers.

His Excellency hesitated at this point, and appeared uncertain whether he should allow his clemency to go any farther or not; and it was not until the Colonel had made another earnest appeal, urging him to release the whole tribe, and recapitulating the reasons already given for this act of justice in which he was supported by the Acting Head of the Native Department, that he at last consented unreservedly. His speech, pardoning the whole Putini tribe, and granting them permission to return to their own location, was carefully translated and explained by the Acting Head of the Native Department to the listening pioneers; and so my Colonel's cause was won, and his exertions rewarded in the way which he desired.

Upon clearly understanding that their whole tribe was free, and might safely go back to their own homes, with one accord the ninety pioneers lifted up their voices in the royal salute, '*Bayete!*' Then they marched up to the Fort, where every man received from the Colonel the sum of money for their wages of which he had previously spoken to me.

But before my Chief rode up to the Fort himself, he dashed down the town, calling to me to follow him. As I came up with him, far down the street, he said, 'I have not a moment to spare, but I must get my friend Brookes to send out word to the Bishop of what is done.'

I knew nothing of the town, nor of where we might be going, until we drew rein at a pretty little house quite at the lower end of Pietermaritzburg. Through its gate, held open by a native servant, the Colonel rode, calling to a friend within, while I remained in the street, from whence, however, I could distinctly hear what passed.

'Well, I've done it!' exclaimed my Chief, speaking through an open window, with an eager excitement taking the place of his usual calm.

'I'm glad to hear it!' replied a pleasant hearty voice from within, the owner of which I could not see. 'But what have you done with your rebels?'

'They are all free! and I want you to tell the Bishop, for I have not time to go out myself.'

'Have you their freedom in writing?' inquired the invisible voice.

'No; but it has been promised me for the whole tribe, in the presence of several important witnesses. Shall you be going or sending out to Bishopstowe today?'

'Yes; one or the other. But won't you come in and tell us all about it?'

'Thanks; not now. I have not a moment to spare; but I will come down again this evening. Goodbye.' And he rode out again, and we galloped away through the streets up to his quarters and the expectant pioneers.

After receiving their money they were dismissed into the town to make their purchases. As I rode through Church Street that afternoon I saw parties of our men at every turn, five or six together, and all easily to be recognised by a certain uniformity of costume. Each party, apparently, was escorted by native friends and acquaintances, who must have been either servants in the town, or else have come in from the adjacent country upon business. Our people were all very busy, providing themselves with such necessaries and comforts as they could afford. Their purchases appeared to consist chiefly of blankets and cooking vessels; and they seemed to have too much good sense to expend their little stock of money upon anything not strictly necessary. The men appeared to be thoroughly cheerful and hopeful, yet most of them must have felt very uncertain as to where they should find their women and children, or what was to become of them all when found. Probably their faith in our Chief, and in his power and willingness to aid them, had something to do with their happy looks.

I had my orders already, and was directed by the Colonel to hold myself in readiness to start up-country, taking with me our ninety, as soon as ever they were ready to go. I was to march them back by the same way as that by which we had just come down. We were to strike across country, and to avoid the main roads, as my Chief did not wish the return of the pioneers to their own location to attract general attention until they should be completely and quietly settled. Indeed we were quite aware that the colonists would be violently opposed to the proceeding, and might even create some disturbance.

The Colonel had already sent off his Basuto after-rider, with a note from the Acting Head of the Native Department to the Magistrate who had been especially appointed to look after the deserted locations, informing him that the whole tribe had been released and permitted to return to their homes. I was directed to hand over my men to this Magistrate, as it was advisable that a register should be kept of their number, and also that it should be quite plain that my Chief was doing all in order.

The Colonel had also been requested to take upon himself the business of collecting the remainder of the scattered tribe from the different white men's farms and houses, where they had been 'given out' to service, as also from the kraals of some of the native chiefs, and to make proper arrangements for their return home. Indeed he offered to undertake the management of the whole, thinking, and thinking rightly, that the faith which these people had in him would enable him the more easily to carry out the matter in the quiet and orderly way which was so particularly desirable under the circumstances.

At daylight upon the morning of the 6th July, the pioneers were duly paraded at the Colonel's quarters. Not a man was missing from the number, and all were fully equipped for their return to their desolate homes. Each man carried a blanket, rolled and worn in true soldier fashion, over one shoulder and under the other, and bore besides a huge bundle, consisting of his sleeping mat and blankets, his cooking pot, and other necessaries, purchased upon the previous day.

The Colonel addressed them through an interpreter, telling them that on their return to their location they must at once busy themselves in erecting huts, and cultivating mealie gardens, and must settle down immediately as a quiet and industrious people. They must always, he said, pay the greatest attention and respect to the magistrate set over them, whom they were to regard for the present in the light of their chief, to whom they were to refer every matter for decision and advice. To this address they replied, in spite of the Colonel's repeated admonitions, by one simultaneous shoud of '*Bayete!*' and then the party moved off with cries and exclamations in honour of my Chief, all denoting their great respect, but the translations of which sound odd to English ears. '*Inkos*! *Baba*! [Lord and Father!] oh! great wild beast! oh! great black one! oh! lion! oh! tiger! oh! great snake! oh! chief, your face is white, but your heart is very black!' (an especial compliment)—all, except the reference to the 'white face,' being terms commonly applied to the Zulu king by his warriors.

CHAPTER XVII

ESCAPES AND DISASTERS

After handing over my men to the Magistrate according to my orders, I went on to our camp at the Bushman's River Pass, with despatches for Captain ——— from the Colonel. I found all well in camp, and the work upon the mountains progressing satisfactorily, but still a long way from its completion. The Colonel had desired me to return to him in a fortnight's time, with full information about what was being done, and what had yet to be done. Accordingly I spent much of my time in going backwards and forwards to the different spots at which separate parties of men were at work, at distances of three, four, and in one instance of ten miles along the top of the Berg. Here there was fair riding ground, after the first long steep pull from the Bushman's River Pass—that is to say, one could ride at the rate of six miles an hour.

Of these passes the one at the greatest distance from our camp, and indeed not three miles from the Giant's Castle, had been newly discovered by the Basuto, Windvogel, and a party of some half-dozen soldiers were encamped near at hand for the purpose of scarping it, as it was too far for them to come and go daily from the main camp. My horse having fallen slightly lame one day, I started for this pass on foot, and reached the place so late that I determined to remain with the men for the night and return upon the following morning. Indeed by this time I had become so thoroughly inured to our rough life that it mattered little to me whether I slept in a patrol-tent or marquee, in a sheltered cleft among the rocks or in a kafir hut, as long as I could go from a good fire to a thick blanket or rug. The little patrol-tents occupied by the party at this new pass were pitched close under the mountain crest, where the projecting cliffs afforded some shelter from the piercing blasts.

After sleeping soundly in one of these through the night, I woke about sunrise, dreaming that I was a small boy again, visiting the monkey's cage at the zoo. It was a vivid dream, for, even after I opened my eyes, the noise made by the animals still sounded in my ears. Oddly enough, it grew louder and louder, until the air was filled with chattering, screaming, and hoarse angry sounds. This could be no dream, and, peeping out through the slit at the end of the tent, I beheld the most remarkable sight my eyes ever fell upon. The patrol-tents, as I have said, were close beneath the cliff; and surrounding them, in the form of a crescent or half-moon, hundreds of dog-faced baboons had collected in hostile array, apparently exceedingly angry to find strange creatures upon the mountains which they had hitherto regarded as their own. These animals exist in great numbers upon the Draakensberg, and are very large and excessively fierce. I have heard that they will attack the leopard, or tiger as it is called in Natal, whenever they see him, regardless of the numbers they may lose in the contest. There seems to be a blood feud between them, and it is said that, if once tracked by the baboons, a tiger never escapes them in the end.

It may easily, therefore, be conceived that they would prove formidable antagonists to the six or seven men whom they now appeared disposed to attack. Our rifles would have been of little service to us, for we should only have time to fire once ere we should be seized and torn in pieces by the disgusting monsters—than which I can hardly imagine a more revolting fate.

The baboons formed an army, in fact, for they were led by an old male of great size and grizzled with age. He was so evidently in command of the party that he was immediately dubbed 'the General' by us. While we were all peeping out and watching the angry gestures of the animals with some anxiety, one of the men said that he had heard that, although enraged baboons were not to be scared away by the loss of any number of what might be called their rank and file, yet that the death of their leader was always the signal for instant flight. This, we thought, might possibly be the case, and, at all events, the movements of the enemy now became so aggressive that we decided to try the plan as our only chance of escape. The men seized their rifles, and one of them covering 'the General,' fired and killed him upon the spot. To our intense relief and satisfaction, his followers immediately turned and fled upon seeing him fall, and vanished over the mountain, their howls and screams echoing amongst the rocks long after they had passed from our sight.

I am no coward, I hope, but I confess I felt for the moment almost overcome by the thought of our certain fate had the mass of enraged brutes persisted in their attack.

After a breakfast of hot coffee and biscuit, which was most acceptable in the keen mountain air, I thought I would find my way back to the camp down the pass in which the men were engaged, instead of along the mountain top, over which I had walked or ridden so often that I was quite tired of it. Accordingly, accompanied by the trusty Windvogel, who had come with me as guide, I started down the mountain. We had a terrific scramble for part of the way, down along the bed of a dried-up watercourse; but I had become accustomed to that sort of descent, and looked upon it as a matter of course.

After a long and toilsome walk we at last approached the camp, which lay round a sharp corner or shoulder of hill, so that it was not visible to us until we were close upon it. As we came in full view of it, but at a considerably higher elevation, from which we looked down upon it, I saw, to my great consternation, the guard hut suddenly burst into a blaze. The guard and a few soldiers left in camp immediately rushed to the powder magazine, and carried the powder barrels to the riverside, so that they could be thrown in should the fire spread in that direction, and then all set to work to strike the tents as rapidly as possible. Fortunately, the grass had been carefully cut for a considerable distance round each tent; but the wind, blowing strongly at the time, carried the flame from the guard hut right across the tributary stream to the Bushman's River, and in one moment the whole hill side was in a blaze. The long grass and bush at this time of year was as dry as tinder, so that when it once caught fire nothing could stop its burning. The flame ran up the hill, and coming to the mouth of a deep ravine, turned, and, sweeping again across the stream, seized upon the hill side above the camp. Soon the whole valley, as far as the eye could reach, was a raging sea of flame—a grand sight truly, but an awful one to witness.

Thanks to the precautions taken for the protection of our camp from fires, in the broad belts of closely-cut grass which surrounded us on every side, no damage was done either to life or property, except the destruction of the guard hut where the mischief began. But for some time we were in considerable danger, as at any moment a stronger gust of wind might drive the flame across our safeguards. In the course of one half-hour our pleasant grassy valley, with its numerous evergreen bushes, was reduced to a cinder, presenting nothing to the sight but a blackened surface, dotted with charred and smouldering stumps.

Had Windvogel and I been but a little later in our return to camp we should assuredly have been overtaken and destroyed by the flames, for the spot upon which our camp remained, looked afterwards like an oasis in a desert of black, which surrounded it on every side. As it was, we had barely time to gain our lines before the hill we had just quitted was one sheet of flame.

So for the second time in the course of a few hours my Basuto friend and I were preserved from a dreadful death—first, by the hands and teeth of the infuriated baboons; and, secondly, by the breath of that element, so useful when restrained, so incomparably terrible and deadly when once set free.

Our party met with another accident a few days later, which unfortunately proved less harmless than that already related, although it directly affected two only of our company.

One morning I was, with a working party, employed in blasting, when an explosion made some of us turn to find that two soldiers who were engaged in boring a hole in the rock had been blown to a little distance from it, and were lying on the ground with injured eyes and faces. The hole had been charged upon the previous day, but had missed fire, and the men, under the impression that it had been 'drowned,' had set to work at it again. The powder, however, was dry and fit for use, and hence arose the accident. It was one of those pieces of carelessness which men so often commit when they have been long enough employed upon perilous materials for their sense of danger to become blunted by custom.

The poor fellows were immediately conveyed to the camp; we sent off a mounted orderly to Estcourt for a doctor; and meanwhile did what little we could to made the sufferers comfortable. The doctor arrived next day, and, after making his examination, he pronounced that the sight of the man who was most seriously hurt would not be permanently injured, although it would be a long while before he recovered the use of it. His comrade was simply burnt, and was doing well. We sent the former down to headquarters at Pietermaritzburg as soon as he was fit to travel, and I am happy to say that when I saw him last he was perfectly recovered from the accident.

I will close this chapter of escapes and disasters with an account of a curious accident which occurred to an attendant of some English visitors to our camp, who were upon a shooting expedition amongst the mountain spurs, and came to us for a night's lodging. They had been out after elands, which, however, they had not found, and had been benighted, and obliged to lie out the night before they came to us. The accident to their servant occurred as follows. He happened to be a 'head-ring man,' which, as it turned out, was a fortunate circumstance for him. In the darkness of the night he had walked clean over a precipice, some thirty feet high, falling upon his head-ring, the interposition of which saved his skull, which was not cracked, as it must have been had it been unprotected. The ring itself was not broken, although the hair was almost torn out by the roots, and the head much cut. Yet, when his injuries were dressed at our camp, the man obstinately refused to part with the cherished ornament, which was only attached by some half-dozen hairs. Wrapping a handkerchief round it, he appeared to be far more concerned for his head-ring than for his head.

CHAPTER XVIII

THE PUTINI TRIBE AGAIN

Despatches received from the Colonel detained me at the camp some days longer than I had expected, and it was not until the 23rd of August that I returned to Fort Napier, where my Chief received me with his usual hospitable kindness. When off duty his manner to me was uniformly that of a friend rather than master, and by this time I had learnt to be thoroughly at home at his quarters, where my dog, my horse, and I were his guests as long as we remained in Pietermaritzburg .

Upon the morning after my return we had just finished breakfast when a native servant appeared at the door, and called the Colonel's attention to him by the usual salute, '*Nkos!*'

'Well, John, what is it?' inquired his master.

'Putini men come; want speak *Inkos*,' replied John in his broken English.

'Putini men!' echoed the Colonel in some surprise. 'What can they have come down again for, I wonder!' and immediately went out to make the inquiry. I, of course, followed to hear what was going on.

Outside the garden gate waited some half-dozen natives, who, upon being summoned by John, came in, and crouched down in the usual native attitude of respect, exclaiming '*'Nkos! Baba!*' as they did so.

With the aid of John as interpreter they then gave the Colonel a piece of information which astonished us both considerably, and which brought the momentary expression into his eyes which I had learnt to recognise as the one sign of his being greatly moved which he could not altogether repress. The men said that they had come back because they and all their tribe, with the exception of the ninety pioneers, had been told by their Magistrate that their having been set at liberty was a mistake. There was no such order from Government, they were told. Only the ninety were pardoned, and all the others must go and live upon white men's farms as servants. In fact they must be 'given out' again. They had now come, said the men, to ask their own '*Inkos*,' in the name of the tribe, what they were to do next.

The Colonel's temporary answer to this question was to hand the envoys over to John, with orders to feed them and to keep them with the native servants of the establishment until further notice. He made no comment to me upon what we had just been told, but I heard him ejaculate, 'This will reflect the deepest discredit upon the Government.' And then he ordered his horse, and rode away towards the town, with an expression of countenance that made me avoid asking questions, or getting in the way to offer officious services of any description whatsoever.

For my own part I spent an idle morning. The Colonel had not yet set me to work, and, as I had not a single acquaintance in the town, there was not much open to me in the way of amusement beyond what the Colonel's precincts afforded. I had no wish to make acquaintances, or my Chief would readily have introduced me to the officers of the regiment stationed in Pietermaritzburg. My old disinclination to bring the fact that I had lost my proper place in the world before the notice of others of my own kind clung to me still, in spite of the Colonel's kindness in entirely ignoring my antecedents. I could not face the inevitable inquiries concerning myself and comments upon my career, which my introduction into Pietermaritzburg society would certainly involve.

'Wylde? Atherton Wylde? Who is he?'

'He has been in the Service, has he? the Engineers?'

'Oh! *that* Wylde! I've heard of the man. He made a fool of himself, and came to awful grief at Gib. in such a year.'

Such would have been the remarks made upon my name, and I did not care to encounter them. I should have clerical work to do for the Colonel shortly, but he had left me no orders on this particular morning except to look after myself, and to remember that there would be luncheon upon the table at half-past one. I believe I spent the greater part of my leisure in the company of Jack and Charlie, the two baboons who had an establishment of their own in the courtyard, and were a never failing source of amusement to me. Each of them had a pole of his own with a cross-bar at the top, to which he was attached by a long chain fastened at one end to a collar round his neck, and by the other to a ring which slid easily up and down the pole. They had each a brick-lined bath or well of water for their own use, and the stump of a tree beside it as a seat or table. Jack was a huge fellow who was pleased to be very friendly with me, and would throw somersaults for the reward of a peach or apple almost as readily at my command as at that of his master. But Charlie, who was rather smaller, and was an older inhabitant of the yard than Jack, would have nothing to say to me, nor, as far as I ever saw, to any other stranger, reserving all his marks of regard for the Colonel, to whom he was greatly attached. The length of their chains gave them ample room for exercise and amusement, and, being well out of the way of all tormentors, they appeared as happy as possible. Nevertheless, upon the one or two occasions when Master Charlie got loose, he showed all the inclination of his kind for mischief, and was with the greatest difficulty prevented from stripping the house of slates. Looking at Jack's great teeth and powerful limbs, and remembering my experiences at Windvogel's Pass, I came to the conclusion that I very much preferred the company of a couple of chained baboons to that of some hundreds of wild ones at large.

When I was tired of Jack and Charlie, I returned to the Colonel's sitting room (or office, for it did duty as both), and taking a book from the shelves, I deposited myself in a remarkably comfortable lounging chair for a quiet read. My book was a novel, the scene of which was partly laid in Hong Kong. I had just come to the conclusion that the writer was a woman, and had never been out of England in her life, when I fell asleep, and was only roused from my slumbers by the clank of the Colonel's spurs as he entered the room at half-past one.

I believe I first stammered something about the monkeys and Hong Kong; but, quickly recovering my senses, I sprang out of my chair with apologies for my want of manners. The Colonel picked up the book, which had fallen from my hand to the ground when I was overcome by sleep, but made no remark except to ask me whether I was ready for my luncheon, and we presently sat down to table.

I noticed that he looked grave and anxious; but as the impatient expression which had kept me aloof in the morning had entirely vanished, I ventured to put some questions concerning the results of his inquiries.

He told me then what I could hardly have believed possible—that, having seen and questioned most of the officials present at Government House upon the day on which the Putini tribe was released, he found that they by no means agreed in their recollection as to how far the Governor's clemency had extended, and as to whether the whole tribe, or only the ninety pioneers, had been set free. Some supported his views as to the universality of the pardon; others asserted that the pioneers only had received their liberty; while others, again, pleaded uncertainty upon the matter, on the grounds that they had arrived late upon the spot, and had not heard all that had passed.

'Surely, sir,' I exclaimed with much heat, 'you cannot believe a word of that? No one who was present at all can have the slightest doubt as to what occurred, or that the whole tribe was set free?'

'Since these gentlemen say so, I cannot do otherwise than believe it,' replied my Chief, with just a *soupçon* of reproof in his tone, which reminded me that I had been speaking of the officials of a Government under which he himself was serving at present. 'My own impressions are quite clear, I admit,' he continued, 'and I must do all I can for these people, for my honour is concerned in the matter. I, at least, know that I have promised them liberty in the name of the Government, and that promise myst be redeemed or————.' But he did not say what would be the consequences.

'What shall you do next, sir?' I inquired.

'I must write to the Acting Head of the Native Department, who is at present away, and who himself gave me the letter to Mr. ———— (the Magistrate). Then all I can do is to await his answer or return.'

And 'wait' indeed we did, for another month, to the inevitable detriment of the Putini people's crops. Meanwhile all was in confusion and uncertainty in the location, and many of the people were 'given out' afresh as servants to the white families up-country.

During this month I spent my days between the two offices belonging to my Chief, as Colonial and as Commanding Engineer, and in taking long rides, either alone or in company with the Colonel. In the latter case we were usually bound for some road party or other which he wished to inspect; for he never left them longer than he could help to their own devices, knowing that sudden and unexpected visits to his workmen were highly conducive to industry and order. But although I was leading a busy and contented life, I resolutely refused to make any acquaintances; so that when I left the colony a month or two later, I had not one farewell to make save to my Chief, to his human and four-footed dependents, and to my own horse and dog.

At last the Acting Secretary for Native Affairs returned, and the Colonel immediately had an interview with him. It then appeared that Mr. ————, the Magistrate, had only acted under orders, as a second letter had been sent to him within twenty-four hours of the first which was given to the Colonel, entirely contradicting the contents of that as far as it referred to any besides the ninety pioneers. Of this second despatch no mention whatever had been made to my Chief, so that from the 5th of August to the 24th—when the Putini men began to return—he was left under the impression that the promises made by Government, and through himself, were duly being carried into effect. The Acting Head of the Native Department was at first inclined to dispute the fact that the whole tribe had ever been pardoned, or that he had translated anything of the sort to the pioneers. But the Colonel reminded him of all that had passed in so exact and detailed a manner, that he finally withdrew his objections. And now, impelled thereto by the Colonel's energetic and forcible representations, he wrote upon the spot another order to the location Magistrate, contradicting the second letter, and repeating the instructions contained in the original despatch. This order, without any reference to his Excellency the Lieutenant-Governor, he signed and gave to the Colonel, who, having only waited to obtain it before going up-country again, started at two o'clock the same day, bearing the message of freedom, and attended of course by me and his usual Basuto after-riders.

We took our old course across country to the Bushman's River Pass, sending a messenger from Hlubi's to Mr. ——— with the precious despatch, and arriving at our old camp about midday upon the 22nd September.

The next day was spent by the Colonel in inspecting the passes, which were now all closed, every possible loophole having been rendered impracticable. He got through the whole business in one day, which astonished even me, accustomed as I was by this time to his rapid movements and amazing capacity for work. Indeed he could not spare one unnecessary hour, for his hands were full of other colonial works, and he had as much to get through from one month to another as he could possibly manage. He expressed himself satisfied with the present condition of the passes, and upon the 24th of September we finally broke up our camp, and left the Bushman's River for the last time.

I confess that I felt a lively regret at taking my final departure from this place. Great as had been the hardships which we had encountered upon the mountains, I had come to regard our camp beside the Bushman's River as something more like home than any other spot within the colony of Natal. The shanty, which we left standing for the use of any future benighted travellers who might pass that way, had a friendly homelike look to me. All its little comforts and conveniences were our own contrivances and the work of our own hands, and we had an affection for them not to be shared by ordinary doors and windows, tables, chairs, and chimneys. Never again were those who had sat round the blazing shanty fire, and who, thanks to mutual difficulties and endurance, had grown into close companionship there, likely to meet under such circumstances. For my own part, I had been less lonely amongst those wild deserted hills than there was any probability of my being elsewhere in Natal; for I could not hope to be constantly with my Chief in future; and of other friends I had not one. Here I had had work, a position of trust and responsibility, the goodwill of all our party, black and white, to most of whom the mere fact of my being the Colonel's aide-de-camp, as I might style myself, was enough to secure me respect and attention; and, more than all, I had had, during the greater part of every day, the companionship and confidence of my Chief. All this I might not find in any other part of the colony.

So that it was with a somewhat heavy heart and dejected mien that I turned from a last look at our deserted camping ground and followed the Colonel, who was already riding far ahead on his way down the valley of the Bushman's River.

CHAPTER XIX

CONCLUSION

We camped that night ten miles away, not far from some ruined kraals which had been destroyed at the time of the expedition. When we came in sight of the blackened desolate remains, the Colonel told me of a scene which he had witnessed there when on patrol, shortly after the place had been quitted by the Government forces. It appeared that on exploring a kraal and entering a hut which was still standing, he had come upon a shocking sight. A native woman—or rather a young unmarried girl, as was evident from the fashion in which her hair was dressed—upon her knees in the centre of the hut, was the sole occupant of this deserted spot. Did she fear the return of the native attacking force, who, in their permitted violence, spared neither sex, nor age, nor youth? Was she imploring the protection of the merciful white man, who had found her there alone? Not so; the spoiler and destroyer had no more terrors for her, and she was safe in the hands of the Father of all Mercies—for she was dead. A riem was round her neck; she had been hanged, or had been driven to hang herself, from the centre-pole of the hut!

Nor was this all. A yet more sickening proof of the scenes of awful violence which must have taken place was found in a cattle-kraal hard by—a human leg, not merely severed from the body, but dragged out at the hip-joint by main force!

Enough of such horrors; one's blood runs cold at the repetition of them, but burns with shame and indignation at the thought that they were inflicted in the name of an English Government upon an innocent and helpless people.

Next day we were marching through the Putini location again, where the people were beginning to settle, the brown beehive huts to reappear, and the thin blue smoke of their fires to rise once more into the moist spring air. The Colonel had sent word beforehand to the men of the tribe to meet him on his way through their location. Accordingly they all flocked round him during the day's march, when he repeated to them his original caution as to their conduct, and assured them that their freedom was now a settled thing. It is worthy of remark that from this time forwards there were always from one-hundred to one-hundred-and-fifty men of the Putini tribe at work upon the roads who voluntarily engaged themselves as labourers, whereas it is a well-known fact that, with this one exception, all the road parties in the colony are supplied with forced labour.

We spent the night of the 25th at Cathkin—where old Mr. ——— was loud in his praises of the quiet and orderly behaviour of those very 'rebels' whom he had feared so much when they were first marched up to the mountains—and a few days later we were at Estcourt.

Here I met with one last incident of the feeling up-country concerning the coloured races. It happened that the Basuto Jabez, who was still in attendance upon the Colonel, had been sent down by him to the Estcourt inn with a note to the landlord, requesting a supply of certain provisions required by our party. Jabez, who was a stranger in the place, went to the door of the taproom, and, seeing a white man within—the landlord in question—he entered to give him the note. The landlord, looking up at his entrance, immediately called out, 'Get out, you! No black man comes in here. Go round to the backdoor.' Jabez, however, who looked upon the paper in his hand as a safe-conduct anywhere, and naturally supposed that the man did not perceive it, still advanced, holding out the note to be taken. Whereupon the landlord, without more ado, rushed upon the harmless messenger, struck him, and pushed him out of doors.

Now Jabez is a man of spirit, and in a fair fight would dearly have liked to avenge the unmerited insult put upon him; but he is also a man of sense, and knows but too well that fair fight between white and black there will never be in his time. So he returned to the Colonel, and reported what had befallen him while upon his master's errand. The Colonel was never likely to allow his helpless dependents to be injured; and on this occasion he immediately went down to the inn himself, and inquired of the landlord what he meant by striking his servant. The man was civil enough in speaking to my Chief, but stuck to his point. It was his custom. No black man could be allowed to enter by that door without paying for his presumption.

The Colonel remonstrated. 'How is a strange black man to know your regulations?' he said.

To which the landlord's only reply was, 'Can't help it! That's my rule. They can go to the back-door.'

Whereupon the Colonel, finding it of no avail to talk to the fellow, left him, saying, 'I do not allow my servants to be beaten with impunity, and shall have the matter brought before the Resident Magistrate.'

Unfortunately for us the next day was a public holiday, and there was no magistrate's court sitting. The Colonel could stay no longer, for he was obliged to return to Pietermaritzburg, where his Excellency was anxious to see him upon business. He put Jabez's affairs into the hands of a friend, asking him to attend the court and to see that justice was done. He then saw the Acting Resident Magistrate (our old acquaintance Mr. ————), so as to leave nothing undone which could assist his servant's cause. The old gentleman in his turn promised to do justice in the case, and we started for Pietermaritzburg, leaving behind the disconsolate Jabez, who, indeed, implored his master to take him with him, saying that he knew very well that he should get no satisfaction. The Colonel, however, hoped better things, and would not allow him to relinquish the case. But poor Jabez's apprehensions proved quite correct, for, when the case came on, the Magistrate decided in favour of the white man, saying that he had a perfect right to make and to keep rules in his own house. So much for our second attempt at getting justice done to a native at Estcourt.

Well! we were once more at Fort Napier. My Chief had carried the main point for which he had laboured and suffered through the winter months of 1874, and the people whom he had rescued were at peace. The chief point was settled, although he had yet to insist upon the justice of restitution, or at all events upon the immediate wants of the tribe being supplied by Government until their first year's crops should have ripened—and there remained also the question of the restitution of cattle to be settled.* All this the Colonel hoped to effect in time, but I was not to see the fulfilment of his purpose, for my life in Natal, and my connection with my Chief was just at an end when I returned to Pietermaritzburg. The winter was fairly over; the grass began to have the appearance of green velvet, owing to its black underlying layer of last year's burnt crop; the lengthening days grew hot, and the short hours of the night were warm and pleasant; my existence in the colony was about to vanish like the winter's snow upon the Draakensberg.

An English mail had just arrived, and my letters awaited me at the Colonel's quarters. Amongst them was one from my father, full of affection for his

---

*   *Restitution to the Putini Tribe.* Since writing the above I have learnt the following facts:—Sir Garnet Wolseley, when he 'settled' Natal, being unable to obtain any certain information concerning the amount of cattle taken from the Putini tribe, decided to restore to them £12,000, the estimated value of 4,000 head, which was half of the sum realised by Government by the sale of the cattle of both tribes. This would seem to be a fair decision, but for the fact that it was put down in black and white by the military authorities at the time that over 8,000 head of cattle, besides horses, sheep, and goats, were taken from the Putini tribe alone. But even this meagre £12,000 has not as yet been really paid. I understand that £3,000 was voted by the Legislative Council as compensation to the Putini tribe for 1875, and for the following year an additional sum of £1,500 under the head of 'Relief in cases of individual distress amongst the natives.' And this is all that they have yet received. Will fuller justice ever be done?

prodigal son, and begging me to return home by the first steamer from Natal. It seems that my letters to him had convinced him of the welcome fact that I had thoroughly forsaken my old wild and thoughtless ways, and had really settled down into a steady useful member of society. It so happened that a warm friend of my father's, General ———, having a post to fill up 'for a young man of sense and energy,' bethought himself of his friend's son, whom he had known as a lad. He had a conversation with my father, the result of which was that he promised to give me the post in question, on condition that I reached England by a certain date, and that I brought with me a satisfactory letter from Colonel Durnford, my present Chief, as to my steadiness and general good conduct while working under him.

There could not be the slightest doubt in the mind of any sensible individual as to what my course should be on receipt of this letter. Here was such a chance for me as I was never likely to meet with again—a return home, and restoration to my proper place amongst my fellow-men. It was now in my own power to wipe out and cancel by an honourable future the foolish reckless past. My wildest hopes of advancement had never reached such a height as the opening now offered me. Surely no man in his senses could hesitate? Yet hesitate I did, and in the cause of my hesitation was the tie, single but powerful, which bound me to Natal—the regard I had for my Chief. Could I have been assured of remaining in his service to my life's end, I would have asked for nothing better, even although I should remain a small colonial official for the rest of my days—so long as I worked under and with him.

There was no time given me for consideration. I must either go at once or not at all, for no later mail would reach England in time for me to take up the appointment. I had read my letter, sitting opposite to the Colonel, who was similarly engaged, in his room after dinner that evening of our return from Estcourt. When I had finished reading, I sat watching him, and thinking over the question before me, until he laid down his last paper and looked up at me.

Something in the intentness of my gaze must have attracted his notice, for with his usual ready attention he said, 'Well, Atherton, what is it?'

For all answer, I handed him my father's letter in silence.

When he had read it he very naturally began to offer me his warm congratulations upon my good fortune, but stopped short in amazement at my dissatisfied look.

'What is the matter now?' he inquired, 'does not the offer please you?'

I could not say that it did. I could not tell him why at first, and I think he began to suspect me of having committed the folly of falling in love in the colony, before it dawned upon him that he himself was the attraction. I believe the discovery took him very much by surprise. Not the undemonstrative Basutos themselves had been more chary of expression of devotion than I. I had obeyed my Chief implicitly, and had done all that he desired me to the very best of my ability. But probably he put all that down to my natural disposition, and had no idea that it had taken all his influence and all my desire to win his approbation to transform me, from the idle good-for-nothing youngster that I had once been, to the steady trustworthy man I can honestly say that I had now become.

While I blundered on from one incoherent sentence to another, saying that I had no such friends anywhere as I had in Natal, yet admitting in the same breath that I hardly knew a soul to speak to except himself, that I preferred the work here to any other as long as I served under him, and so on, growing more and more confused and annoyed with myself for a sentiment which I feared would appear absurd in his eyes; he looked at me almost in silence with an expression which gradually softened from its original bewildered astonishment to one of great kindness. And then I fairly broke down, and implored him to keep me in his service, in however humble a capacity it might be, assuring him that indeed I cared to serve under no other than himself.

Doubtless I was supremely ridiculous in my fancy, and was old enough to have grown out of such romantic notions. Nevertheless, my Chief had saved me, and had made a new man of me, and my life was at his command.

He, at all events, did not despise or laugh at my devotion. It seemed to me that it touched and did not displease him.

A moment's silence followed upon my outburst, and then he put out his hand, and laid it upon my shoulder.

'Look here, Atherton,' he said, 'I should be doing excessively wrong were I to keep you with me now, although there are not so many to care whether one lives or dies in this solitary place that one can afford to throw away a friend. But for your own sake it is impossible that I should do what you ask.'

I made a gesture of impatient dissent.

'No; listen to me,' he went on, checking the folly that I was about to utter. 'Supposing that I were to consent to your throwing away this excellent offer, and staying on as you are now, what would be the result? My action in the Putini affair will lose me my present post of Colonial Engineer. In another year, at the utmost, the appointment will be filled up from England, and then all I could do for you would be to recommend you to the favourable notice of my successor. That, I imagine, would hardly meet your wishes. Well, I shall probably receive orders for some other station soon after my colonial appointment ceases, and our connection will come to an end as surely as though you had taken the chance now offered you—with the difference that, in the one case, you remain in a subordinate position in a colony which I am never likely to revisit, whereas in the other you will return to the life and condition to which we both properly belong. No, Atherton; there is not even a choice before you, although, even if there were, you should choose the right, and do your duty—which is, obviously, to make up to your poor old father for all that he has suffered on your account, and, if only for his sake, to regain the position which you have lost.'

I had not a word to say in answer to this reasoning. It was perfectly conclusive —everything upon one side, nothing but sentiment upon the other. I was silent, feeling somewhat abashed; and my Chief continued with increasing kindliness of tone, 'Don't think that I undervalue your regard, my boy. Perhaps I have not given you sufficient credit for it hitherto; but, believe me, now that you have given me so conclusive a proof of it, I shall not forget it. What has passed between us this evening will leave me with one pleasant thought at least connected with a place which has not been a particularly gay one to me.' The rare softening of a nature which was usually so self-repressed, and which was capable of being so stern, touched me greatly, and those few words from my Chief were recompense enough for a life's devotion, had fate allowed me to bestow it.

But, being both Englishmen, we naturally found sentiment, expressed between ourselves, a most awkward and inconvenient circumstance. I had recovered my self-possession, and, highly as I valued each word that he said, it was an actual relief to me when, suddenly resuming his ordinary tone and manner, he said, 'And now, about your arrangements. There is no time to lose, for you must go down to Durban by post-cart tomorrow.'

He literally packed me up and sent me off next day, for with his natural administrative faculty he settled and attended to everything himself. He sent me into the town early next morning with a list of necessary purchases made out by himself; and, with an apparent utter distrust of my own powers in that line, he sat by and superintended the packing of my portmanteau by his servant.

To the last it was, 'Now, Atherton, have you a good brandy-flask? No. Then take this one of mine!' or 'Where is that rug of yours? You will want it on the voyage.' 'Now, are you sure that you have money enough to take you home comfortably?' and so on. For once in my life I made a start without forgetting anything.

I was but just in time to catch the steamer, and had no leisure for regrets until I stood upon the deck; and watching the blue lines of the shore fading away as we left it, I thought that, with all its faults, Natal will always be dear to me, for the sound of its name must ever be connected in my mind with that of— MY CHIEF.

FIVE YEARS LATER

A SEQUEL TO

MY CHIEF AND I.

BY FRANCES COLENSO.

CONTENTS.

INTRODUCTION

I cannot tell the story of my Chief's last days from my own personal knowledge; for I was not by his side in 1879, or I might lie there now. Others who were strangers to him shared his death, and his undying fame; but for me, who knew and loved him, no such honour was reserved.

Surely it was some intuitive knowledge of what was to come—some faint and far-reaching vision of the future—that made me so deeply, almost unaccountably, unwilling to part with him when my own brightening prospects obliged me to do so. Science explains away all such fancied spiritual impulses by the mere physical reaction of sense-organs and nervous centre, or by the hardly more attractive mental analysis of the psychologists. But, beyond the most perfect theories of man as an exquisitely adapted mechanism and nothing more, there remains to each one of us the certainty that, at one time or another in our lives, from beyond our conscious selves, a soundless voice has spoken to us whose warnings can be disregarded only to our endless regret. Say that such notions are but illusions—it matters not; that which we believe, is what is true to us, and what other measure of truth have we in this world of illusions? Such warnings as these, from whatsoever source, had they been obeyed, would have led me to Rorke's Drift on that fatal morning of January 22nd 1879, when my Chief rode out for the last time. But it was not within my power so far to guide my destiny, and I am left to tell the story of his death as accurately as the most careful sifting of all available evidence will enable me to do. No circumstance shall be related of which there is not proof amounting to certainty, and references, in notes so as not to break the continuity of my tale, will give the authorities for what I say upon contested points.

Atherton Wylde
June 24, 1882.

FIVE YEARS LATER

CHAPTER I

PEACE OR WAR?

To those who were best acquainted with the native mind in South Africa nothing seemed less likely than war, when, in March 1877, after an absence of nine months, Colonel Durnford returned to the colony of Natal.

Yet war was brewing, not in the thatched huts of the Zulus, or the mud dwellings of Kafraria, but in the council-chambers of British rulers, and in the mind of the High Commissioner, Sir Bartle Frere. War!—not indeed the desperate struggles, with enormous waste of British blood and treasure, which actually ensued, for who could guess that the savages would defend their own with such determined courage!—but war by which, with a moderate expenditure and flourish of trumpets, a few shots exchanged perhaps, with just enough risk of one happening to come each man's way to supply the name of war, and reason for a shower of military rewards, those native races, whose inconvenient independence stood in the way of the grand South African confederation, might be coerced, frightened, and forced into owning the supremacy of England. The first step had already been taken, and rumours had been spread of expected disturbances without any real foundation, indeed, but made to appear serious by trifling inaccuracies and discoloured statements. Who does not know with what ease such rumours produce the very thing they profess to predict! A white trader or visitor travelling through the country of an independent chief, and carrying with him the conviction of his dominating birthright of colour, gives offence by some careless or arrogant disregard of native feeling, and receives in return a quiet hint to take his departure. No violence is used towards him; he departs safe in person and property; for the chief, though he may justly despise the individual offender, knows that the latter has England at his back, and will not lightly displease that powerful nation. But our traveller's dignity is injured, and he takes care to inform his fellow colonists that the chief in question is a 'cheeky old beggar,' who thinks himself as good as a white man, and will give trouble one of these days. It takes but little to transform such petulant sayings into a serious report, on the authority of a trader just returned from the country itself, that this chief is meditating an attack upon his white neighbours, and that serious disturbances may shortly be expected. It reaches the ears of some minor government official, who interviews the man, perhaps, and questions him. The latter, very likely, has no deliberate intention of producing false alarms, but his sense of importance is flattered, and he really begins to think that there *was* something suspicious about this and that little circumstance which, at the time, he had known to be perfectly innocent. Imagination once let loose in the direction of danger from the natives, there is no end to its extravagances, and, if our important trader happens to be able to say that messengers from any other powerful chiefs arrived during his stay—*ostensibly* about the purchase of dogs or monkey-skins—there can no longer be any doubt that the aborigines of South Africa are secretly combining against the whites. When a mixed population of whites and blacks of all degrees of civilization and intelligence lives side by side with a race of pure barbarians, it is absurd to suppose for a moment that any feeling prevalent amongst the whites of the former country can be prevented from reaching the inhabitants of the latter in a more or less garbled form. Accordingly, the groundless uneasy feeling aroused in the manner described, or under similar circumstances, soon produces a like suspicion in the mind of the independent chief. Then comes the beginning of the end. We prepare to defend ourselves. Our *defensive* operations bear a very close resemblance to *offensive* ones, so close, indeed, that the hitherto friendly chief feels that it is high time *he* took defensive precautions also, and summons his warriors around him. 'At last,' we exclaim, 'he has thrown off the mask! We must crush him before he has time to strike the first blow, and before other chiefs (doubtless in his confidence, through the medium of those suspicious dogs and monkeys) have time to join him.' And accordingly we do so, not, however, always finding the passive strength which we have chosen to stir up into active resistance quite so easy to deal with as we expected, and never again, perhaps, so harmless as before.

Some such rumours of disturbances in Kafraria had reached England, growing more serious and definite with every mile of distance, before Colonel Durnford started, causing him to leave the steamer at Port Elizabeth, and run up to the supposed scene of action. Having been stationed there before he went to

Natal, and having travelled much amongst the people, he knew them and their country well, and was more surprised at the reports of disaffection which he had heard, than he was to find quiet reigning amongst the Kafirs. He satisfied himself by careful personal inquiry that the suspected disturbers of the peace were as innocent of any such intentions as he was himself, and, report next giving the Natal and Zulu border as the probable scene of military operations, he hurried back to the port, and reached Maritzburg on March 22nd to find all quiet within and beyond her bounds.

The annexation of the Transvaal was just then taking place, and one of the undoubted results of the current rumours of a Zulu rising was to cow the Boers, against whom it was supposed to be directed, into temporary submission to the British yoke. Cetshwayo, it was said, was sending, nay! had actually *sent*, a large army to the Transvaal border, ready to fall upon the Boers at the least sign of resistance to the British rule personified by the Zulus' old friend, Sir Theophilus Shepstone.

No more striking illustration of illusory belief has occurred in our times than the assumed existence of this Zulu army, the purely mythical character of which has only very recently been discovered. The supposed fact was credited alike by friend and foe to the Zulu King, the former stating that it had been despatched to the border, if not at the actual request of Sir Theophilus Shepstone, at least with his private approval, and solely for his protection against the threatening Boers. And Cetshwayo's friends reasonably pointed out that—as, during the three weeks through which this army was (supposed to have been) assembled on the Transvaal border, not the smallest report was heard of violence on their part, of injury done by them to life or property, and as the whole body (was reported to have) quietly dispersed immediately on receiving Sir Theophilus Shepstone's message to them to the effect that he did not require their assistance—the Zulu King's action could not possibly be unfriendly to the English.

Cetshwayo's ready detractors, on the other hand, asserted that enmity to the Boers, and hopes of plunder in case of war, alone attracted the Zulu warriors. Sir Theophilus Shepstone, they said, had never summoned them to his assistance, but, on the contrary, had sent to command them to disperse, and Sir Garnet Wolseley's favourite simile of the 'black war-cloud hovering on the borders' of Natal, was drawn from this (imaginary) incident in the annexation of the Transvaal. Thus the army was as much an acknowledged fact as the battle of Waterloo, though it was afterwards observed that no one, black or white, ever professed to have seen it, or traces of it. Colonel Durnford, paying a flying visit to Pretoria on the day following the annexation, heard of its presence, and addressed a strong remonstrance to the new Administrator against its being allowed to remain there another day, and young Shepstone, it was asserted, was sent to disperse it.

But what appears to have been the actual fact? No Zulu army was sent to the Transvaal border on this occasion at all. Cetshwayo, it appears, had received some message from Sir Theophilus Shepstone, just before the annexation, informing him of his intended visit to the Transvaal, from which message the King understood that his assistance might be wanted. He therefore ordered the *abaqulusi*, who lived on that border, to be on the watch, and hold themselves in readiness to assemble immediately if required; and doubtless, had Sir Theophilus Shepstone been slain by the Boers, he would speedily have been avenged. But, as the change in the government of the country passed off quietly and without bloodshed, the *abaqulusi* were never called out, nor did Sir Garnet's war-cloud 'hover'.

My Chief would not have been himself had he remained quietly unconcerned at a distance when stirring scenes might be expected, and fighting was in the air. Discretion with him went hand in hand with ardour, and, while his calm sagacity was always on the watch to prevent collision, and to smooth the way for peace, where peace could rightly be preserved, his ready valour was as prompt to strike the blow when that should prove advisable or necessary. Truly he did not wait to let the grass grow beneath his feet at this critical period in South African history, and in Maritzburg, Newcastle, Pretoria, the people stared to see him reappear in an incredibly short space of time. A letter from one of my very few colonial acquaintances and correspondents at this time gave me an amusingly characteristic account of some of my Chief's proceedings in the Transvaal, at which I laughed outright as I read it, wishing I had been there to see:

> The Government House party (at Pretoria) were looking rather blue that day when the Colonel dropped down upon them as unexpectedly as a sudden flash of lightning, but a vast deal more welcome. Indeed it was not just as bright a look-out as we could have wished; for our troops in Pretoria were a mere handful, Colonel Pearson and the Buffs were nowhere within hail, and the Boers were growling under their breath. It would not have cost them much to chew us up, soldier and civilian too. The Governor's body-guard of Mounted Police had been drawn in from the open ground, and had their tents pitched in the garden round Government House; and there was a general feeling about that there was a little more thunder in the air than was quite agreeable. The Colonel came in like a fresh breeze, and our great men looked as glad to see him as if he

had brought a thousand men at his back. He took in the situation at a glance, and dashed off again in a few hours' time to hurry up the loitering troops. Up they came, in double quick time, and I wish you had heard their account of it all—how the Colonel swooped down upon them 12 miles or so from the border, crawling along at a snail's pace and, P—— said, 'thinking no evil!' They were in no hurry; the Boers were sure not to fight, it was only a demonstration. So they hadn't even got reserve ammunition with them, waggons were short, and those they had were loaded-up with stores. Colonel Durnford, they say, pitched into the officer in command in his quietly forcible way, saying, 'Look here sir! I daresay the Boers won't fight, and I'm sure they don't want to, but, mark my words, if they *do*—! They are dead shots at game at 500 yards and are all mounted men.' Strongly recommending them to push forwards, he went on himself to Newcastle. Young P—— was there; he swears by the Colonel, you know, and is always good to carry out whatever he wants done. The Colonel got in at midnight, and the moment he saw P—— he called out, 'you're the very man I want! I must have so many waggons before eight o'clock tomorrow morning.' 'Very good Sir,' says P—— hugely delighted, 'if it were anyone but you, Colonel, I should say it couldn't be done.'

'All right,' says the Colonel, 'so long as you don't say it to me.'

At dawn they were out scouring the neighbourhood, but not a thing on wheels was to be had for love or money. Coming back to the camp, 'What are these?' inquired the Colonel, looking at a row of waggons standing ready packed for starting. They were all loaded up with officers' heavy baggage, which was to follow them up to their new quarters in the Transvaal. 'Time enough for that,' says he 'when the Transvaal's made secure,' and in a very short space of time he had them all empty, and loaded up again with ammunition etc. He and P—— and a company of infantry started off with them soon after 2 P.M. that same day, and caught up to the rest of the troops next evening. Of course some of the fellows whose goods were left behind grumbled a good deal, and said afterwards that it would have done just as well if the Colonel had let them alone. That's all very well, *as it happened* that there was no collision with the Boers, but we have had good reason since to know that the Colonel was right in his estimate of possibilities, and, though the happy-go-lucky South African style of doing things may pull people through nine times out of ten, it usually happens that the miserable results of the tenth are enough to outweigh many times over the cost and trouble of precautions in the whole ten.

My Chief's life for the next few months must have been much to his taste, for, from all accounts, it comprised as much active exercise, management of important matters, and useful occupation, as could well be crowded into the time, with sufficient excitement and chance of personal danger to give an agreeable flavour to the whole. To do the utmost human foresight and energy could to avert strife and bloodshed, and to be in the thick of it if, nevertheless, it came, was, as ever, his ambition. The undoubted discontent of a portion of the Boer population subsided for the time, though, as the Colonel always said of them, 'they simmer;' but, after careful investigation of the various current rumours of the enmity of the natives, he was satisfied that they were quite groundless. His opinions on this subject, of great value as coming from one both well acquainted with the natives, and also to a certain extent behind the scenes in British South African politics, are thoroughly set forth in Colonel E. Durnford's last book, *A Soldier's Life and Work in South Africa*, but it does not come within my scope to do more than allude to them in passing.

The breaking out of the Kafrarian war towards the end of 1877 was the first circumstance which, to casual observers, might seem to throw discredit on Colonel Durnford's judgment concerning the peaceful intentions of the native races of South Africa. But a little inquiry proves quite the contrary; for the Colonel certainly never said that the white authorities could not bring about a war on any of the colonial borders if they chose to do so, and the Galeka war was forced by us upon the blacks. That his conclusion, 'there will be no war' (between white and black in South Africa at this time), proved incorrect was the result of his starting with a mistaken proposition, namely, the assumption that the Englishmen in authority in South Africa were as just and righteous in all their dealings as he was himself. He *knew* that the one side had no wish for war; as a true Englishman, a brave soldier, and a wise statesman he judged others of his own rank and class on the other side by himself, and his inference was one worthy of himself, but inapplicable to them. That is how I, who knew him well, have read the riddle, and his own words, quoted in the book alluded to above, bear me out in an opinion formed long before I read them.

Without doubt one of our chief misfortunes from a military point of view, with regard to the Zulu War, was its having been immediately preceded by the campaign in Kafraria, and undertaken by the men who had there met with their first experience of active warfare and of South African life. Lord Chelmsford and his staff came up to Natal in 1878, not merely with no true idea of what war with the Zulus would mean, but with a fixed, false impression of the comparatively small amount of difficulty and danger entailed by a South African campaign. Not a single engagement had taken place in Kafraria worthy of the name of battle, and, that on one occasion a man standing at no great distance from General Thesiger himself had actually been struck by a hostile missile was looked upon as a fact worth mentioning as a proof that the campaign was not without some element of danger. The remark attributed to Lord Chelmsford which went the rounds in Natal, and of which I heard from several quarters, 'if they (the Zulus) will not fight, we must *make* them fight,' was a fair sample of the infatuated spirit which possessed him and his men. They had won their honours and promotion lightly in Kafraria, and expected as easy a harvest from the Zulus; nor were they likely to be persuaded out of their confidence by what they heard in Natal from those with whom they *chose to take counsel*. I emphasise my words because it is plain to me from what I hear that they did *not* choose to consult those whose opinions did not please them—those, therefore, who really knew something of the Zulus, and knew that they might be expected to fight, if we actually invaded their country, and forced them to turn at bay.

In point of fact the colonists generally stood in no great awe of the Zulu armies. They (the Natalians) were only persuaded by Sir Bartle Frere and his friends to look upon them as foes at all; for, unconsciously to a great extent, no doubt, they judged of probabilities by the standard most usual to humanity, that of their own experience. For twenty years or more they had found the Zulus friendly neighbours, without the employment of the smallest defensive precautions—in 1874–5 there was not a vestige of a fort along the whole 200 miles of open border, nor the least pretence of a border-guard—and the solitary Zulu 'scare' on record, that of 1861, was well known to have been all moonshine. Since the early days of Natal, before English, Boers, and Zulus had settled down within the limits which they now occupy, there had been no stories told of Zulu attacks on other tribes, no exploits by which the Zulu fighting temper could be judged. A few ancient Boers (like the one whose earnest entreaty to Lord Chelmsford on the General's first entrance into Zululand that he would laager his camps, was laughed at and disregarded by that unlucky officer) may have known better; but the general opinion was that expressed as follows by a correspondent 'with the Carbineers,' to one of the Natal papers. He writes from Zululand on the 18th January, 1879, four days before the disaster, 'I imagine they (the Zulus) are much like the other natives—very great at bragging, but easily depressed and panic-stricken by any sudden reverse . . . . from all I can see, I hardly think there will be much fighting.'

CHAPTER II

WAR IF POSSIBLE

The war in Kafraria had not come to an end before plans for a Zulu campaign to follow it were laid. As early as August 1878 the Zululand coast was reconnoitred from the sea-board side with a view to the possible landing of our troops there, while the King was assured, upon Sir Bartle Frere's advice, by a neat little tale of merchant vessels, and a big English man-of-war to protect him from—the Russians? This fact in itself is enough to show that the war was a preconcerted scheme on our part, for at that time we had not even the semblance of a case against Cetshwayo. We wanted to pick a quarrel with him, and were lying in wait for a chance, but had found no pretext as yet. I think my Chief knew by this time that certain people in power looked upon the subjugation of the Zulus as the next move on the political chessboard, and that they meant to bring it about if they possibly could. But he knew that the Zulu King was too wise a man, and too friendly to the English, to behave in such a way as to give the latter a fair and justifiable *casus belli*, and—still judging others by himself—he did *not* imagine that Englishmen of high rank and position, and of noted piety into the bargain, would stoop to the fabrication of an imaginary offence where none existed. Once more the mistake which led to his disbelieving in a Zulu war up to the very last reflects more honour on himself, than credit on his colleagues or superiors. In support of his opinion, however, it must be remembered that that of his immediate (civil) superior officer (Sir Henry Bulwer) was evidently from first to last dead against the Zulu War, and that probably my Chief was well aware of this at the time, although he does not appear to have betrayed his knowledge to the world.

The point of view from which the matter was chiefly looked at by those on the spot appears to have been as follows: that, having annexed the Transvaal, we took over all its quarrels and claims, right or wrong, with it, and were bound to subjugate the Zulus in order to pacify the Boers, and in order to put an end to the much talked of 'standing menace' on the part of the Zulus, while an unusually large proportion of Imperial troops were in South Africa. [N.B. As far as I could ever learn, the 'standing menace' never meant more than the power—without the will or intention—on the part of the Zulus to injure Natal.]

Others, again, held that the subjugation of the Zulu nation would destroy the balance of power between Boer and native, and would set the former free to take up arms for their own independence against ourselves. But this point of view was not popular, and still less so was that of those few who believed or maintained that strict truth and justice on our part was all that was needed to preserve the peace between us and the various coloured natives of South Africa. To this latter extremely small class belonged, I am sure, my Chief, and his last action before the war was one especially calculated to produce that effect. I allude, of course, to the Zulu Border Commission, of which he was a member. The two other gentlemen who composed it with him were barely known to me by sight, nor did I ever exchange a dozen words with either of them; it will therefore easily be understood that I intend no reflection upon them in alluding more particularly to my Chief's share in their common labours. One of the two was the 'Acting Head of the Native Department' from whom Colonel Durnford had with so much difficulty obtained the order for the release of the Putini tribe as related in a previous chapter of this book.

The dispute, upon the merits of which these three gentlemen were sent to decide, seems to have been a simple one enough when once the political cobwebs spun over it by interested officials had been cleared away. The Boers and Zulus each laid claim to a certain strip of land between the two countries acknowledged as Transvaal and Zululand. The Boers asserted that the Zulus had sold or given it to them, and the Zulus positively denied that any such transaction had ever taken place. So far it would seem a matter of hard swearing on both sides, but of course the Boers had got to prove their case, since, as has been pointed out before, the other side could not be called upon to prove a negative. Against the Boers, also, there were the well-known facts concerning their usual practice of obtaining land from the natives, by a process which to English ears sounds little short of swindling, and that nearly the whole of the country in dispute was, as it had always been, actually occupied by Zulus,* although cut up on paper into farms which had all been sold or granted to Boers *by their own Government*, but never occupied—showing that at no period during the twenty years or so of dispute had the Zulus acknowledged the Boer claim. But the discovery which settled the justice of the question beyond a doubt was that the deeds and papers on which the Boer delegates professed to rest their claims proved to be either untrustworthy documents in every sense, or else too incomplete to prove their case, while some were plainly forged. Need I say that the decision of the Commissioners was in favour of the Zulu claim, with

---

* *Authority for this statement*: Sir Theophilus Shepstone quoted by Sir Henry Bulwer in a Blue Book of Feb. 23rd, 1878, No. 2100, p. 67.

a suggestion that the Transvaal Government should compensate the Boer farmers for the loss of the land which it had no right to sell to them. I do not assert that the prompt and honest execution of this judgement would have prevented the Zulu War since Sir Bartle Frere was resolved that war should be waged—though it does not appear that there was at any time any chance of an invasion of our territory by the Zulus unless we attacked them first; but it has since been amply proved that it would have had a most salutary effect on all the native tribes, quieting at one stroke that too well-founded distrust in British sincerity which is the most dangerous feeling that we can arouse. But, although the Commissioners had finished their work, and sent in their report by the middle of June, the award was withheld from the Zulus until Dec. 11th when it was delivered at the same time as the Ultimatum which Sir Bartle Frere sent, as he remarked himself beforehand, to 'put an end to pacific relations with our neighbours.'* Under such circumstances, it could, of course, have no effect whatever, since the Zulus must naturally have been entirely taken up by the news that they were to be attacked in thirty days' time, unless they fulfilled before them conditions which were perfectly impossible within that or a much longer period.

But the broad fact of the decision being in favour of the Zulus was known in Natal before then, and it was as unpopular as it was unexpected. The connection between the Natal colonists and the Transvaal Boers, both by marriage and business relations, is close enough for the sympathies of the former to be entirely with the latter on any subject in dispute between them and the coloured races, not to mention the bond of *colour*, which seems to be stronger in proportion to the lack of cultivation of those who feel it.

I take for granted that the three Commissioners were equally concerned in their report, as it appears to have been unanimous; but, judging from the remarks of the press after the nature of that report was made known, the old colonial tendency to lay blame upon my Chief had its way again. Certainly, with the one exception of the *Natal Colonist*, those publications never missed an opportunity of throwing an evil word at Colonel Durnford during his life-time, and, though there has been a great change since, and both writers and readers probably regret the past, their repentance came quite too late to do good to anyone but themselves. One of the worst of these papers speaks on Feb. 3, 1879 of 'the *mischief-making* award,' and of 'the unfortunate Commissioner who ignored Christian oaths† which were in conflict with Zulu pretensions,'

---

*   This will be found in the Blue Book No. 2220, p. 280, and has since been quoted in several accounts of the Zulu War.

†   Christian oaths! *Boer forgeries* rather.

alluding, of course, to the Colonel, and showing to what lengths perfectly unreasoning spite may carry a writer and editor. In order to find another expression of blame to apply to the soldier whose death had not quenched their causeless ill-will, they 'ignore,' not only the facts that the award never had a chance of doing either good or harm, and was certainly not calculated to make mischief between us and the Zulus, but also the trifling ,circumstance that Colonel Durnford was one of three in that matter. But, judging from the usual tone of the journal in question both before, and during the war, we may reasonably conclude that in this particular case *'mischief*-making' is merely synonymous with *peace*-making.*

Stronger still than the personal feeling of the Natalians against the award was the disgust of those leaders of the game who looked upon it as a false move upon the political chessboard. These politicians desired to subjugate the Zulu nation; but they knew the temper of the British public well enough to desire also a plausible excuse for their intended hostile operations. According to their ideas the decision should have been entirely in favour of the Boers, although given with all due regard to appearances of impartiality and justice. To such a decision the Zulus surely would not quietly submit after their many years of patient faith in England. Some outbreak would be the consequence which would oblige us to take 'defensive precautions,' and we all know what *that* means. Some such argument, though doubtless expressed (even inwardly) in more elegantly delusive terms, must have been the cause of Sir Bartle Frere's palpable chagrin on receiving the Commissioners' report. In fact they had put him in a hole. He had trusted them to stir up the Zulus into a temper which would lead to war, and had therefore expressed full confidence in their decision beforehand. Instead of which they had done what made war less likely than ever, unless we began it ourselves, manifestly without provocation. Under the circumstances he could hardly refuse to ratify their award because it turned out different from what he had expected it to be. The only course left open to him, except that of abandoning his schemes of conquest altogether, was that of delaying the delivery of the award as long as possible, in hopes that the uncertain and expectant state of mind in which the proceedings of the Commissioners unavoidably left the Zulus, might be irritated by chance, or by the delay itself, into furnishing some sort of an excuse for the projected war of invasion.

* Although such was certainly the impression given by the general tone of what I heard in the colony in 1874–5, and have gathered from Natal newspapers since, it is only fair to remark that I know there were exceptions to the rule, and that, besides the many poor and unimportant human beings who have special cause to remember my Chief with grateful affection, there are, here and there throughout the colony, men who always understood his worth.

Unhappily causes for offence are seldom far to look for when the stronger of two parties is anxious to discover them, and Sir Bartle Frere had not long to wait. The Zulu King might keep his own temper under provocation, and might restrain the ardour of his council and of his soldiers; but he could not keep every household in his dominions in order, nor prevent young women running away from their husbands if they had a mind to do so. This is what occurred. Two wives of a Chief living near the Natal border eloped with their lovers, and took refuge in Natal. They were followed by members of the family, carried back into Zululand, and put to death, poor creatures, by the severe law of their land. It is not my intention to express an opinion upon the action of the young men who carried out this terrible retribution; were I to do so, my remarks might hit some of our civilized customs as well as those of the savages. But that question has nothing to do with the case in point, which consisted in the offence against the British Government in the fact that the women were captured on the Natal side of the border, a practice which until within 2 or 3 years had been not only permitted but encouraged by the law of Natal.* The act was one of private vengeance, and the 'King knew nothing' at all about it at the time. When he heard of it he expressed his great regret, and offered to pay a fine for his subjects' offence, which was not accepted by Sir Bartle Frere.

This was Sir Bartle Frere's first cause for complaint. The second was that a government surveyor, having been ordered to inspect a certain road down to the Tugela on the Natal side, had not the sense to carry out his instructions to go upon his errand alone, and to act with great discretion so as not to alarm the Zulus on the other side. He took a companion with him, and, by behaving in an odd and unusual manner, 'taking no notice' of questions put to them by the Zulus etc., they aroused the suspicions of the latter, who seized them in the river, and detained them as prisoners for an hour-and-a-half, but eventually allowed them to depart uninjured.

This happened, of course, altogether without the knowledge or authority of the Zulu King, who would without the slightest doubt have made the fullest apologies and amends for this act also, had he been allowed the chance of doing so. These two cases actually comprise the whole of the direct offences towards the English attributed to the Zulu King; but the list was swelled by the addition to it of the acts of the independent robber-chiefs Umbilini and Manyonzoba, who, living in some natural fortresses to the north of Zululand, proved themselves from time to time inconvenient neighbours to the Boers, Swazis,

* Refugee Law for the rendition of *women and cattle*, since repealed.

and Zulus alike.* As to the breaking of the so-called 'Coronation Promises' on which Sir Bartle Frere laid so much stress, it is a matter hardly worth alluding to since it has been treated with contempt by all parties. The said 'promises' could only have been voluntarily and conditionally made, and as they had nothing whatever to do with British lands or British subjects, we had no right whatever to enforce them. But, indeed, there is no proof offered of their ever having been broken. Stripped of all high-sounding but meaningless phrases, and reduced to a plain honest statement of proven facts, the provocations upon which we undertook the disastrous war of 1879 become painfully and absurdly small, and, in fact, amount to no more than the saying that 'any stick is good enough to beat a dog with.'

So much for the causes of the Zulu War, of which I have not ventured to give this brief account without first carefully studying all that has been said upon the subject in official and other writings. And although no doubt my mind has been to a certain extent influenced by my previous knowledge of my Chief's views and opinions, I believe that I am sufficiently able to take an impartial view of what I read and hear, to have been struck by any *proven fact* against the theory which I have formed. But no such proof has been produced on behalf of Sir Bartle Frere's policy, and of mere unsupported assertions I make no account.

Passing from this short preliminary account to my Chief's share in the war itself, I take up the tale at the time when, having done all that he could do as a politician to prevent the war, he turned his attention to his duty as a soldier, and endeavoured to leaven with his own share of experience and commonsense the singular ignorance (of the Zulus and all their ways), and obstinately cheerful misconception of the task before them, which characterised Lord Chelmsford and his Staff.

---

* My Chief personally reconnoitred one of Umbilini's caves, and told me that six men could hold it against an army, so that the surrender of Umbilini, called for by one of the clauses of the Ultimatum sent to Cetshwayo, would not have been an easy term to comply with.

CHAPTER III

WAR

General Thesiger and his Staff landed in Natal early in August 1878, and from that time forwards preparations for war—that is to say for an invasion of Zululand by our forces—were as steadily carried on as though there had been no question at all as to whether it should take place or not. Probably this was precisely the case, and no conduct whatever on Cetwayo's part would have averted the evil, short of a voluntary and unconditional surrender of himself and country into the hands of the British. Yet up to the very last Colonel Durnford doubted its actually coming to pass. We had no grievance, and he could not believe that we should really proceed to extremities without one. Nevertheless the offence might yet come, and there was no doubt at all that, if it did, it would be eagerly seized upon by Sir Bartle Frere. It was, therefore, even more than usually incumbent upon the superior officers of Her Majesty's forces in Natal to see that the said forces were in good order for any service which they might suddenly be called upon to undertake. So thought my Chief, and threw himself with ardour into schemes for avoiding the mischief which he had himself seen arise on a previous occasion (see p. 42 *et seq*) from the employment, as troops, of half-armed, undisciplined bands of natives, led by their own chiefs, and fighting in their own fashion. Such 'troops' had hitherto proved of no use whatever in the hour of danger, while it had been found next to impossible to prevent their committing excesses in that of victory. Colonel Durnford, being the only officer of rank in Natal who had much experience of, or influence over, the natives was deputed by Lord Chelmsford to raise a Native Contingent in Natal some 7,000 strong, to be divided into three regiments. Only a third of the whole eventually came under his personal control. But I have it on the authority of Englishmen who served through the campaign, that the Native Contingent of Colonel Durnford's column was the only one that remained steady throughout the war, or did any really good service. He had but a very short time in which to give them any training, but he threw his whole soul into the work during that time, and many of the men, both cavalry and infantry, who were with him, had learned beforehand that personal confidence in their Leader which goes so far in carrying troops, whether black or white, through difficulty and danger without flinching. 'Not a man of us but would have followed him unhesitatingly wherever he chose to lead,' said one of his European officers,* afterwards asserting his conviction that all his brother-officers would say the same, and from my own experience I can readily believe his words. The month spent in drilling his men at that fine breezy spot, Krans-Kop, where my Chief's column was encamped, must have suited him—to use an expression of his own—'down to the ground.' His political work was over; he had done his best to make war unnecessary, and it was now no part of his duty to question the determination of those under whom he served. The Ultimatum had been delivered, and, at the end of the time of grace allowed, the troops were to cross the Tugela into Zululand. That was a settled matter now; but still, the Colonel thought, judicious conduct on our part, and strict adherence to the policy professed by Sir Bartle Frere and Lord Chelmsford, of abstaining from all unprovoked violence, and marching steadily but quietly forwards, might result in a bloodless campaign, and a mere 'military promenade,' enforcing our conditions. It is useless to speculate upon what might have been the result of such a course, for it was never put in practice for an hour. Almost while the words, promising security for person and property to all Zulus who would remain quietly in their homes, were on the General's lips, the troops which he accompanied in person were seizing herds of cattle from their peaceful owners, and firing upon those who objected to the appropriation.

Lord Chelmsford crossed the Tugela on January 11th, and Colonel Durnford's orders brought him, with part of his Column (No. 2) to Rorke's Drift on the 20th. Except the officers and the artillery belonging to the rocket-battery, his troops were all natives; but, in the five troops of Basuto and Edendale horse, he commanded what was at that time about the best cavalry at Lord Chelmsford's disposal. The General, indeed, was short of cavalry—a necessity in such warfare as that in Zululand—the Home Government, not intending to be responsible for an invasion of Zululand, had persistently declined to respond to his petitions for a larger supply, considering those already in the colony ample for all *defensive purposes*. Lord Chelmsford had always appeared to think that, should an actual battle with the Zulus take place, this want of cavalry would place him at a disadvantage, and no doubt he was well aware how invaluable under such circumstances would be a body of light cavalry, so well disciplined, so fleet, and so inured to fatigue as were 'Durnford's Horse,' while it was well known that their leader's powers of endurance in the saddle were hardly to be matched in Natal. Of my three friends of former days, Hlubi, Jabez and

---

* The officers of the Native Contingents were all white men.

Windvogel, the two former were certainly with my Chief in 1879; but I heard nothing of the third, although probably he was there as well.

On January 17th Lord Chelmsford made a reconnaissance into Zululand as far as the hill of Isandhlwana, a mere name at that time, misspelt and mispronounced in a half-dozen different ways. Here the General selected the site of that camp—'more defenceless than an English village'—the position of which has since been described as one which 'seems to offer a premium on disaster, and asks to be attacked,' and concerning which all who have visited it since have agreed in wondering on what possible grounds the choice could have been made. About a mile away was a spot suitable in every respect; many better ones than the slope of Isandhlwana hill might have been found close at hand; whilst it would hardly have been possible for ingenuity to discover a worse. One can only charitably fall back upon the supposition that Lord Chelmsford's head was still affected, through the whole of this disastrous period, by the fall from his horse upon it, which he is reported to have had a few days before. The camp at Isandhlwana has so often been described that I need give but the briefest account of it here. The tents, with the waggons in their rear, were scattered along a front of about half-a-mile, across the slope which ran up to the crest (inaccessible from the camp side) of the Isandhlwana hill. This crest formed a wall, open at both ends, and accessible from behind, while the slope in front on which the camp was pitched is commanded by high ground on either side, more especially on the right, where a small stony hill, afterwards named Black's Kopje, overlooked the camp at less than 100 yards' distance from its top to the nearest tents. The only part of Isandhlwana hill that is inaccessible is just the ledge of rocks at the very top. All the base of the hill—lying between the camp and the ledge—is a great grassy stony mound, that men can rush all over, affording excellent shelter and thoroughly commanding the camp at a distance of from 150 to 200 yards. In this veritable trap Lord Chelmsford contentedly placed the camp of No. 3 Column on January 20th, and spent that day and the next in comfortable ignorance of the five-and-twenty thousand armed Zulus who were meanwhile collecting at their rendezvous, just beyond the range of hills that half-encircled the solitary Isandhlwana mountain, and was connected with it in the rear by a broad neck of land.

The General had started with minute instructions (prepared in November, 1878) to his officers concerning 'laager,' entrenchments, and other defences to be formed at every camp in the enemy's country;* but he appears to have

---

* His 'Regulations' of February 1879 even went so far as to direct that troops, when halting for a few hours only, 'should invariably form a waggon laager,' but this was after he had profited by sad experience.

laboured under the delusion that his personal presence obviated the necessity of all defensive precautions, and he certainly took none at Isandhlwana. Colonel Glyn wished to laager or entrench the camp; but the General replied that it was not worthwhile as they should leave it so soon. No attempt was made to search the country, except in the one direction in which he intended to move on; and neither Black's Kopje on the right of the camp nor the shoulder of the hill (also thoroughly commanding the camp) was even occupied by picquets during the two nights the force was there. 'Not a single step was taken in any way to defend our new position in case of a night or day attack from the enemy,' says one who was present; and the most extraordinary proof of the General's strange conviction of security lies in the fact that, although small bodies of Zulu scouts were observed on the 21st upon the hills behind which, as afterwards appeared, lay the whole Zulu force, no attempt was made to reconnoitre the country in that direction beyond the immediate vicinity of the camp. Two parties were, however, sent out on the 20th to reconnoitre a place, known as Matshana's stronghold, some twelve miles distant; and, during the night of the 21st the leader of one of these parties (who were bivouacking out in the open) sent back reports of having marked the Zulus down in a kloof in considerable numbers. This decided Lord Chelmsford to go out himself at dawn next day in that direction, with Colonel Glyn, the 2nd Battalion 24th Regiment, the Mounted Infantry and four guns, and 50 Natal Native Pioneers. A message was sent off to Colonel Durnford at Rorke's Drift, and Lieut.-Colonel Pulleine 1.24th was left in command of the camp 'during the absence of Colonel Glyn.' Plainly the General anticipated no danger to the camp; for not only did he leave it 'more defenceless than an English village,' but, when he had ridden some miles away from it, he enquired 'what orders had been left for Colonel Pulleine?'

Colonel Durnford's movements had been arranged beforehand, Lord Chelmsford's despatch of January 14th mentioning where he was intended to place his battalions of infantry, 'while he and the mounted men and rocket-battery were to join me with No. 3 Column,'* and a later despatch (of January, 19th) repeats much the same thing, 'his Mounted Natives will co-operate with us.' Accordingly the order sent off to him by Colonel Crealock at daybreak on the 22nd was briefly this:

> You are to march to this camp *at once*, with all the force you have with you of No. 2 Column.

---

* See Blue Book No. C. 2242.

Major Bengough's Battalion is to move to Rorke's Drift as ordered
yesterday.

2/24th, artillery and mounted men with the General and Colonel Glyn
move off at once to attack a Zulu force about 10 miles distant.*

This plainly refers to previous instructions, as also did Colonel Durnford's
remark, as reported by Lieut. Cochrane, 32nd L.I., when he received it. 'Ah!
just what I expected. We are to go on at once. The General has gone out to attack
an *impi*.' There can be little doubt that the intention with regard to Colonel
Durnford's movements upon that fatal day was that he should come up with his
cavalry and rocket-battery, and render such active assistance to the General's
force as occasion suggested. The boldly asserted fiction that the order sent to
him that morning was 'move up to Isandula Camp at once with all your mounted
men and rocket-battery; *take command of it*,' which the discovery, in Colonel
Crealock's note-book, of the copy made at the time of the actual order (as given
above) has lately refuted, was only consistent with a degree of anxiety about the
safety of the camp which the General clearly never felt. But it was so
completely out of keeping with all the known events of the day that Colonel
Durnford's friends doubted it from the first.

The Colonel had crossed over into Natal on an expedition to obtain waggons
when the General's order arrived and was sent after him by Capt. George
Shepstone. He returned immediately to Rorke's Drift and marched for
Isandhlwana with the least possible delay. At about 10.30 A.M. as he approached
the camp at the head of his mounted men, he was met by Lieut. Chard R.E., who
told him that Colonel Pulleine's troops were then in column outside the camp,
as bodies of the enemy had been seen on the crest of the distant hills. They
seemed, he said, to be working round so far to the left† that he feared they might
be going to make a dash at Rorke's Drift, and he was hastening back to his post
there to prepare for emergencies. He took orders from the Colonel to Major
Russell to hurry up with the rocket-battery, to detach a company of natives to
protect the baggage, and for all to 'look out to the left.'

On reaching the camp, between 10.30 and 11 A.M., Colonel Durnford found
that, though bodies of the enemy had been seen moving about the crests of
the distant hills, and one column was reported as moving towards the General,
no definite information had been obtained as to their strength, position,

---

* From copy of the order made at the time in Colonel Crealock's note-book which was afterwards
found on the field of Isandhlwana.
† That is, to the left of the party advancing from Rorke's Drift.

or movements, that they 'are retiring in every direction' being the latest report.*

Colonel Durnford being in command of another column, and having (as is now acknowledged by Colonel Crealock) received no orders to take command of No. 3 Column camp—now told Lieut.-Colonel Pulleine that he should not interfere with his command, and proceeded to do what he could to 'co-operate' with the troops which were supposed to be actively engaged with the enemy. Manifestly there were two things to be done; to ascertain, for the first time, the strength and position of the enemy behind those unexplored hills, and, if possible, to cut off the column moving towards the General, so as to prevent their joining the (supposed) main body of the Zulus with which he was thought to be engaged. Probably it had not yet occurred to any man of either Column No. 2 or 3 that the General had *left his foe behind* him, and was pursuing phantoms in the distance, 'a Zulu force that fell back from hill to hill as we advanced, giving up, without a shot, most commanding positions.'†

Accordingly Colonel Durnford sent one troop of Natal Native Horse to reinforce his baggage guard; two troops, under Captains Shepstone and Barton, to the hills on the left—one to move along the crest of the range, and the other to search the valley beyond. He himself, with the remaining two troops of horse went out to the front to prevent that 'one column' joining the *impi* with which the General was supposed to be engaged. The rocket-battery, with its escort of a company of Native Contingent, followed him; but Lieut.-Colonel Pulleine had seemed so unwilling to spare two companies of infantry which Colonel Durnford asked him for as an additional support, that my Chief decided to take his own men only. And so he rode out with his hundred men, across a long low rolling country, intersected here and there with small gullies and water-courses, straight towards that part of the hilly amphitheatre (which made a semicircle round and behind the Isandhlwana hill) up the other side of which one end—the left horn—of the great Zulu army was even then advancing. The Zulus say that they had not meant to fight that day,‡ but that they were roused at this end of the great, waiting half-circle by the movements of Lord Chelmsford and his troops. They saw the General leave the camp in the early morning and heard the firing of his guns. Excited by the sounds of combat, they could refrain no longer, but

---

*   Colonel Pulleine had sent a message to warn Lord Chelmsford of the first appearance of the Zulus, and several later messages seem to have been sent, with increasing urgency. The latest being that received soon after 12 A.M., 'Come in every man, for God's sake. The camp is surrounded, and will be taken unless helped at once.'

†   Colonel Crealock, Blue Book No. C. 2260, p. 99.

‡   The day of the new-moon, their Sabbath or holy-day.

rose and advanced upon the camp, appearing over the ridge as Colonel Durnford approached, so suddenly that without a moment's warning he found his little band face to face with an immense attacking force. Simultaneously with the discovery, firing was heard behind the hills to the left of the camp where Capt. George Shepstone's troops were reconnoitring, and a trooper came dashing across from thence to report to the Colonel the presence of an immense *impi* in that direction also. Roughly speaking the direction taken by Capt. Shepstone was at about right angles with that followed by the Colonel; but the curve of the hills and of the Zulu army behind them approached nearer to the camp at the former point, and Capt. Shepstone's men came right upon the Zulus at close quarters. Fire was opened on both sides and Capt. Shepstone retired down the hill, leaving one dead upon the field. The whole Zulu army now showed itself, advancing upon the doomed and defenceless camp; and Capt. Shepstone, having withdrawn his troop, galloped back to give the alarm to Colonel Pulleine and his men, who, however, being unable from the position of the camp, to see the approaching peril until it was close upon them, appear to have been incredulous of its magnitude.

But my Chief, whom I have left, four miles from camp, and facing with his little handful of staunch supporters an attacking force of many thousands of brave and determined warriors, how fared it with him meanwhile? He knew the defenceless condition of the camp, and how inadequate were the forces at Colonel Pulleine's disposal to protect that scattered array of tents and waggons* as they now stood. Clearly the best service he and his hundred horsemen could render would be to keep back the enemy's approach as long as possible, and so give time for those in camp to attempt forming a laager. No easy matter this in a hurry, let me tell you, when the waggons are too heavy to be moved without their oxen, as anyone versed in South African waggon travelling will agree, even where, as—according to Mr. Brickhill†—was the case in this instance, the oxen had been driven into camp early, and were tied to the yokes, though not inspanned.‡ The incredulity with which Captain George Shepstone's report

---

*   Inadequate *under the circumstances* only; doubtless in a less hopeless position, with *plentiful ammunition*, and a simple waggon laager, the men would have held their own at Isandhlwana, as their comrades did at Rorke's Drift.

†   Mr. Brickhill was interpreter to No. 3 Column.

‡   Each ox has a heavy thong looped round the base of the horns by one end, with about a yard-and-a-half of thong left by which, when the ox is inspanned, the yoke is bound to the horns. Before the oxen are inspanned the whole number—18 to 24—may be tied up in a circle by the loose ends of their thongs, or 'reims', as no doubt was the case in this instance, leaving, therefore, a considerable amount of work to be done before the oxen could be used to move the waggons into place.

was received in camp appears to have prevented any attempt being made to profit by what little time there was to spare. But, indeed it was too short to be of any real service, for, though Colonel Durnford's action delayed the approach of the left horn of the Zulu army, the 'chest' was steadily advancing, and was soon engaged with the camp force under Colonel Pulleine, while the right horn was swinging round the Isandhlwana hill, so as to attack at close quarters at that end of the 'open wall.' I needed but a slight sketch of what my Chief did that day in order to understand it all as well as though I had been present; for I knew him, and could judge correctly of what he was likely to do on such an occasion as this. But one of my old Basuto friends, who was with our Chief that day, wrote me a detailed account of all he could remember, which, as it substantially agrees with every other tale from trustworthy sources, may be regarded as true. When the presence of the immense Zulu force was made known in the appalling manner already described, the Colonel galloped back with his troops to the first ground suitable for a stand which they had passed on their way out, a water-course with broken ground beyond it. Here he dismounted and placed his men in a single line right across the country between the camp and the Zulus, who were now pouring over the ridge in numbers, and moving towards the camp. The hundred men placed thus, each at a little distance from the other, fired upon the great advancing mass of the foe with deadly effect the moment they came within range of their rifles, and long before the Zulus could throw their assegais to any purpose.* The instant they had fired they sprang upon their horses by the Colonel's orders, and galloped back a few dozen yards, dismounting there to repeat the same manoeuvre, and so disputing every foot of ground that lay between them and the camp. Lithe and rapid, and instantly obedient as were the Colonel's men to every sign from their gallant leader— who was no more ruffled by the great and sudden danger than if he had been commanding at a holiday parade—an enemy must have fallen to every rifle that opened fire upon the serried ranks of the many thousand Zulu warriors, but never a man lost he, he was too quick for them—always out of range of their flung assegais before they could recover themselves from the last fire. But they numbered more than a hundred to one, and this could not go on for ever. At last they reached a stream not far from the camp itself, with much broken stony ground beyond it, forming the best cover they had yet found. Here a long stand was made, for there was no more vantage ground between that and the nearest tents, and the enemy still pressed on in countless numbers. Fast as they could

---

* Some of the Zulus were armed with guns, but mostly of an inferior description. Their assegais did far more mischief upon this unhappy day.

load our men poured in their deadly fire, knowing that the moment they relaxed, the enemy would sweep on, while the Colonel rode up and down their line, cheering and encouraging each man with voice and smile. 'Fire, my boys! Well done, my boys!' he cried, as, careless of his own safety, he passed amongst them to and fro. 'Keep back, Sir,' exclaimed one and another of those who knew and loved him best. 'Keep behind us, or you will be hit,' for now the Zulu shots and spears were falling perilously near.

'Nonsense!' he answered. 'Fire away! I am all right,' and laughed at their fears for him. 'Never before,' said my informant, 'in all the years I had been with him, had I seen his face so bright and glad as then, when, as now I understand, he knew his death was coming near.* We shall all remember his voice that day, and how he seemed to give us each his own brave spirit as he went along our line, so that not one of us wished to flinch, or fall back, though we could not see how this should end without our death.'

How long this donga might have yet been held, if ammunition had held out, we cannot guess. My Chief had sent a message back to camp for more as soon as the last halt was made. But the man who took it did not return, and presently the Colonel sent another and another, but still with no result. While they were still fighting here, and when the whole camp-force had become engaged, the day suddenly darkened, a strange shade fell over all, and the sunlight shone red and dull. It was the hour of the great eclipse which lasted throughout this unhappy battle of Isandhlwana, passing at its close.†

But, at last, the fire from the donga—before which, at its hottest, the Zulus had wavered and lain down, began to slacken. The cartridges were done. Another moment and the fact would become apparent to the foe, and, finding it useless to expect ammunition from the camp, the Colonel bade his Lieutenant hasten back with the men to their own waggons—which, coming from Rorke's Drift, had not yet entered the lines of the camp—and get out their own stores as rapidly as possible. As he sent them on their errand he spoke a few words of

---

*   So Wordsworth says of 'The Happy Warrior'

         . . . who, if he be called upon to face
        Some awful moment to which Heaven has joined
        Great issues, good or bad for human kind,
        Is happy as a Lover; and attired
        With sudden brightness, like a man inspired;

    The whole of this poem is singularly applicable to the character of my Chief.

†   The *Natal Almanac* for 1879 gives the eclipse as commencing at 1 h, 9 m, 30 s. P.M. and lasting
    until 3 h, 50 m, 10 s, which is in almost startling coincidence with the hours during which the
    combat was maintained.

warm praise of their conduct hitherto, saying that, if he lived to do so, he should report it to the Queen. And those were the last words they ever heard him speak; for, as they went off in one direction towards their waggons, and he turned in the other and rode up into the centre of the camp, the great wave of Zulu warriors, hitherto held back at this point by the fire from the donga, swept onwards and upwards between him and them, and they saw him no more.

And what happened there, at the camp? No one lived to tell the tale, but it has since been plainly told by the dead themselves. Four long months later, the ground was searched at last, and the true story was revealed of the gallant stand there made, and the glorious death of him whom I have called 'my Chief.' All honour indeed, to those companies of infantry who died in their ranks, fighting steadily to the last. But still greater praise is due to those who, with my Chief, and inspired by his example, disdained to seek in flight that safety which their horses might readily have afforded them, and, deliberately leaving them at their picquet-posts, took up their position, with him at their head, upon the one spot which experienced soldiers have since decided to be the only one which could have been held for any length of time. The main body of our army was in full flight by this time, followed closely by a foe from whom there was no escape on foot. Not a man of the infantry escaped alive, and many of the riders fell as well. The fugitives' best chance seemed to be for those who remained to hold the neck of land on which the Colonel had taken his stand; but this devoted attempt to cover their retreat was rendered futile by the immense number of the Zulu force, a mere fraction of which, doubling round the Isandhlwana hill, was enough to destroy the flying troops, even while the main body was kept at bay by the little band upon the neck. Meanwhile around them pressed a countless foe, eager to make an end of such a small impediment, and, so many were there of the Zulus that whole regiments were held back from action, our soldiers being soon surrounded. Formed into a square, they fired so rapidly from every side upon their assailants, that the advance-guard of Lord Chelmsford's tardily returning force described the firing as they saw it from a distance, as 'like incessant lightning.' Speedy assistance would have saved this little band of heroes yet, but none came, and once more their ammunition began to fail, while every moment assegai or bullet made their number less by one. Still the brave voice of their leader was heard and noted by the attacking force,* commanding and encouraging his men. But at last that voice was silent, for a Zulu bullet† had

---

*   Account given by a Zulu prisoner.

†   Evidence of Mr. Longhurst, Vet. Surgeon, K.D.G., who found the bullet in May 1879, when Colonel Durnford was buried, and sent it home.

sent my Colonel's noble spirit to its rest.* There was no more firing from the rifles now; the ammunition was spent to the last cartridge, and a few revolvers only remained. But the struggle was over. The assegais of the Zulus made but short work, and in a few minutes more, as the lurid shadow of the eclipse passed from off the land, the end had come for all.

---

* Twenty minutes to four. The time is fixed by the evidence of Colonel Durnford's watch, which was stopped at that hour by his death wound. The account given by members of the General's advance-guard, shows that the end must have followed immediately.